ECONOMICS FOR EXECUTIVES

Economics for Executives

ERIC CHALMERS, M.A.

JOHN MURRAY

*Printed in Great Britain by
Cox & Wyman Ltd.,
London, Reading and Fakenham*

CASED 0 7195 2591 8
LIMP 0 7195 2592 6

To my parents

Preface

As its title implies, this book is expressly designed to offer an easy introduction to economics for those actively engaged in the everyday business world. The treatment is therefore purposely light, with not too much abstruse theory. Through simplicity and readability the aim has been to provide what could perhaps be regarded as 'economics for the tired businessman'. A special concern has also been to relate the subject matter directly to the business decision-making process, describing those contemporary economic policies and institutions that form the inescapable background to management activity. Particular emphasis is placed on the character of the economic cycle and how this should be taken into account in business planning.

Economics for Executives will be found useful to students preparing for those general economics papers included in so many professional examinations. In this context, the syllabus for the Institute of Chartered Accountants' final examination General Paper has been particularly kept in view when planning the contents of this book. In all these professional examinations importance is rightly attached to candidates exhibiting a knowledge of recent economic and financial developments. As those drafting the syllabuses recommend, this can be obtained by regularly reading a good national daily newspaper. But even where the student does so conscientiously during the years leading up to examination, his memory will scarcely be able to retain accurately the multitude of economic happenings, even when they are explained fully in the newspapers, not merely reported upon. Press cutting files can be valuable aids to memory but it is unlikely that the busy professional student will have either the time or the self-discipline to adhere faithfully to a system of keeping them. The present volume, with its considerable stress on contemporary economics, offers to solve this problem by providing, in addition to traditional economic theory, a convenient record, as well as some explanation and interpretation, of the economic scene in Britain over recent years.

ERIC CHALMERS

Contents

Contents

PART ONE

The Firm in the Economy

I

Economics and the Business World

RELEVANCE OF ECONOMICS

No author of a book on economics can be expected to neglect the economic aspects of his own efforts. He will therefore naturally endeavour to address himself to the largest possible audience. For this reason, many of the elementary introductions to the subject have tended to be written principally for the sixth former and the first-year student at university, as well as for the general reader; all these providing a potential readership of some tens, if not some hundreds, of thousands. Books written for such readers are chiefly concerned to explain clearly and simply the theoretical basis of the subject, giving the definitions and the economic laws. But in seeking simplicity, realism is often sacrificed and the examples given to illustrate the principles seem to come from a world far removed from that which the businessman knows today. Many of the theoretical concepts in economics are by their nature rather abstract. And even when contemporary institutions are described, these tend to be mainly in the financial sphere. To the business executive such introductions to economics must seem to have something of an Alice in Wonderland flavour. Those who occasionally take up the study of the subject, feeling that a knowledge of it might help them to become better managers, tend to find little resemblance between the theoretical economist's dreamworld and their everyday business experience. Not surprisingly, the usefulness of the subject tends to escape them.

PRACTICAL USEFULNESS

It is the prime purpose of this book to show that economics does have a very real relevance to the business decision-making activity. Economics can be useful to the executive in many different ways. First of all, it provides him with terminology and principles representing convenient generalisations of the countless

3

individual instances making up the business scene. When the particular cases come along, he can more readily identify them for what they are; be aware of their most usual features and tendencies; and in certain cases approach them much more sympathetically, this being particularly so in the field of industrial relations. Secondly, economic theory highlights the most usual pattern of cause and effect relationships, both in the immediate industrial environment as well as throughout the economy generally. This enables the course of economic cycles to be intelligently anticipated and the various features likely to impinge upon the firm can be taken into account in business planning. These same economic principles operate in other countries as well and thus also give a guide to developments in export markets. Lastly, provided that it is presented in an up-to-date form, economics can explain contemporary institutions and government policies facing the businessman. In this way he becomes aware of the general configuration of the whole economy and where his particular firm fits into the picture. This also helps in tracing likely cause and effect relationships and in anticipating possible repercussions on himself, his suppliers, his customers or his competitors.

REAL WORLD APPROACH

The onus of indicating the relevance of a knowledge of economics to the management activity cannot be evaded if the approach to the subject is made from the direction of the actual business world. Instead of dwelling chiefly on the theory, with the occasional illustration from an ideal world, we should instead start with the areas of management decision-making and show how these are influenced by the general economic environment in which they must inescapably be made. Underlying economic principles, provided these are strictly relevant, may then be introduced. This indeed is the way economics started; from an observation of the contemporary industrial and commercial scene by eighteenth-century writers like Adam Smith, who generalised from the thousand and one particular cases to create the theory of economics. Today, a book on economics for business executives must be written in terms of consumer booms, investment cycles, unemployment, growth, inflation, money supply, credit

4

squeeze, incomes policy, balance of payments, devaluation, floating exchange rates, and so on.

ECONOMIC BACKGROUND

There are some people in management who try to ignore the economic background factor. This, they argue, is determined by the Government and nothing can be done by businessmen about it. In their planning, they therefore tend to assume that things will more or less continue as they are, unless the Chancellor does something to stop it, and who can be expected to plan for this unknown factor? Others argue that their products are so specialist and technical, serving a restricted market, that they are relatively unaffected by any variations in the level of the activity in the economy as a whole. In some cases this of course is very true, the 'ethical' pharmaceutical market being perhaps the best example. But there are not nearly as many of these unaffected areas and products as is sometimes claimed.

Although it may often appear so to the businessman, the actions of Chancellors are not intended to be either arbitrary or capricious: they are usually a reaction to underlying economic forces. These forces can be identified and their development closely watched. In this way Government restrictive measures may be anticipated and the necessary avoiding action taken in order to mitigate adverse effects. Should the expected Government policies be in the direction of expansion, then the firm can prepare to raise production and stock levels in order to take full and early advantage of the economic upturn when it comes.

BUSINESS DECISION AREAS

Although there are many types of business decision, they are, or should be, all concerned with the same goal, namely profit maximisation. The total amount of profit may be increased by improving the profitability of existing operations, either by cutting costs or increasing prices; or by extending operations, in terms of selling more of existing products or by developing into other areas, in other words by 'growth'. A very large part of management decision-making in the twenty-five years since the Second World War has been concerned with the growth of the firm and its products. This growth has been sought in order to gain the economies that go with size, or quite simply for its own sake, as a means of personal fulfilment for those in command, who have identified themselves closely with the business. Growth may also have been a defensive reaction, to avoid being swallowed up by larger rivals.

SALES EXPANSION

Increased sales of existing products may be achieved because total demand in the economy has increased; or at the expense of competitors, by capturing an increased share of the market. While sales growth by the first method is necessarily linked to the general expansion of the economy, growth by the second method is probably also more easily achieved in such a climate. Market share improvement is very hard to accomplish in a static or contracting market, unless conditions are so bad that competitors are being forced out of business: but at such a low level of activity increased market share may still mean that a firm's total sales volume is no greater, and may even be less. In planning any major sales growth it is therefore better to ensure that the increased marketing expenditures and production build-up coincide with an expansion phase in the economy, or at any rate in that sector of it forming the market. By so doing the highest return per £ of marketing expenditure may be achieved.

Achievement of this correct timing in business planning involves being aware of the key economic indicators. It also requires a knowledge of the character and sequence of the various stages in an expansion phase of the economy. The upturn in demand for consumer goods generally occurs first, followed a year to eighteen months later by increased orders for capital goods. The nature of some consumer goods means that the demand for them normally expands faster or contracts more than the general movement of consumer expenditure; while the more basic items keep fairly closely to the overall consumer expenditure growth rate or, if they are very basic, to the population growth rate.

PRODUCT PLANNING

The total value of sales can be increased by the introduction of new items into a firm's product range. This may, in addition,

6

be motivated by a desire to pull out of contracting traditional markets, or to achieve diversification to guard against the risk of having too many eggs in the one product or market basket. The finding of new products is frequently left to research, development or technical departments to come up with something new. But a more sensible preliminary activity is to study the broad economic and social trends operating in the country, together with Government policy pronouncements. A study of the growth rate of industry sectors also gives some indication of the more rapidly growing industrial markets, as also does an awareness of government regional development policies.

PRODUCTION FACILITIES

In planning expansion of the firm's production facilities, the existence of a cycle in fixed capital formation should be taken into account, since to place orders for new equipment, at the same moment as everyone else, is to risk delay in delivery and possibly higher prices. In the period of slack, after the peak in the investment cycle, equipment can often be obtained much more quickly and with greater certainty of delivery on the due date. If the economy is in a slight recession phase, with a good deal of excess production capacity, second-hand plant can sometimes be obtained quite cheaply, as may factory space.

RAISING CAPITAL

Enlargement of sales volume and production facilities may also be achieved by the take-over of, or merger with, other companies. In the case of take-over, this can obviously be carried out more cheaply at times when ordinary share prices are low, and this again follows the pattern of the economic cycle. When a company requires additional capital, care should be taken in the timing of an issue of new shares, for when ordinary share prices are high, new equity capital can be successfully raised on the basis of a lowish yield. But when the outlook for equities becomes clouded and interest rates are high, then the raising of new money by debentures can place a heavy fixed charge burden on the company's future earnings, particularly if the rate of inflation slackens. With new projects, because of their complexity, having to be planned increasingly far ahead, it should not be difficult to choose the best moment for raising new funds, even if this means going to the market long before the money is actually needed. After all, with Britain's highly developed capital market, particularly for short-term funds, there should be no difficulty in finding interim employment for the money raised.

INDUSTRIAL RELATIONS

In the field of industrial relations, intelligent anticipation by management is also useful, and again can be achieved by economic forecasting. When the economy is expected to enter an expansion phase, then, along with the build-up of stocks, new operatives can be recruited and trained before the labour market becomes tight again. Once the expansion gets well under way, the un-employment percentage will fall progressively, the bargaining power of labour rise accordingly, and therefore in cost-estimating exercises provision should be made for a somewhat faster increase in wage costs. During such times, strike action is likely to be threatened more frequently. Wage demands will also be stimulated by a faster rise in the cost of living (a feature of such periods) and by evidence of rising profits and dividend increases.

Sufficient has perhaps now been said to show that the economic facts of life do have a very definite relevance to the making of business decisions. So far, only the most superficial outline has been given; it is the purpose of later sections to fill in the picture in more detail. When doing so, as much illustration as possible will be taken from contemporary statistics; in this way the theory can clearly be shown to be borne out in practice.

2

Factors of Production:
Land and Labour

Economics is unashamedly an intensely materialistic subject, having little to do with the finer things in life. Instead, it concerns itself almost exclusively with wealth. This makes it for some people a very absorbing subject: it also makes it a highly topical one. In Britain today the maximisation of human happiness is increasingly and unquestioningly equated with the creation of more and more wealth. There has been indeed nothing less than a national obsession with 'growth' in recent years. This desire to create more and more wealth, at an ever-increasing rate, would of course be wholly admirable if the wealth so produced were used to alleviate hunger and misery throughout the world. But this is not in fact the end-use of the greater part of the national product of the advanced countries. It is frequently stipulated that economics is not a moral science: it merely studies the means, passing no judgement as to what should be the ends. This of course can be questioned. In being a party to the means, it is arguable that the economist cannot be completely absolved of responsibility for the ends.

WEALTH

Economics is then the amoral science of wealth. Wealth is anything which is scarce and which people want; and is therefore anything for which they are prepared to pay money. Thus, services as well as goods are embraced within the term 'wealth'. The scope of economics is seen to be even wider when we go on to say that it is concerned with the production, distribution and consumption of wealth: all these activities being measured by money value. Thought of in terms of the wealth-creating unit, namely the firm, this means that the wealth produced is the sales value (on an ex-factory basis) of, for example, the washing machines turned out.

9

This sales value is distributed in payments to suppliers, salaries and wages to the employees, with the residual profit being ploughed back or distributed to shareholders. Suppliers, in turn, will make the same sort of distribution of their sales receipts. Ultimately, the wealth finds its way to those owning the resources required to produce it, namely the land, labour and capital, about which more will be said below. These final recipients of the created wealth will either consume it or invest it, the latter being just a slower consumption process. Thus, all the many forms of economic activity can be categorised as having to do with the creation of wealth, the distribution of wealth produced, and the final consumption of that wealth. Wealth not consumed immediately, but used to create more wealth, is termed 'capital'; but ultimately it too gets consumed or worn out.

FACTORS OF PRODUCTION

The creation of wealth invariably involves bringing together and using what are termed the three factors of production: land, labour and capital. These three single words are a convenient shorthand for natural resources, including the tremendous variety in the location and fertility of land; all the different skills and crafts of labour; the buildings, plant and machinery (fixed capital), as well as materials and stocks (working capital). Every firm employs these three factors, in some form or another and in varying proportions, in its production activity. The person bringing the factors together for this production process used to be termed the 'entrepreneur', although this word is little heard nowadays.

LAND

Land was defined by Ricardo* as the 'original and indestructible powers of the soil'. Cultivated land is therefore not solely land, but a mixture of land, plus the labour expended upon it; together with the capital used to improve fertility, such as fertiliser, or capital used to assist labour, for example, a tractor. For the firm the factor land is usually the site of the factory and offices; that is,

* David Ricardo was an early nineteenth-century economist and a leading member of the 'classical school' of economic thought.

the ground on which the firm's employees work. Land has two characteristics distinguishing it from the other factors of production: It is fixed in supply and it is also immobile. In general land cannot be created, although we could perhaps recognise an exception to this in the case of land reclaimed from the sea. But it could also be argued that the land reclaimed from the sea was there all the time, so that nothing new has really been created. The fixity of supply of land is to some extent got round nowadays by putting more on each square foot of it, by building higher and higher. Nevertheless, ultimately there is a limit to the supply of land in a way that there is not in the case of labour and capital.

The second characteristic of land, namely its immobility, fosters this fixity of supply and scarcity. High prices for land in a certain part of the country cannot attract more land to that area. The immobility of land also means that, if a certain site is uniquely suitable, then the other two factors must move to it. Since the mobility of capital is hardly ever a problem, talk about mobility usually centres on labour.

Payment for the use of the factor land is termed 'rent' and, even where the freehold is owned, in calculating production costs a notional allowance should be made for rent. Because of the fixity of supply of land and the uniqueness of each particular site, the owner of a piece of land has something in the nature of a natural monopoly and rent is therefore sometimes regarded as a 'monopoly' price. This aspect is well illustrated in Britain today by the soaring values of town and suburban properties.

There is now a growing practice whereby firms not only lease land but also the factory premises on it. For many of the larger institutional investors. like insurance companies and private company pension funds, direct investment in property is an attractive alternative to portfolio investment and these institutions are often prepared, sometimes in partnership with developers, to provide office and factory buildings, as well as the land, on a leasehold basis. By this arrangement the factor land, and some of the fixed capital as well, is clearly seen to be supplied to the entrepreneur and therefore to demand its price.

LABOUR

The factor labour is the one of whose existence management is generally most aware. Since it is the 'human' factor, perhaps it is inevitable that it should cause the greatest headaches. Although we talk about labour in general, it is more common in practice to think in terms of various types of labour: for example, manual and clerical, skilled and unskilled, direct and indirect, and even productive and non-productive labour. Similarly, the rewards for these different varieties of labour are given special names: for example, wages, salaries, fees. But whatever name these rewards go by, they are all the price for that particular type of labour and, as we shall see later, like any other price the level is fixed by the interaction of supply and demand in what may be a free, or a less than free, market. The greater the skill and the longer the period, of training required, then the higher is this price likely to be; for in such cases there will usually be in addition an element of scarcity as well as high supply cost. Sometimes this scarcity will be contrived, no less among professional bodies than among skilled and semi-skilled workers. Although this is defended on the grounds of maintaining professional standards, it is often simply protective.

DIVISION OF LABOUR

Modern production processes are usually on the basis of a division of labour into specialised tasks. Instead of making a product from start to finish, today's industrial worker performs only a small part of the total manufacturing process, but does so over a large number of units. On the assembly line an individual worker's role may be no more than a tightening up of half a dozen nuts, but he will do so on many hundreds of units as the line moves past him. The advantages of such a breakdown of the overall labour function into many separate tasks is that it develops skill in the specialist and may make the best use of his natural aptitudes; it certainly saves time not having to shift from one process to another and changing tools; and lastly it makes mechanisation of labour an economic proposition, since the specialist machine in the worker's hands will be almost continuously in use. Disadvantages of the division of labour, especially when carried to extremes, is the monotony it imposes on the worker and destruction of craft pride. On a wider scale there is the vulnerability of the whole factory's operation to a stoppage in any one part of what may be a very long continuous production line, as in the case of the automobile industry. A too rigid adherence by the men themselves to a division of labour gives rise to the problems of over-manning and demarcation disputes.

LABOUR SUPPLY

The supply of labour available to industry and commerce is dependent upon many factors. The basic determinant of growth in the labour force is the underlying rate of increase in the total population, which in Britain in recent years has been around half of a per cent each year. But uneven population distribution between age groups will sometimes cause a faster increase of working population; for example, when birth-rate 'bulges' reach school-leaving age. Such natural growth rate factors are, however, not usually of a sufficiently large magnitude to be significant. More noticeable increases in the supply of labour arise from a change in the net migration position; from more people coming from overseas to work in this country than are leaving it to work abroad. Provided that there are no resulting social problems, particularly in the sphere of housing, such a pool of available foreign labour is economically useful. It can help to prevent a full employment situation generating too much wages-push inflation. The supply of labour in this country may also be increased by any tendency for wives to continue working, or through a greater use by industry of part-time labour—not only female but also retired males.

As the production process becomes complex, more of the factor capital is normally used in conjunction with labour. In this way the available labour supply also becomes less of a limiting factor in the expansion of production. Indeed, sometimes fears begin to be expressed that a too rapid supplanting of labour by capital, such as results from the spread of automation techniques, may render a part of the working population redundant.

PRODUCTIVITY AND WAGES

We have seen how the limiting factor of the actual number of people of working age available can be got round by substituting wherever possible machinery for men. This will also result in the output of each worker in employment being higher, either because with a machine (or a bigger and better one) he can now produce more; or because with a greater utilisation of machines the total output of the factory can be increased with the same number of men, or with a reduced number. In all these cases the total value of output divided by the number of workers will give a resultant higher output per man than previously and this output per man is what is termed 'productivity'. (More sophisticatedly it may be defined as output per *manhour*.) There are, however, some subtle distinctions as to the ways in which productivity can be increased, and such distinctions are not always appreciated.

In few cases is the worker asked to work any harder as a result of the introduction of new machinery. although he may have to exercise greater skill. The use of machinery may render working conditions more or less pleasant: the old coachbuilders probably had better working conditions than those existing in our motor factories today; on the other hand, conditions in our modern chemical factories are far superior to those of fifty years ago. When a man is given a machine, or a better machine, he may as we have said be called upon to exercise greater skill in using it and for this reason he has some claim on the greater output achieved. But he does not have a claim to all the increased output, because extra capital had to be provided in the form of the machine and this has to be paid for. There is therefore a problem of allocating the fruits of the extra output among the factors contributing to it. If no extra space is required then of course the factor land will get nothing and the extra output has then only to be divided between labour and capital. But how is the extra skill which the workers are called upon to exercise to be valued? Despite the development of job evaluation techniques, it is true to say that there is still no completely satisfactory way of doing this, and indeed in all the talk about productivity nowadays it is quite obvious that no very precise calculation is envisaged by the parties concerned. Trade union officials are apt to argue quite simply that if productivity goes up by 5 per cent, then wages should also be increased by 5 per cent. If there is any attempt at all to make a more intricate calculation than this, it is usually the reward of capital which is calculated first, since this can more readily be done. Approaching the problem from this angle means of course that the 'residual' in the productivity increase goes to labour, although traditionally profit has always been regarded as the 'residual' reward.

A calculation of capital's share in the increased productivity can be attempted first of all by breaking down the cost of the new machine over its expected life, or more usually over the number of years which the Inland Revenue is prepared to agree that it may be written off. Secondly, provision must be made for some reasonable return on capital employed. When the share of the factor capital has been calculated in this way, what is left of the additional production created may be paid out in higher wages. If there is very little left, the workers' representatives will undoubtedly prefer the relatively crude method of granting to their members the same percentage increase as was achieved in improved productivity. In any case, it must be admitted that the more precise calculation of what capital should get is not really as cut-and-dried as it would appear. It contains, for example, certain assumptions that might easily be challenged by the workers' representatives. The depreciated life of a machine, as agreed by the Inland Revenue, is usually in practice much shorter than the machine's eventual working life: but to say this one also has to take a view on obsolescence, as well as physical wear and tear. It is also possible that the 'accepted' return on capital employed may be unacceptable from the workers' point of view—it may be regarded as being too high. What is a reasonable return on capital employed is not something about which many opinions are volunteered.

There are occasions when a machine is introduced which almost entirely replaces the worker; for example, the automated engine block line in a car factory. In such cases it cannot be represented that by being prepared to learn a new skill the productivity of any particular worker has been raised and that he is therefore entitled to some share in the extra product. Indeed the activities of the other workers (that is, other than those who were entirely replaced by the automated machinery) may be completely unaffected: they may continue to use the same machines and the output from these machines may remain unaltered. Nevertheless, by the conventional method of calculating it, productivity would have risen. So, if there is not to be a good deal of confusion and disagreement, some other way of measuring productivity must be devised. The present method smacks too much of the labour theory of value,* since it expresses output increase solely in terms of one of the factors of production, namely labour. Indeed, productivity has become something to which lip-service is paid in order to make wage demands appear respectable. Productivity thus becomes not an end in itself but simply a means of obtaining higher earnings. This attitude is laid bare in years when industrial earnings rise very much faster than productivity. There are in any case large areas of industry and commerce where any sort of productivity measurement is wellnigh impossible and where, therefore, increases in the reward to the factor labour must be related to something other than productivity.

MOBILITY OF LABOUR

It has already been noted that land is a completely immobile factor. We must now consider the extent of the mobility of labour. On the face of it, it would seem that, especially in this age of easier communications, the mobility of labour should pose no problem. However, because of the three it is the 'human' factor, its movement is subject to all sorts of restraints. Probably the most important of these is the understandable disinclination of the worker to uproot himself and his family and move to a new social environment; for doing so interrupts his children's schooling and for himself and his wife involves the building up of new friendships. This disinclination towards geographical movement (except at holiday time) has been further reinforced in the post-war period by the housing shortage. But even when new housing is provided there is still frequently an unwillingness to leave 'the valley'. In addition to these social factors, labour mobility between trades and areas is hindered by lack of capacity to learn a new trade, particularly among workers in their fifties, or through lack of training facilities. There may also be union regulations limiting entry into a particular trade.

---

* Ricardo and Marx believed that the value, and the price, of goods depended upon the amount of labour expended in their production. Capital was regarded merely as 'stored-up' labour.

REGIONAL UNEMPLOYMENT

Because of these restraints on the mobility of labour there is in consequence considerable unevenness in the labour supply throughout the country. Certain trades and industries are always short of skilled labour, while in others labour is 'laid off' as soon as there is any downturn in the economy. In some geographical areas the unemployment percentage is always well below the national average; in other areas unemployment is high even at times when throughout the country as a whole there is effectively full employment. In a year of relatively high national unemployment regional unemployment percentages can range from 1·5 per cent to 8 per cent; while in a full employment year the percentage still ranges from 1 per cent to 6 per cent.

If workers cannot, or will not, move to places where there is work for them, then the alternative is to move industry to the areas of relatively high unemployment in order to reduce it. The object of regional development policy is to bring about a more even spread of employment opportunities throughout the country; so that a given percentage of unemployment nationally will not mean extremely high rates in some parts of the country, with still comparatively low rates in others. If this can be done it will then be possible, without undue hardship, to run the economy on a basis of a slightly higher level of unemployment and so lessen the forces of wage-push inflation.

COLLECTIVE BARGAINING

Just as the owners of the other two factors have the right to offer, or not to offer, them for sale; so the worker has the right to offer or withhold his labour. This right is not in these modern times exercised on an individual basis, but is done collectively, as part of the process of collective bargaining. The workers' agents in this bargaining are their trade union officials. Of the total labour force of 23 million workers, just under 10 million of them are organised in just over five hundred trade unions. When, in a particular firm or industry, the workers act in concert regarding the terms upon which they will offer their labour, they are in effect creating a sole supplier or monopolistic situation. They do so on the grounds that they themselves are faced with almost a sole buyer situation for their labour: there being many thousand workers facing only one or at the most a few employers. If the workers were to act individually in wage negotiations, they would be in the impossibly weak position of many competing sellers of labour but only one or two dominant buyers. This situation is also of course affected by the other employment opportunities there may, or may not, be in the district.

The collective bargaining process is primarily aimed at improving the workers' conditions; so that it is their representatives who generally take the initiative in opening negotiations. But in driving the bargain, the employers may also take the opportunity to obtain agreement on the introduction of certain changes in working practices. The degree of success attained by either side in these negotiations will be influenced by their relative bargaining strengths at that point in time, and this in turn will depend very much upon the prevailing economic climate. When unemployment is low and new workers hard to get, the bargaining power of labour is at its strongest. Times of full employment are also times during which business is good: employers can well afford to offer less resistance to wage increases, and may even be prepared to bid against one another for scarce labour. The large amount of overtime working in periods of high demand also boosts industrial earnings. If the employers do not yield to the workers' demands, strike action, both official and unofficial, may be more readily threatened, and just as readily feared by employers, who will not wish to lose production and markets. Conversely, when unemployment is high, employers will not give in so easily to wage demands, and indeed may not be able to afford to. At the same time the workers will be more fearful of losing their jobs and may not be quite so ready to threaten strike action.

PHILLIPS CURVE

What is known as the 'Phillips curve' represents in graph form this relationship between the level of unemployment and the rate of change in money wages, the latter being greater when the former is lower. In other words, there is a certain trade-off between unemployment and the rate of wages-push inflation. In most recent years, however, with a marked rise in the level of unemployment, but no deceleration in the growth rate of industrial earnings (indeed quite the reverse) it has been questioned whether the Phillips curve still applies. But what appears to have happened is that the existence of unemployed outside the factory gate has become less of an inhibiting influence upon the wage demands of those still in employment inside the factory gate. With higher unemployment and social benefits introduced during the second half of the sixties, the fear of being unemployed has not been as great; and due to the same factor there is also a greater preparedness to go on strike in support of wage demands. Union practices and workers' solidarity nowadays prevent the unemployed posing much of a threat to those still in employment. It has however been argued that these developments do not invalidate the Phillips curve but merely shift it upwards; so that unemployment has now to be that much higher to achieve a given reduction in the rate of wages growth.

Looking at the years from 1960 to 1967, the correlation between low percentages for unemployment and high rates of increase in industrial earnings can be clearly seen. The incidence of strikes does not, however, fit into the pattern quite so neatly; for example, the peak level of industrial stoppages in 1962 occurred in a year of fairly high unemployment, although the average duration of stoppage was a good deal shorter than in previous years. From 1968 onwards the number of strikes increased markedly, despite the rising level of unemployment. Perhaps the explanation for the pattern of industrial stoppages, in relation to unemployment and the rise in industrial earnings, lies in the fact that when labour is in its strongest position to strike, it does not need to do so, for the employers are quite ready to grant wage increases. When unemployment is high, the strike stands less chance of success; the employers, being quite happy to reduce their wages bill when the demand for their products is slack, are more prepared to have a show-down with labour, and the unions will often unwisely accept the challenge. Another feature of such periods is an attempt by the government to enforce some sort of wages restraint, and this not only encourages the employers to take a tougher line but also incites the workers into making their protest against such a policy by taking industrial action.

UNEMPLOYMENT, WAGES AND STRIKES

	1960	1961	1962	1963	1964	1965	1966	1967	1968	1969	1970
Unemployment: Percentage of labour force	1·6	1·5	2·0	2·5	1·6	1·4	1·5	2·4	2·4	2·4	2·6
Industrial Earnings: Percentage increase over previous year	8	6½	4	3½	8	8	7	3	8½	8	14
Hourly Wage Rates: Percentage increase over previous year	4	6½	4½	4	5	6½	6½	4	6½	5	10
Industrial Stoppages: Workers involved ('000)	814	774	4,420	590	871	869	530	731	2,255	1,654	1,775
Working days lost ('000)	3,024	3,046	5,798	1,755	2,277	2,925	2,398	2,787	4,690	6,846	10,970

Source: Monthly Digest
Annual Abstract of Statistics
H.M.S.O.

Factors of Production: Land and Labour

WAGE DRIFT

It will be noticed from the table that the rise in industrial earnings in expansionist years, like 1960 and 1964, is usually much greater than the increase in hourly wage rates. This is not solely the result of greater overtime working; it also reflects the willingness of employers to give special incentive and overtime payments, as well as bonuses, in order to retain or attract scarce labour. The extent to which average hourly earnings, ruling out the effect of overtime, exceed average hourly wage rates is termed 'wage drift'. The degree of this 'drift' is calculated twice a year by the Department of Employment and shows the position at April and October in relation to the same month in the previous year. The extent of wage drift over the past ten years can be seen in the table and it will be noticed that wage drift was greatest in the years of low unemployment and rapid industrial expansion, namely 1960 and 1964/65. The year 1969 was, however, an exception to this rule, being one of slow growth but with a high degree of wage drift.

INDUSTRIAL RELATIONS ACT

Following an extremely militant period of exorbitant wage claims, supported by a record number of strikes, the Conservative Government decided to enact in 1971 an Industrial Relations Bill. The Government's broad objective was to carry out a widespread reform of industrial relations in Britain, providing a framework of law such as existed in other countries, to better protect the interests of the community as a whole, as well as individuals. Workers have the right to belong or not to belong to a union and in general 'closed shops' can no longer be operated. Unions have a right to recognition by employers, but, unless registered, lose their legal immunities. The Act made legally enforceable all agreements arrived at through collective bargaining, unless the parties specifically desire otherwise and there is selective statutory enforcement of procedural agreements. Unions' rules are vetted by the Registrar of Trade Unions and individual workers may complain to him about treatment by their union. The Act lists 'unfair industrial practices', giving those injured a right of compensation. Workers are safeguarded against unfair dismissal. There is a system of industrial relations courts: problems at lower

WAGE DRIFT

Percentage Increase over Corresponding Month in Previous Year

	April	October
1960	+2·0	+1·8
1961	+0·3	+0·5
1962	+1·1	+0·2
1963	+0·4	+1·3
1964	+1·6	+2·4
1965	+2·7	+2·2
1966	+1·7	+0·9
1967	+0·3	−0·3
1968	−0·9	+0·3
1969	+1·5	+2·5

Source: Department of Employment Gazette.

levels are dealt with by Industrial Tribunals; higher matters come within the province of the National Industrial Relations Court which has High Court status. To help operate the Act the previously set up Royal Commission became a statutory Commission on Industrial Relations. Lastly, under the Act the Government can call for a cooling-off period whenever an industrial dispute threatens to create a national emergency and in these and other circumstances unions may be required to ballot their membership before taking strike action. A Code of Industrial Relations Practice was published to give general guidance on the conduct of labour relations.

3

Factors of Production: Capital and Enterprise, Combining the Factors

CAPITAL

Capital is the most mobile and probably also the most impersonal of the factors of production. As has already been said, capital is wealth that is not consumed immediately, but which is used to create more wealth. Capital raises the productivity of labour and improves the fertility of land: capital is the machine in the hands of the worker or the fertiliser on the land. Capital may be regarded as the youngest of the three factors of production. Originally, there was only labour and land, but as man increasingly set aside part of his activity to tasks other than those satisfying immediate consumption needs, such as making weapons, implements, etc., so a store of capital grew up. Nowadays, we tend to think of capital as money, and indeed this is how most of our capital originates. Instead of spending all their money, people save part of it and lend this either directly or indirectly to industry, where it is used to purchase new machinery or materials or hire labour.

SAVING

The supply of capital depends on the level of saving in our society, but this saving can assume many guises, some of which may not immediately be recognised as saving. If the Government uses tax revenue to finance a capital project then this is a form of compulsory saving. If the money for the capital project is instead obtained by the sale of government stocks to the public, this is a more usual form of saving, in much the same way as when people buy stocks and shares to provide capital for companies. In addition to private persons, there are also large institutional investors, like insurance companies and pension funds, who in

24

fact provide a great part of the capital used by industry today. But the funds invested by these institutions have their origin in the contractual saving of the ordinary members of the public, through insurance premiums and pension fund contributions. The insurance companies and the pension funds are therefore merely standing between the savers and the ultimate users of capital, and for this reason they are often referred to as 'financial intermediaries'. The banking system also lends to industry and commerce by way of advances, although this is primarily intended to cover working capital needs. But by far the greater part of the capital used by companies comes from their own retained profits, through provision for depreciation or by distributing less than the possible maximum to shareholders.

The table below shows the sources of capital funds used by industrial and commercial companies in 1970:

	£ million
Undistributed income	2,762
Capital transfers (net)	511*
Bank lending	1,078
Other loans and mortgages	212
Capital issues by quoted companies (net)	226
	4,789

Source: Financial Statistics, H.M.S.O.

RISK AND LOAN CAPITAL

Although the capital supplied by savers in the form of money is as such homogeneous (to an extent to which the other two factors by their very nature can never be), nevertheless the terms on which the savings are offered (and of course accepted) can vary considerably. Some savers are prepared to lend for a considerable period and thus supply 'long-term capital'. Others will lend only on a short-term basis and such saving satisfies mainly working capital needs. Often, the longer the lending, the greater is the degree of uncertainty and, allied to this, the degree of risk. Risk can also be a factor on its own and savers do supply capital (or the money with which capital assets can be bought) on the basis of varying degrees of risk. Some savers may wish to supply capital

* Including £473 investment grants.

only on a secured basis (for example, a secured loan stock) at a fixed rate of interest, with repayment of the sum lent at a certain specified time in the future. At the opposite extreme, other savers may be prepared to lend on the basis of a share in the equity (ownership); there being no guarantee either of income or that they will ever get their money back. Savers lend on such a basis when they purchase ordinary shares on the Stock Exchange. The reward for providing risk capital is, on average, a higher return than on the basis of fixed interest investment; but the risk of loss is always present to a greater or lesser extent, depending on how well or how badly the company is doing. We should not forget, however, that the provider of loan capital also faces a risk: that inflation will considerably reduce the real value of the annual fixed interest payment and the repaid capital sum. Indeed, it is because of this that in the post-war years, with an average annual rate of inflation of 4 per cent, fixed interest stocks have been a very cheap way of financing company operations. Over the years, with prices and profits geared to inflation, the real burden of fixed interest charges has been reduced.

INTEREST AND PROFIT

For each of these two types of capital, 'risk' and the more secure 'loan', there are distinct rewards. The person who lends on the basis of a guaranteed eventual return of his capital, and in the meantime a fixed annual income, receives interest as the reward for his type of capital. Where there is an element of risk, then the reward for success is 'profit' and for failure 'loss'. The factor capital has therefore two types of reward, namely interest and profit. But profit is not just compensation for running a risk: it is also regarded as the reward for enterprise. In our modern circumstances this may not seem to accord with the reality. The ordinary shareholders of the company are certainly its owners; they appoint the directors and have a legal claim on the profits and assets after prior charges have been satisfied. But by no stretch of the imagination can the ordinary shareholders of the modern large public company be regarded as exhibiting 'enterprise'. The shareholder's role today is almost as passive as that of the supplier of loan capital.

The allocation of profit as the reward for enterprise is more readily understood and accepted when the active directors running the company also have a controlling interest in it; so that substantially the profit goes to them rather than to the passive shareholders. In the earlier stages of our industrial history this was the basis upon which the greater part of industry was financed and operated. The man of enterprise (the entrepreneur) came along and with his own capital and, in addition, some borrowed capital (but borrowed on such terms as to retain for him a controlling interest) he hired or bought the factors of production and started up his business. If the business was successful, the bulk of the profits went to the entrepreneur as the reward for his enterprise. Those who lent him the money were still, even in those days, not actively participating in the enterprise, although the element of risk was certainly there and to a greater degree than today. With the modern large 'blue chip' companies the element of risk has been considerably reduced. However, since the saver supplies capital through the purchase of the companies' shares on the Stock Exchange, and since share prices may fluctuate in that market, then the saver is in this sense subject to an element of risk, which need not in fact always be directly related to the fortunes of the particular company concerned.

ENTERPRISE

Some people like to think of enterprise as a separate fourth factor of production. The difficulty in doing so lies in the fact that there is no distinct separate reward for it. In the case of the entrepreneur, who supplies the bulk of the capital himself, his reward, as we have seen, is a share of the profits as a major shareholder; he may in addition pay himself a salary as the senior executive. Thus, his total remuneration is a combination of the recognised rewards for capital and labour. But, in the larger companies of today, those exhibiting the enterprise and taking the decisions are often the salaried executive directors and senior managers, whose rewards are directors' fees and salaries. The owners of such firms, namely the shareholders, do not participate in the decision-making, which nowadays represents the enterprise function. Nevertheless, the residual profits belong to the shareholders, although part of it is usually held back by the directors, with the approval of the shareholders, to provide part of the firm's need for finance to replace the company's worn out or obsolete capital assets.

COMBINING THE FACTORS

Having described the nature of the three factors of production, we now examine some of the features arising from their combination in the production process. The initial 'mix' of factors is of course basically determined by technical and indeed physical considerations. There is a certain minimum of each required, in a certain ratio to one another, to do the job at all. The production of a quantity of an article will require one machine (capital) one operator (labour), both standing on so many square feet of covered space (land and capital). To achieve a greater output either the number of such production units must be increased, and in so doing certain additional economies of large-scale production may be achieved; or more of one particular factor must be used in the basic production unit. The method of larger scale production will be considered later, when dealing with the growth of the firm.

LAW OF DIMINISHING RETURNS

The second way of trying to achieve greater output, namely to increase the amount of some of the factors in the 'mix', brings us to the first of our economic 'laws'. Such 'laws' are simply generalisations based on observation of what happens most frequently in certain circumstances, unless there are extraneous factors operating to prevent it, as indeed there often are. When more of one factor is applied to the production process, with the quantity of the other factor or factors remaining unchanged, there will almost certainly be some increase in output. This increase may, particularly at first, be as much as or even more than that which the original equal quantity of that factor produced. But further additional applications of that factor will eventually give a decreasing extra amount of production. This tendency is described in economics as 'the law of diminishing returns or increasing costs'. It may help to accept that this should be so, if one remembers that for each additional unit of one factor there is less of the other factors to go with it.

The law of diminishing returns is traditionally illustrated by reference to the case of agriculture, although it applies equally in the industrial situation. For ease of explanation, we will follow custom by taking the agricultural case first and then consider examples of the operation of the law in the more usual industrial circumstances we live in today. Consider therefore first of all the case of a piece of land, the working of which enables one man to produce a crop to the value of £100. A higher value crop, or even more of the same crop, might be obtained from the same piece of land if our first man is joined by a second in the cultivation of the land. The value of agricultural output might then be £200 or even £210; if the latter is the case the second unit of labour will have brought about an output increase *greater* than the value of the output achieved by the first, and we therefore say that the law of increasing returns is operating. However, if the total value of output from the land was £180 as a result of the employment of the second man, then the law of diminishing returns would be operating.

So far, we have dealt solely with the factor labour in combination with the factor land in an increasing proportion. The law also operates with the application of increasing doses of capital to the same piece of land. The capital may, for example, be applied in the form of fertiliser. If the one man working the land, which produces £100 of crop, applies fertiliser he may raise the output to £120; but a second and equal dose of fertiliser may cause output to rise to only £130. Instead of thinking of capital in terms of fertiliser, we can also think of it in terms of machinery and equipment, thus coming nearer to the industrial example we will next consider. The purchase of a cultivator may raise the value of output from a piece of land by £50, but the purchase of a small tractor, costing twice as much, may raise the total value of the output by only £75; and not twice as much as would be required for the increase to be proportional in relation to the extra expenditure of capital. Thus, the law of diminishing returns in relation to land can be summed up by stating that the more labour and capital are applied to a fixed piece of land, the smaller ultimately becomes the increase in the crop obtained from it.

As already said, this law of diminishing returns also applies in the factory situation. But here the fixed factor is not necessarily always land, as it usually must be in the case of agriculture. If you give a cotton mill operative more machines to look after, the area of mill space that he has to supervise will also be larger, so that both capital and land are being increased in relation to labour. You can keep on giving a worker more and more mechanical aids to do his job and thus increase his output; but after a certain time the rate at which his output further increases becomes less per extra £50 worth of capital, in the form of mechanical aids you put at his disposal. The question then arises: when do you stop providing more of the factors in the 'mix'? As a first answer, it would seem that it was worthwhile doing so as long as the sales value of the extra amount produced exceeded the cost of the additional factor. Here we come close to the theory of marginal costs which, however, it will be more appropriate to deal with later when we talk about pricing.

Let us just note before concluding this section that the answer to the question: 'When do we stop applying more of the factors of production?' is not as simple as the theory of marginal costs. It may be that using the factor elsewhere will give a higher return and this brings us into the realm of 'opportunity cost'. The theory of 'opportunity cost' suggests that the real cost of using a factor of production in any particular activity is what it would have earned had it been employed elsewhere. The level of opportunity cost is therefore what would have been earned by the factor in its most remunerative alternative employment. This probably seems a rather nebulous concept, but in fact we often use it in everyday life, as for example when we decide not to employ our capital in a certain project because it will give no higher return than would possibly be obtained by investing the money in stocks and shares.

4

Broad Sectors of the Economy

NATIONAL WORKSHOP

So far most of Part One has been spent in describing the basic ingredients of the production process and introducing some of the principles operating in it. In this remaining chapter, we will look at the overall shape of the economy. In doing so it will become clear that, in all that has been said so far about the factors of production, we have not been dealing with mere vague theoretical concepts. To prove that this is so, it is now possible for us to leave the world of abstraction and to identify these factors at work in the national workshop. The amount of each factor employed, what in combination they produce, how this is distributed; all these things can be put in concrete terms, with the aid of official government statistics.

THE NATION'S FACTORS OF PRODUCTION

We start by looking at the magnitudes of the resources available in this country for the production of goods and services, the total value of which is currently £42,000 million. To produce this vast amount, we have, out of our total population of 56 million, a working population of just under half that amount, namely 25 million people, leaving out of account those in the armed services. Within this work force, employers and self-employed are just under 2 million, while 23 million are employees. Women now account for about one-third of the working population. The total wages and salaries bill for the work force comes to £33,000 million, including just over £3,000 million for self-employed persons.

Turning now to the factor land, in this country there are nearly 60 million acres or 93,000 square miles of it, leaving out of account inland waters which cover 750,000 acres or 1,200 square miles. This gives about one acre per head of total population, or two acres per head of working population. It is difficult to give a value figure for the country's total supply of the factor land. Much of our land provides the site for houses and factories and any figures available naturally relate to the combined value, and not to site value alone. Mr. Jack Revell* gave his estimated values in 1961 for land as £2,360 million, dwellings (including land) as £25,468 million and other land and buildings at £22,759 million.

Since capital can assume a much greater variety of shapes and forms than either labour or land, often being combined with the latter, a global figure for this factor is probably about the hardest to get. Revell put the total value of physical assets (including land) in 1961 at around £80,000 million.† Since the output of goods and services at that time was £24,000 million, this is equivalent to a 30 per cent return on capital employed. When compared with the average return on capital employed achieved by companies, this may seem to be a somewhat high rate and suggests that the estimate for the total value of physical assets may unavoidably be on the conservative side.

NATIONAL INCOME

The value of goods and services produced over a given period (usually a year) by the factors of production, and exchanged for money, is called the national income. The country's national income can be worked out in three ways:

(1) By adding up all the incomes received by the factors of production for producing the goods and services—*the incomes method.*
(2) From the total amount spent in buying goods and services—*the expenditure method.*
(3) By adding together the value of what is produced by various industries—*the output method.*

The major categories of factor incomes under the first method are: wages and salaries of employees, together with those of

---

* *The Wealth of a Nation,* Jack Revell, Cambridge University Press, 1967.

† Later work provided a more up-to-date figure of nearly £138,000 million for total physical assets in 1966. See 'National balance sheets and national accounting – a progress report', Jack Revell and Alan R. Roe, *Economic Trends,* H.M.S.O., May 1971.

self-employed; trading profits of private sector companies and surpluses earned by undertakings in the public sector, like public corporations, nationalised industries, etc.; and lastly rent. Other forms of income, such as social benefits, pension, dividends, etc. are excluded since they are 'transfer payments' from the incomes of others and therefore already included.

By the expenditure method of estimating national income we take the total spent on goods and services for consumption and for investment (that is, for creating more wealth). Ordinary private consumption is termed 'consumers' expenditure'; that by national and local government is labelled in the national income statistics 'public authorities' consumption'. Again investment may be either private or public sector, and be in respect of machinery, factory buildings or houses, spending on these being known as 'fixed capital formation'; or if in the form of raw materials and stocks of semi- or finished goods, are regarded as 'investment in stocks'. When expenditure on British-made consumer or capital goods is by overseas buyers, then this is covered in the export figure: imports are deducted.

The last of the three methods of calculating national income is to take the sum of the value of industry products. Under this method it is only the value added by each industry that is summated; the cost of materials and labour supplied by other industries or imported from abroad is subtracted from final sales value.

The totals for national income derived from each of these three methods should be the same, but due to unavoidable inaccuracies and omissions in the vast network of national accounting a 'residual error' item has to be added to square up the totals. From these national accounting exercises three concepts can be derived: GDP, GNP and NNP. *Gross domestic product* is the total of goods and services actually produced in the country, valued on the basis of the prices at which they are sold, and therefore including purchase tax and customs and excise duties, but excluding subsidies. To get 'GDP at factor cost', indirect taxes are deducted, but subsidies added. This gives a closer approximation to what the producer actually receives and is an appropriate basis on which to calculate trends in domestic unit costs of production. Since Britain has substantial overseas investments, the income enjoyed by its citizens does not derive solely from domestic output. There must also be included interest, profits and dividends received from abroad to give *gross national product* at factor cost. When gauging national income in terms of the flows of goods and services we must take into account the extent by which capital assets are being worn out in producing it: in other words, the extent of capital consumption or depreciation. Deducting this from GNP gives *net national product* or national income.

NATIONAL INCOME 1970
(approximate figures)

£s million

INCOME METHOD		EXPENDITURE METHOD	
Income from employment	30,400	Consumers' expenditure	31,100
Income from self-employment	3,200	Public authorities' consumption	9,000
Gross trading profits of companies	5,000	Gross fixed capital formation	8,700
Surpluses of public enterprises	1,500	Value of physical increase in stocks	500
Rent	3,000	Exports of goods and services	10,900
TOTAL DOMESTIC INCOMES	43,100	TOTAL FINAL EXPENDITURE AT MARKET PRICES	60,200
less stock appreciation	−900	less import of goods and services	−10,600
Residual error	−200	GROSS DOMESTIC PRODUCT AT MARKET PRICES	49,600
		less taxes on expenditure	−8,500
		Subsidies	900
GROSS DOMESTIC PRODUCT AT FACTOR COST	42,000	....	42,000
Net property income from abroad	500	....	500
GROSS NATIONAL PRODUCT AT FACTOR COST	42,500	....	42,500
less capital consumption	−4,100	....	−4,100
NATIONAL INCOME	38,400	....	38,400

Source: National Income and Expenditure, H.M.S.O.

SECTORS OF THE ECONOMY

There are several possible ways of splitting up the economy into major divisions. It can for example be divided into the public sector (that is, central and local Government, including state undertakings) and the private sector (companies owned by private individuals, including shareholders). Today about 40 per cent of our total national economic activity is in the public sector, with

60 per cent in the private sector, and thus we have what is termed a 'mixed' economy. The state-owned 'nationalised industries' are in the main either heavy basic industries, like coal and steel, or the public utility type like gas, electricity, railways, etc. In most cases the state undertaking has a monopoly, but in some areas, like airways and road services, it competes with private enterprise.

The total production activity may also be broken down in terms of goods and services and the table below shows the extent of the contribution of the major industries and economic activities towards the total national output of goods and services. It will be seen that the value of services produced is nearly as great as that of goods. This is a normal condition for an advanced country, whose citizens spend just as much on service items as they do on basic goods items, such as food and clothing.

CONTRIBUTIONS OF MAJOR INDUSTRIES TO GNP

GOODS	£ Thousand Million
Manufacturing	13·3
Construction	2·6
Agriculture, forestry and fishing	1·2
Gas, electricity and water	1·4
Mining and quarrying	0·7
	19·2
SERVICES	
Distributive trades	4·2
Public services*	4·3
Transport and communication	3·3
Insurance, banking and finance	1·3
Other services	5·1
	18·2

Source: National Income and Expenditure, H.M.S.O.

Goods can be further split into extractive, capital goods and consumer goods industries. The first two categories are what are

* Public administration, defence, health and education.

often referred to as 'heavy industry'. The capital goods industries produce our stock of national capital: that part of wealth set aside to produce more wealth for the future. In the main these descriptions are self-explanatory, but in the case of the division into consumer goods and capital goods there often arises difficulty when classifying a particular industry. There are, for example, firms which sell not directly to the consumer, but to another industry. However, the products of some of these firms can hardly be regarded as capital equipment, being in the nature of light materials, although they can be regarded as supplying working capital items. In some cases the same product may equally be sold direct to the consumer, or to another industry. The solution to this problem of classification may be to restrict the designation 'capital goods' to the traditional heavy industries, such as iron and steel, engineering and shipbuilding; and to classify everything else as consumer goods, with the word 'consumer' embracing industrial consumers as well as the ordinary private consumer.

The work force of 23 million is spread over the broad sectors of industry and commerce as shown in the table below. It will be seen that only 39 per cent of the labour force is actually employed in manufacturing, while 45 per cent is taken up by service indus-

DISTRIBUTION OF NATIONAL WORK FORCE

		Million
Manufacturing		9·0
Services and utilities		10·4
Transport and communications	1·6	
Distributive trades	2·8	
Catering and hotels	0·6	
Financial, professional and		
scientific services	3·7	
Miscellaneous services	1·3	
Gas, electricity and water	0·4	
Construction		1·5
Mining and quarrying		0·4
Agriculture, fishing and forestry		0·4
Government—national and local		1·4
		23·1

Source: Monthly Digest of statistics, H.M.S.O.

tries. Although, as has already been pointed out, this large 'service' element in the total economic activity is a normal feature of an advanced country, nevertheless in the case of Britain such a development is not without its dangers to the balance of payments position. Services tend by their very nature to be more for home consumption and less exportable than goods; so that too great a 'services' activity means that the economy is inevitably less geared to exporting. The Selective Employment Tax introduced in 1966 was an attempt to encourage some correction of this imbalance in the proportion of the labour force employed in the supply of services as opposed to goods.

HOW RESOURCES ARE ALLOCATED

Having seen how our resources are distributed over the various industrial sectors and the contribution of each of these sectors to the national product, one might wonder how this all comes about. How do the factors of production find their way to these various industries and how do the industries themselves know what, and how much of it, to produce? Is there a master planner behind the scenes controlling it all, or does it just happen?

THE PRICE MECHANISM

Today, of course, it is a bit of both. The master planner is present in the Government. Although there is still about 60 per cent of the economy which is left to private enterprise, its activities are also increasingly being influenced by the Government through fiscal measures or through the 'little neddies'. By and large, the private sector is still, however, relatively unplanned in any overall sense. Before the Government started to play such a predominant role in our economic affairs, the system did seem to work, almost of its own accord, with a sort of inbuilt automatic pilot. This automatic pilot or regulator was the price mechanism, which by Adam Smith* was almost deified as the 'invisible hand' controlling our economic destinies.

The starting point under the pricing mechanism was human needs and wants and the willingness to pay a price for the goods

* Adam Smith was an eighteenth-century economist and author of the famous *Wealth of Nations*.

and services necessary to satisfy them. This willingness to pay a price attracted the attention of producers or entrepreneurs and induced them to supply goods and services at these prices, since they could make a profit by doing so. The entrepreneur in turn bid for the factors of production at a level of price which allowed for a margin under that which the consumer was willing to pay, so that he made a profit. If the consumer wanted more of the product, he offered a higher price; and if he wanted less he lowered his price, or more probably he reduced his purchases. This in turn caused the entrepreneur to increase or reduce his call upon the factors of production, by increasing or reducing what he was prepared to pay for them. The preparedness on the part of the consumer to pay a higher price usually initially, at any rate, meant a higher profit for the producer and this was his incentive to produce more. Thus price was what rationed the national resources: the price the consumer was prepared to pay and the price, therefore, which the producer in turn could offer to the factors of production. This seemingly theoretically perfect system did not, of course, always work out in practice, as the widespread depression of the 1930s showed.

There were some essential lubricants of the pricing mechanism which had to be present for it to operate efficiently as a self-correcting mechanism. These prior conditions were free competition (as a safeguard against exploitation of the consumer by the producer) and an absence of restrictive practices, together with a high degree of mobility of the factors of production. It was these conditions which gave the pricing mechanism its flexibility and when they were absent, the resultant rigidities often threw up widespread unemployment and unused resources, alongside still unsatisfied human wants.

The human needs which started the whole economic process going had to be backed by purchasing power or else the pricing mechanism would not work. This is what Keynes meant by 'effective demand'. When there was a shortfall in available purchasing power, production exceeded demand and had to be cut-back. This in itself, through reducing employment and incomes, caused a further reduction in purchasing power. So a vicious spiral was set up, which could bring the economy down to a very low level of activity, at which it stayed until something

—possibly an increase in Government spending or war, or recovery of business expectations—came along to generate incomes and employment once more.

The exponents of the pricing mechanism argued that the 'locking' of the automatic pilot on to a downward course resulted from imperfections, rather than from a failure of the system itself. They argued that if demand for a product fell, the ability to make a reduction in price in order to stimulate demand again, or to find new markets, was sometimes restricted by a refusal of the factors of production, and especially labour, to accept a reduction in their price or to be moved elsewhere. In such circumstances the factors might prefer the level of output to fall permanently, and they might even go on strike. In both cases there would be a fall in their purchasing power, which would add to the downward trend in demand. The labour released by the cut-back in production might be unable or unwilling to seek employment elsewhere, in other words, there might not be present the essential ingredient of mobility. The spending power of this section in the community would therefore drop to the level which their 'dole' and savings (if any) could support. This would have a chain reaction effect on the level of employment and incomes in other parts of the economy. If such were the pattern of events, then the blame could not be placed on the pricing system itself; but instead upon the rigidities and inflexibilities of some of the participants in it. However, it can also be argued that if, for its perfect operation, the price mechanism has to have conditions which are unlikely to prevail in practice, then this is grounds for departing from such a system.

STATE INTERVENTION

The alternative to leaving everything to the natural operation of the pricing mechanism is to have varying degrees of state intervention. Government action may be directed at helping the pricing mechanism operate as it should do, by adding the essential oil and removing the grit. Alternatively, government policies may be aimed at dispensing with the operation of the price mechanism, if not entirely, at least from a substantial section of the economy. Government policies which help the pricing mechanism to function more perfectly are those aimed at increasing competition:

D

by attacking monopolies and restrictive practices, or by lowering tariff barriers and thus bringing international competition into play, or by encouraging consumer associations. The mobility of the factors of production may be fostered by retraining schemes and redundancy payments; or by investment incentives to encourage the movement of capital to areas where economic activity is lower. When the pricing mechanism shows signs of heading the economy downwards to a rock-bottom level of activity, the state can step in with 'pump-priming' spending, such as on public works. The employment thereby created in the construction industries generates incomes which are spent on the products of other industries.

Although the pricing mechanism brings about an allocation of resources throughout the economy, this does not mean that socially it will be the best possible allocation. There are certain spheres where the consumer is not always given the opportunity to express his scale of preferences by the offer of a price. If say, a new roadway or hospital is required in a certain area, it is unlikely that this can be brought into being by the pricing mechanism. It may be argued that this is an unfair example, since these are areas where the state traditionally operates. But very often it was because the pricing mechanism did not work in such areas that the state had to step in. Moreover, people will often not offer, or not be able to offer, a price for the things which it would be better for them to have, or which they subconsciously want. By leaving it entirely to the price mechanism, we can get a situation in which shiny cars are parked outside dilapidated slum housing. In such cases the state has to step in and see that the people get what they really want, or ought to want. Economic man, it should be noted, is not always rational. Because of this, the state may take over the provision of certain goods and services which would not be adequately supplied under the pricing mechanism. It has been the policy of the Labour Party that the state may also take over industry sectors which are considered to be basic (and which therefore must be under the control of the state) or sectors which have 'failed the nation'. With the exception of steel nationalisation, however, the desire for state ownership by the Labour Party appears to have lessened in recent years. Instead, it is argued that the same objectives can be achieved through indicative planning and state participation, rather than state monopoly, in areas which are thought to require wakening-up or encouraged to form larger and more economic working units (the former Industrial Reorganisation Corporation was set up to this end). Sometimes government intervention has been directed at the reorganisation and modernisation of a whole industry, as for example in the case of the Lancashire cotton and shipbuilding industries.

NATIONAL PLANNING

Economic planning in this country became formalised with the publication of National Plans. The overall objective of these was to bring about a higher rate of growth in gross national product, that is, in total national output of goods and services. To help achieve this, target rates of growth were set, so that firms in industry could make their own growth plans with reference to these, and also that any areas of possible shortage might be highlighted, as a result of thinking through the detailed implications of overall growth rates for the economy. More will be said about national planning and the work of the National Economic Development Council and the former Department of Economic Affairs when we come to consider 'growth' among government economic objectives in Part Three.

REGIONAL DEVELOPMENT

It will, however, be convenient at this point, since we have been considering the distribution of the factors of production throughout the economy, to look briefly at how the Government seeks to influence the location of labour and capital. Ever since the thirties, Governments in this country have had some kind of policy with regard to the location of industry. In the thirties the dominant problem was one of extremely high unemployment concentrated in what were known as the 'depressed areas', but which were later given the official designation 'special areas'. These areas were in the main the centres of the older declining heavy industries like coal, shipbuilding and steel, as well as lighter declining industries like cotton textiles. During the war heavy industry was again fully employed, so there was no regional unemployment problem. Throughout the post-war years there has been a great deal of legislative action to ensure that the conditions of the thirties did not return, and the accidentally high unemployment of the severe winter of 1962/63 accelerated such measures.

Nowadays, government regional development policy has two aspects. It is not solely concerned with the areas of traditionally high unemployment, but also seeks to prevent too much industrial concentration in other areas. Current regional planning is made up of measures designed to encourage industry to move to areas industrially underdeveloped and in which there is above average unemployment, as well as steer it away from areas where there is already an excessive pressure on available resources.

The industrial development certificate is the chief means whereby this second objective is pursued. In the Town and Country Planning Acts 1947 it was stipulated that no planning permission could be given for the erection of industrial buildings above a certain size, unless the application was accompanied by a certificate from the Board of Trade confirming that the proposed project was in keeping with the proper distribution of industry. Gradually, by introducing an element of discrimination, the i.d.c. also became an instrument for steering industry towards the areas of high unemployment.

The inducements given to industry to set up in the development areas are numerous, but are only given if the move will add significantly to the employment opportunities in the area. The boundaries, and even the designation of these areas, have frequently been changed; but currently the development areas embrace five broad regions: most of Scotland and Wales, the northern region, Merseyside and most of Cornwall and North Devon. Investment in these areas by companies receives particularly generous tax allowances. In addition, there is a good deal of assistance available under the Local Employment Acts: factories for rent or sale on favourable terms, building grants, loans and grants for other purposes, together with help from the Department of Employment in training labour and paying workers' removal expenses. Financial help may be given to the local authorities in the development areas for the clearing of derelict land and also for the improvement of basic services.

These considerable inducements and deterrents have succeeded in bringing about some notable shifts of industry into the development areas: for example, the setting up of parts of the motor industry near Liverpool and in the Scottish lowlands. On the spot help and supervision is provided by regional Economic Planning Councils and Boards.

Towards the end of 1967 a further inducement was given to industry to move into the development areas by the payment of a Regional Employment Premium. This amounted to a government subsidy of the wages bill of manufacturing industries in development areas. The R.E.P. scheme was to operate for not less than seven years; in 1970 the Conservative Government indicated that it would not be extended beyond this initial period.

PART TWO

Where the Money Comes From

5

Value of Money

A time-honoured definition of economics is that it is concerned with the production, distribution and exchange of wealth. We have just been looking in Part One at the factors involved in the production of wealth and how it is shared out between them. People nowadays are not generally sharing out amongst themselves that which they have been a party to producing. What they produce is sold, exchanged into money, and with their share of the money proceeds they can then acquire the items of wealth they want. We saw also in Part One that the ordering of much of our economy, the allocation of resources to satisfy our various wants, is achieved through the operation of the price mechanism, itself dependent upon the ability to attach a price or money value to everything.

It is therefore quite appropriate that at this early stage in the book we should be looking at money and at the financial institutions handling it, mainly banks. Every businessman has his friendly (or sometimes not-so-friendly) bank manager, with whom he leaves his cash balances and from whom (usually to a greater extent) he obtains loans to help him get started in business or to supply part of his working capital needs (to pay for materials and labour) for the normal running of the business. When longer-term financing is required for the purchase of fixed assets, like factory space and machinery, our businessman may have to borrow the money in the capital market, and here again a bank, and particularly a merchant bank, can be of help. Money and banking is therefore an important part of everyday business life.

An understanding of the mechanisms of money and banking is also useful from a wider aspect. The relationship in the economy between the supply of money on the one hand, and the physical output of goods and services on the other, plays an important role in determining the general economic climate—whether one of inflation or deflation, rising or falling general price level. Furthermore, much of government economic management is conducted through monetary policy, through money supply and interest rates and operating upon financial institutions. A fuller understanding of government policy in this area, and its likely effect upon the economy as a whole, can be better achieved through a knowledge of the theory of money and banking, together with the practical workings of financial institutions.

NATURE AND FUNCTIONS OF MONEY

Money is something we take so much for granted today that it is difficult to imagine what it would be like without it; this also tends to make us less conscious of the many functions that money does perform. When man was completely self-sufficient he had little need of money, because he did not have to exchange one thing for another in order to satisfy the whole range of his wants. When he did move away from self-sufficiency and began to exchange his surpluses for those of other people and to depend upon this for the satisfaction of many of his wants, he did so at first by means of barter, by exchanging one good directly for another. Barter had many inconveniences. There had to be a double coincidence of wants; each had to be prepared to accept what the other wished to give in exchange. Also there had to be the possibility of achieving acceptable equivalence in reasonable quantities. To solve these difficulties involved in barter, there grew up the practice of using an intermediate good in exchange, for which you exchanged your surplus and from which you could then transfer into what you really wanted. Many objects were used as a medium of exchange, that is as money, and in primitive societies some still are. But gradually it was found that precious metals made into coins served best as money because they had all the necessary qualities: universal acceptability, scarcity, durability, divisibility, homogeneity and portability.

Money is therefore primarily a medium of exchange; something accepted everywhere, without question, in payments for goods and services or in settlement of a debt. But money also performs other functions. It provides a common measure of value: everything's value can be expressed in terms of pounds and new pence, to determine equivalence in exchange, to keep accounts, to record future payments. Lastly, money provides a store of value: a form in which wealth can be kept without deteriorating (although, as we shall see later, money can lose its value). When one stores one's wealth in money, the money has the facility of 'liquidity', the ability to change readily into any other form of wealth.

Because of the security risk and such practices as 'clipping', it gradually became less common for coins made of precious metals to circulate. Instead the gold and silver would be deposited with goldsmiths, who issued certificates of deposit, and it was these that circulated as 'representative' money, being thus the early form of bank notes. However, it should be noted that they represented gold and silver that *did* exist, to the value stated on the paper. Paper money nowadays is not so backed and is therefore 'token' money, as also are coins not containing metal equal to their face value. Today, notes and coins are only the small change of our money supply; the greater part of which is merely entries in bank ledgers, namely deposit and current accounts. The means of payment is increasingly the debiting of the account of one bank customer and the crediting of that of another. Notes and coins pass from hand to hand only for small value transactions. The money supply in Britain today, on the narrowest definition, is around £8,500 million, of which £5,500 million is bank current accounts. Accounts with other financial institutions, like savings banks and building societies, that can almost as easily be used as a means of payment, are termed 'near money'.

CHANGES IN THE VALUE OF MONEY

It has been seen how the value of everything can be expressed in money terms. The monetary unit itself also has a value: the amount of goods and services it will purchase. We say that the value of money is falling when a £ will buy less goods than it used to, because prices have risen; conversely if prices fall, the value of money rises. Change in the value of money is measured by movements in the general level of prices, but we will have more to say about this later in Chapter 9 when we look at the question of the strength and stability of the currency.

The explanation of changes in the value of money lies therefore in what causes the general price level to move. Monetarists, adhering to the quantity theory, argue that this results from variation in the relationship between the quantity of money on the one hand and the physical volume of goods and services on the other (while Keynsians look more at the level of demand). A very simple example can illustrate the monetarists' viewpoint. If A has ten apples to sell and B's only available purchasing power is ten pennies, then each apple will sell for one penny. Should B have twenty pennies, each apple would sell for two pence; should A have only five apples, then again each would sell for two pence. In both these cases the level of price has risen; the value of each unit of money fallen; but, it should be noted, for a different reason in each case. In the first it was because the quantity of money increased, in the second because the volume of goods decreased. Conversely, the value of money would have risen if the volume of apples had increased or there had been fewer pennies; in both cases each penny would have bought more apples.

In practice the relationship between the supply of money and the volume of goods and services is more complicated than this simple illustration. The supply of money is not just a matter of the number of units, but also of how many times each unit (whether coins, notes or bank deposits) performs the function of a means of payment. This is what is known as the 'velocity of circulation' of money.

The relationships determining changes in the general price level, and therefore in the value of money, can be expressed as an equation, embodying the 'quantity theory' of money:

$$MV = PT$$

M = number of monetary units
V = velocity of circulation
T = volume of goods and services
P = price level (the value of money being the inverse of this)

MV therefore represents the money spent; PT equals the sales value of goods and services.

To highlight the aspect of price level (and value of money) the equation can be written as follows: $P = \dfrac{MV}{T}$

This shows that if either M or V, or both, increase in relation to

T, then the level of P rises, that is, the value of money falls. The same will happen if T diminishes, with MV remaining the same. Conversely, if T increases, or MV diminishes, then P will fall and the value of money increase. Thus there are three major variables governing movement of the general price level and therefore determining whether the value of money increases or decreases. But they are not necessarily *independent* variables. For example, if an increase in M causes the price of goods to rise and the value of money to fall, then people are less likely to want to hold on to money and therefore velocity of circulation will also increase.

Some economists have looked at the value of money as being determined, like everything else, by supply and demand; and in the case of money particularly the demand for it. If the demand for money exceeds its supply then its value will rise, that is, prices will fall. If, on the other hand, the supply of money increases faster than the demand for it, then its value will fall, prices will rise. The supply of money is quite simply the number of units. The demand for money depends on the volume of transactions, the length of period between receipt of income and making payments out of it. The desire to hold money may also be influenced by speculative or precautionary motives. If it is generally believed that the price of goods (or stocks or shares) is going to fall, then people will hold off from buying and for the moment keep more of their wealth as money; on a large scale this would undoubtedly help to bring about the expected fall in prices. A feeling that there may be a sudden and unexpected need for cash will also make for the holding of higher money balances. Both these demands for money represent a liquidity preference, a desire to hold wealth as money rather than as goods. Although this emphasis on the demand for money as explaining changes in its value was put forward as an alternative to the quantity theory approach, it will be realised that many of these demand aspects are inherent in the concept of velocity of circulation.

The more extreme exponents of the quantity theory were inclined to regard changes in M (money supply) alone as determining what happened to the price level, the effect of the former upon the latter being direct, albeit after some time-lag. Other economists, including Keynes, regarded the causation between the supply of money and its value as being indirect and uncertain. Should money supply growth go ahead of liquidity preference, with people having more money than they wanted to hold, then they would put the excess into securities like government bonds, thus bringing down interest rates and giving encouragement to investment, itself having a multiplier expansionist effect on national income. If, at the start of this, there is a margin of idle resources, especially of labour, these will be brought into use to expand output. It would only be if, and when, the economy was operating at full employment that the expansion in demand through increased investment and increased money supply would lead to a rise in prices.

We have now given a theoretical framework to explain why the general price level may be rising or falling: in other words, why we have inflation or deflation. The implications of inflation or deflation for the economy will be dealt with later, when we will also examine other causes of general movement in the price level. Here we have been concerned with the role that money plays. It is because of this role that there has been much talk in recent years about the need to exercise control over the rate of growth in money supply and over what has been termed 'domestic credit expansion'. More will be said about this when we come to deal with monetary policy. Let us now see how money supply is created.

HOW MONEY IS CREATED

Nowadays the creation of money is much less a matter of simply minting coins and printing notes. As we have seen, by far the greatest element in money supply is bank deposits; so that our main concern is with how these are created. The short answer is that the banks themselves create deposits (although the extent of this can be limited by the central monetary authority). This is a point of monetary theory which many people always find difficult to grasp. Somehow it seems all wrong; somewhere there is a flaw in the logic. Certainly, an individual bank cannot lend more than is deposited with it, and generally its lending is a good deal less. However, since banks hold only a small percentage of their deposits as cash, as a reserve against sudden withdrawals, the banking system as a whole can create deposits to a multiple of the cash deposited with it. The maximum size of this multiple depends upon the reserve percentage: that is, if a 10 per cent reserve is kept, the banking system can create deposits by a maximum multiple of ten times the initial deposit made with it; if 20 per cent then only five times. The proof that all this is so can be best illustrated by example. In practice, the multiple is usually a good deal less than the theoretically possible maximum.

Let us assume as a starting point that a bank receives a deposit of £1,000 from a member of the public. If the bank adhered to a 100 per cent reserve ratio then its balance sheet would read:

Liabilities		*Assets*	
Deposits	£1,000	Cash reserve	£1,000

This would not be very profitable banking, for the cash would merely be lying idle, earning nothing; so the bank would have to make a substantial charge for safe-keeping and the facility of being able to write cheques. In practice, with a large number of accounts, the banks find that they need keep in cash only a small percentage of the funds deposited with them to meet the possibility of withdrawal by some of their customers of part of their deposits.

For ease of illustration, in our example we will assume a cash reserve ratio of 10 per cent. Our bank would therefore be able to employ the other 90 per cent remuneratively, in granting loans or acquiring interest earning investments like Government stocks. The balance sheet would then read like this:

Liabilities		*Assets*	
Deposits	£1,000	Cash reserve	£100
		Loans and investments	£900
			———
			£1,000

It will be seen that, although with a 10 per cent reserve requirement there is a possibility of expansion of deposits of ten times the original deposit, namely £10,000, our bank itself cannot achieve this. It could only do so if it was the only bank and if people did not draw out cash from it. Since there are in fact other banks, our first bank is bound to experience loss of cash to them in granting loans or acquiring investments.

Our bank can therefore do nothing further until it receives more money. Nevertheless there has been some increase in money supply. Before, the money supply consisted of the public's cash holding of £1,000; now the public owns bank deposits of £1,000 and £900 of the original deposit has found its way back to the public by way of loans to them or the purchase of investments from them. Thus, money supply is now £1,900.

In reality, there are many banks, and it is more likely that the £900 which left the first bank will find its way to these other banks. As the customers of the first bank spend their loans with shopkeepers, etc., the shopkeepers will pay their receipts into their own banks; those from whom the first bank purchased investments will also pay the cheques in their favour into their own banks. Thus, what we may call the second line of banks will receive deposits of £900, of which they in turn will keep 10 per cent in reserve and employ the rest.

Liabilities		*Assets*	
Deposits	£900	Cash reserve	£90
		Loans and investments	£810
			———
			£900

The third line of banks will receive deposits of £810, of which they will keep £81 as cash and lend or acquire investments with the remaining £729. The process can continue until the final balance sheet position of the whole banking system is that deposits have grown to ten times the original deposit.

Liabilities		*Assets*	
Deposits	£10,000	Cash reserve	£1,000
		Loans and investments	£9,000
			———
			£10,000

For this process of multiple deposit creation upon an original deposit to proceed to its maximum, as above, there must be no leakage of cash out of the banking system back to the public either into cash in circulation or into the public sector: if, say, £100 of the original £1,000 did so, then the maximum possible creation of deposits would be £900 × 10 = £9,000.

Four things are therefore necessary for bank deposit creation to take place. The banks must first of all receive additional deposits of cash. Second, they must use the greater part of this to make loans or acquire investments from the private sector, rather than hold excess reserves. Third, there must be people wanting to borrow from the banks or prepared to sell securities to them. Lastly, as we saw in the previous paragraph, the public must continue to leave its money on deposit with the banks rather than increase their cash holdings and so deplete bank reserves.

THE PRICE OF MONEY

The rate of interest is the price paid for borrowing money; in other words the reward received by the lender. Money borrowed and lent is referred to as capital; although the word 'money' is commonly employed in the context of short term lending and borrowing, as in the title 'money market'. As capital, money is one of the three factors of production, and as such receives its reward. Capital in fact has two types of reward associated with it: those lending capital receive interest; those using it make a profit, or loss.

The person parting with his money, lending it to someone else to use, makes a sacrifice in doing so. To have the money to lend he has to have 'saved'. He has *abstained* from immediate consumption, being prepared to *wait* until some future time to do so. The longer the loan, the greater is his waiting (and therefore the higher the rate of interest). Interest is thus the reward for abstinence and waiting. At times when the general inclination is to spend, rather than save, and not be prepared to wait, the greater will be the interest rate inducement that has to be offered.

When the saver lends his money, say by investing in a fixed interest stock, he is parting with liquidity. He is putting part of his wealth in a form that can be less easily exchanged back into something else, at any rate before the loan is due to be repaid. When, for a variety of reasons, people want to hold money rather than anything else, they are said to have a 'liquidity preference'. When this is strong, the rate of interest has to be that much higher in order to persuade them to part with liquidity. The more marketable an investment the more liquid it is, and therefore the lower the rate of interest it need carry. Holding wealth in the form of money has its disadvantages: it earns nothing and its value falls if the price of everything else rises. So, when

E

the rate of inflation is high, there will be a disinclination to keep large idle balances and a willingness instead to lend them at a rate of interest in order to earn something that will help to preserve the real value of wealth.

Sometimes the lender does not receive back the money he has lent, because the borrower has defaulted or gone bankrupt. The saver in lending therefore incurs a *risk*. It has been argued that interest is however only the reward for waiting; that when there is also an element of risk involved the extra reward this warrants is 'profit'. But profit is more associated with the active user of capital. In any case it is seldom possible to have a completely riskless fixed interest investment for which 'pure' interest would be the appropriate reward. Even where the investment is 'gilt-edged', with payment of interest and repayment of principal guaranteed, there is always the risk that real values will be greatly eroded by a higher than anticipated rate of inflation.

Apart from being seen as the reward to the lender for abstinence, waiting and risk, the rate of interest can also be regarded as the price that results from the forces of demand and supply operating in the capital market. The supply of capital depends, as we have seen, on saving; the demand for capital springs from active business investment. If savings exceed investment, interest rates will fall and this will either discourage saving or increase investment, thus bringing the two into equality at a new equilibrium rate of interest. Conversely, if the demand for capital for fixed asset creation is higher, this will push up the rate of interest, which will encourage greater saving, as well as render some investment projects less attractive at the higher cost of borrowing capital.

The rate of savings in a society partly depends upon the distribution of income; the more evenly it is spread the greater will be the overall propensity to consume rather than save. But in a highly developed community there will also be fairly widespread contractual saving: contributions to pension funds and premiums to insurance companies, and much of this will be made available to active users of capital. In retaining a certain proportion of their earnings, rather than paying out as dividends, companies also carry out saving.

In regarding the rate of interest as being the price that must be paid to bring forth the required amount of saving, there is of course an implicit assumption that saving is interest-elastic; that the volume of saving responds to the level of interest rates. Saving takes place from a variety of motives, some of which may be fairly independent of what happens to interest rates. The desire to put something by for a rainy day may be stronger at a time when interest rates are falling through a decline in the level of economic activity. At such times sluggishness in consumer demand may be attributed to this higher 'savings ratio' (ratio of savings to G.N.P.).

The demand for capital is conditioned by its marginal productivity, the return obtained by employing an additional unit of capital. So long as the cost of capital, the rate of interest, is below its marginal productivity it will be worthwhile to employ more of it by engaging in additional projects. The rate of interest cannot rise above the marginal productivity of capital, but if the latter improves through a rise in the level of demand or technological development, the demand for capital will increase accordingly and the rate of interest will be bid up to bring forth the required additional savings.

In considering the response of those supplying and demanding capital, it is very important to bear in mind the distinction between real and nominal rates of interest, as well as gross and net rates. This distinction is particularly relevant in the case of long term rates. Nominal interest rates are the prevailing market rates of return on fixed interest investments. From the nominal rate must be deducted the rate of inflation to arrive at the real interest rate, what the lender is left with, after allowing for the fall in the value of money. In other words, it is the reduced real purchasing power of the rate of interest he received for parting with his savings. Thus, what is a high nominal rate may in fact be quite a low real rate of interest. In America calculations have been made that show a constant real rate of interest in the range of 3-4 per cent. American nominal rates therefore represent merely the addition of the current, or more probably the anticipated, rate of inflation to this relatively unchanging real rate of interest. From the borrower's point of view the true burden of a fixed interest charge upon his earnings is the nominal rate, less the rate of inflation, provided of course that his earnings keep pace with inflation. In calculating the real return and the real burden, account must also be taken of tax. In doing so, in the case of the lender, it is usually found that there is no net real return at all, but indeed a loss. Since business borrowers are allowed tax relief on their nominal interest payments, the real net burden of their borrowing is usually also a minus quantity. In the highly inflationary background of recent times this distinction between real and nominal rates of interest has been of increasing importance, particularly in capital project analysis.

6

Commercial Banks

In explaining how the banks create the largest element in our money supply we have already touched upon some aspects of banking. We now look at Britain's commercial banks in some detail, starting with those accepting deposits from the ordinary public, notably the London Clearing banks, although much of what is said applies equally to Scottish banks.

THE CLEARING BANKS

The London Clearing banks are the major deposit-taking commercial banks in England and Wales, having between them 12,000 branches scattered throughout the country. Britain therefore has a branch banking system, as distinct from a unit banking system, as in America. The Clearing banks derive their name from the fact that they are members of the London Bankers' Clearing House. Their combined deposits total around £10,500 million and they thereby provide the main element in Britain's money supply. The Committee of the London Clearing Bankers, in its monthly summary of financial statements, lists six member banks: Barclays, Coutts, Lloyds, Midland, National Westminster and Williams and Glyn's. However, Coutts is a subsidiary of National Westminster; while Williams Deacons and Glyn's (and also National) have amalgamated as a subsidiary of the National and Commercial Banking Group (of which Lloyds has part-ownership). For a long time it was customary to speak of the Big Five in British banking: Barclays, Lloyds, Midland, National Provincial and Westminster. With the merger of the last two, it has now become the Big Four. On the basis of size of deposits, the ranking of the Big Four is as follows: Barclays (including Martins) and National Westminster come first and second respectively, both with deposits around £3,000 million; Midland and Lloyds occupy third and fourth positions, with deposits in the region of £2,000 million.

Among the services the Clearing banks supply there are two major ones. First of all, they provide a place of safe-keeping where people can conveniently hold their money balances, drawing upon these as required, either by cheque or in cash, to make payment for their purchases of goods and services. The second major function performed by the banks is the provision of credit, by extending loans to their customers. As we have seen, by this lending the banking system itself creates bank deposits and therefore money.

THE MEANS OF PAYMENT

The Clearing banks accept deposits from the ordinary members of the public, as well as from business, and hold these on current, deposit or savings accounts. Just over half of the deposits are held on current account. On these no interest is paid, but attaching to them is the convenience of the cheque facility, enabling depositors to make payments without carrying large sums around with them. Provided the customer keeps a reasonable credit balance no charge is made for this service. The banks are also, of course, a source of notes and coins for making cash payments. For deposit or withdrawal of cash outside normal banking hours, there are night safes, and, more recently, cash dispensers. Interest *is* paid on deposit and savings accounts. On deposit accounts the current rate is 2 per cent under Bank rate, although this could change when the banks abandon their rate agreement. These accounts are not normally used as a means of payment, for cheques cannot be drawn upon them. One week's notice of withdrawal is generally required on deposit accounts, but in practice the banks relax this rule, although there may be a deduction from interest earned.

Providing customers with convenient ways of making payments is a procedure the banks now call their 'money transfer service', which has two main parts.

First, through the bank 'giro', money can be transferred from one customer's account to another, without having to use cheques for each individual transaction. Under the 'credit transfer', the banks will make a number of different payments on a customer's instructions, with only one cheque being required to cover the total value of these transactions. From the opposite side, any regular payments the customer is due to receive can be collected on his behalf by the bank, this service being known as 'direct debiting'. The older arrangement of the 'standing order' (whereby the customer instructs the bank to make on his behalf payments of a recurring nature) also comes within the bank giro service. The difference between the standing order and the newer direct debiting service is that under the latter it is the payee who takes the initiative.

The second aspect of the banks' money transfer service is the traditional method of paying by cheque. The drawing of a cheque brings about the transfer of deposits from the payer's to the payee's bank. But a cheque can only be paid at the branch of the bank upon which it is drawn. The payee, or more usually the payee's bank, must therefore present the cheque for payment. This process of collecting payment is known as 'clearing' and when the payer's bank has paid out on the cheque it is said to have been 'cleared'. Cheque clearing is conducted at different levels. Those drawn on and paid into branches of the same bank are obviously cleared within that bank itself. With branches of different banks, that are in the same locality, some Local Clearing takes place. The Town Clearing handles cheques drawn on branches in the City of London. All other cheques drawn on the Clearing banks go through the General Clearing, although there is some preliminary clearing carried on between the larger banks' Clearing Departments. The Town and General Clearing take place at the Clearing House in London.

BANK LENDING

So much for the provision of the means of payment in a variety of forms. The second major function of the Clearing banks is extending loans to their customers. About half the banks' total deposits are used in this way, in the giving of advances or overdrafts. This lending is of a short term nature (in theory being recallable upon demand, although in practice the banks do not normally insist on this), and loans are generally only given against security. The mechanism of lending to business customers is that the banks extend what are termed 'borrowing limits', these being the amount by which a customer's withdrawals from his account can exceed payments into it, interest being charged only on that part of the borrowing facility actually used (unlike in America, for example, where the customer pays interest on the full amount of the overdraft facility).

Private individuals may also obtain loans from their banks, such 'personal loans' can be for as much as £1,000 to assist in the purchase of large value consumer durable goods (as an alternative to hire purchase). Personal loans may also be extended as bridging finance for house purchase. There are slight differences in the manner in which the various banks operate their personal loan schemes, although the overall cost is roughly the same. Personal loans are usually repayable by instalment within a period of two years or less; but some banks base their interest charges on the whole of the amount originally lent, while others do so only on the amount of the loan remaining unpaid.

Although private individuals provide the greater part of the banks' deposits, it is companies who are the largest borrowers, taking very much more out of the banks than they keep on deposit with them. In this way it may be said that the ordinary members of the public have supplied relatively cheap finance for Britain's business firms. Just over half of bank advances go to production industries, with a further 10 per cent being used in the distributive trades. The second largest category accounting for 13 per cent of the total is 'personal' borrowing, just under half of which is used for house purchase. Just over half of the lending to the financial section is to property companies. Included in advances to production industries are those at a fixed rate for exporting and shipbuilding, loans in these categories making up around 8 per cent of total advances.

The rates charged by the banks to various categories of borrower have traditionally been linked to the prevailing level of Bank rate, lying within the range of Bank rate to 3 per cent above it. Nationalised industries are charged $\frac{1}{2}$ per cent above Bank rate, with a minimum of $4\frac{1}{2}$ per cent. The 'blue chip' rate is 1 per cent above Bank rate (with a minimum of 5 per cent) and applies to local authorities, building societies, insurance companies and first class industrial and commercial borrowers. Other industrial and commercial borrowers, including private individuals, have to pay a rate up to 3 per cent above Bank rate. The lending rate to hire purchase companies is not less that 1½ per cent above Bank rate. Short term (that is up to two years) loans for export, under E.C.G.D. guarantee, are given at ½ per cent over Bank rate. Loans for the medium and long term, also those for shipbuilding made under the Shipbuilding Industry Board Scheme, are given at a fixed rate of 7 per cent, regardless of the prevailing level of Bank rate, plus a 1 per cent commitment fee. Once again all this could change when the banks abandon their cartel agreement on rates.

Apart from the major functions of providing easy ways of making payments and of granting loans to their customers, the banks supply many other financial services: safe-keeping for valuables, travel and foreign exchange arrangements, tax advice, executor and trustee and investment services. Under the 1947 Exchange Control Act, banks are 'authorised dealers', their foreign exchange departments facilitating settlement of international transactions by buying or selling foreign currencies for their customers, as well as for correspondent banks abroad. These foreign exchange operations may be for receipt or delivery now ('spot') or at some time in the future ('forward'). Business is conducted through telephone or teleprinter links with other dealers and with foreign exchange markets throughout the world.

EMPLOYMENT OF ASSETS

So far, we have been looking at the banks from the point of view of the services they provide. But the banks are not simply there to supply services, they are also in business to make a profit. They do this by employing the funds deposited with them in such a way as to earn more than they have to pay for these funds, including the cost of free services provided. It may be remarked at this point that, unlike other forms of business organisation, the banks obtain only a very small part of their resources from their shareholders: the great bulk comes from the depositors.

In putting to work the funds deposited with them, the banks adhere to a 'spectrum of liquidity'—that is, they place their deposits in asset forms that range from the most liquid (namely cash) to less liquid, but more profitable forms. The chosen instruments of official monetary policy have always had an important determining influence upon the asset forms held by the banks: the cash and liquidity ratios, special deposits, lending ceilings and, in future, the reserve requirement. (In May 1971 the Bank of England published a paper indicating, amongst many other things, an intention to replace cash and liquidity ratios and lending ceilings with a reserve requirement, made variable by special deposits. At the time of writing this has not yet happened, so the description that follows will be based on what has been the position in recent years and for the moment still is. To understand the difference that the new system will make for the banks the reader is referred to the later section on monetary policy, page 125, where the proposed new arrangements are outlined in more detail.)

Early experience of sudden demands for withdrawal taught the banks always to hold a certain proportion of their deposits in cash. This natural banking prudence is reinforced by an official requirement that the banks keep to a stipulated cash reserve ratio, for a long time at the level of 8 per cent. This reserve is held either as till money on the banks' premises or as 'bankers' deposits' at the Bank of England. Another requirement of the monetary authorities has been that the banks must keep, in addition to the cash reserve, another 20 per cent of their deposits in a highly liquid form, ranging from call money to bills of exchange of no longer maturity than three months. It is from these liquid assets that the banks can quickly make good any loss of cash in order to adhere to the 8 per cent ratio. To give some margin of safety the banks in fact normally operate for most of the year on the basis of a liquidity percentage somewhat above the stipulated minimum of 28 per cent. Looked at in detail, the liquid assets category can be seen to have three major sub-divisions. The first of these is 'money at call and short notice', which is mainly (but not entirely) money lent overnight. Loans to the discount market come within this category, as also does lending to non-Clearing banks, other operators in the money market, stockbrokers and jobbers and bullion brokers. The banks include in this category of liquid assets their holdings of tax reserve certificates. British government Treasury bills form part of the second category of liquid assets, which also contains bills of Commonwealth and foreign governments. Lastly, in the liquid assets portfolio are held commercial bills, either taken from customers or acquired in the market. That portion of the banks' fixed rate lending due to mature within eighteen months can be counted as liquid assets.

The two remaining asset groups are 'investments' and 'advances'. For these the banks may normally please themselves as to the percentages of their deposits employed in each (although in recent years advances have been subject to official ceilings). Since more can be earned on advances, the banks generally keep the greater part of the remaining 72 per cent of their deposits employed in this way. The banks' investments are almost entirely in those British government securities having a maturity no longer than ten years, with their portfolios being fairly evenly spread over the whole period in order to give a regular flow of maturities (although at times when interest rates are expected to rise, the average life may be shortened in order to lessen risk). Banks normally tend to hold their investments to maturity. The percentage held in investments varies, depending partly on whether they wish (or are permitted) to expand their advances. On average, over recent years the banks have kept 15 per cent of their deposits as investments, although this has sometimes fallen as low as 10 per cent while in the nineteen fifties it was as high as 32 per cent.

At times the monetary authorities have required the Clearing and Scottish banks to place a certain part of their deposits in the Banking Department of the Bank of England, such 'special deposits' expressly not to be included by the banks when calculating their liquidity ratio. These deposits have generally been called for in 1 per cent stages ($\frac{1}{2}$ per cent for the Scottish banks) although sometimes $\frac{1}{2}$ per cent has been the amount asked for. So far the peak level reached has been $3\frac{1}{2}$ per cent. Special deposits generally earn the Treasury bill rate of interest, except when the authorities wish, for some reason, to discipline the banks, when a lower rate may be paid, or indeed no interest paid at all. Special deposits were originally intended to be of only temporary duration for just as long as the authorities wished for restraint in bank lending. However, in the 1967 budget it was indicated that in future special deposits might be called for more often, and this has been the case. In the new monetary policy, outlined in 1971, special deposits are retained as a means of making the reserve requirement variable, and extended to merchant, overseas and foreign banks.

OTHER ACTIVITIES

Apart from their main function as deposit-taking banks in the United Kingdom, the London Clearing banks operate in other spheres, either directly or through subsidiaries or associated companies. Nearly all the Clearing banks have part-interests in hire purchase companies. A more recent diversification has been their setting up of unit trusts.

The remaining major area of Clearing bank operations is the international sphere and here again they work through subsidiary companies. While many of these perform the banking function abroad, as would be expected, quite often 'international' denotes the character of their activity, rather than the geographical area of operation. In some cases so-called international subsidiaries were set up primarily to side-step restrictions imposed on the traditional Clearing bank activity, either by the monetary authorities or by the Clearer's own cartel arrangements.

It is not easy to describe the Clearing banks' international activities in terms of distinct categories. In some cases this can be done geographically. The old 'colonial' banks stand out most readily, operating mainly in Africa and Asia. Some of the Clearers have subsidiaries and associated companies in Europe and the western hemisphere; while others are active in the United States and Latin America.

Apart from the particular geographical area of operation, the financing of foreign trade is still a major part of the international banking activity. When, due to exchange control and other official regulations, the necessary finance cannot come from either the importer's or the exporter's country, there has to be resort to the international capital market, particularly to the euro-dollar market. Trade financing apart, much of the other lending by the international banks is medium term and therefore longer than that normally extended by the Clearing banks themselves.

The setting up of hire purchase and international subsidiaries enabled the Clearing banks to compete through them for the larger deposits by offering rates higher than those available within the strict Clearing bank sphere. The international, as well

as hire purchase, subsidiaries were also outwith official requirements regarding reserve and liquidity ratios and could therefore
employ foreign currency deposits as profitably as some of the
other financial institutions, like merchant banks. This enabled the
Clearers, through their international subsidiaries, to play a part
in the rapidly growing euro-currency market and indeed this was
often the prime reason for setting up some of these subsidiaries.
In the longer term lending part of this market the Clearing banks
operate through international consortia.

Competition between the Clearing banks has been restrained
by their cartel agreement to adhere to the same rates of interest
given to depositors and charged for loans, these rates being
linked by a fairly rigid formula to the prevailing level of Bank
rate: 2 per cent below for deposits and at least 1 per cent above
on advances. As part of the new monetary policy authorities have
now asked the banks to abandon this cartel agreement on interest
rates. The banks argue, of course, that since they are all dealing
in exactly the same product, namely money, competition itself
would inevitably bring about this price uniformity and it will
remain to be seen just how much they diverge in practice when the
cartel is ended. What direct competition there has existed in the
past between them has been largely restricted to the quality of
service they have offered. Part of this service is the convenience
of a widely-spread branch network and indeed the banks have on
occasion been criticised for being too ready to open new branches.

Many of the other financial institutions provide the Clearing
banks with a good deal of competition, particularly in winning
deposits, and over the years the Clearing banks' proportion of the
total money supply has declined as a result. With the ending of
their cartel agreement the Clearing banks may be prepared to bid
more aggressively for deposits (although the authorities have
expressed concern that there might be a danger that this could be
at the expense of the building societies and savings banks, in which
case official limits might have to be set on rates offered by banks
for some kinds of deposits). By and large, the Clearing banks'
lending rates have been quite competitive: indeed bank loans have
usually been a good deal cheaper than most other sources of

finance. It is for the money of those willing to lend (rather than those wanting to borrow) that the other institutions have been better able to compete. To a large extent this is because the Clearing banks offer no interest at all to those placing their money on current account; whereas most of the other deposit accepting institutions give a substantial return on deposits that are in practice just as liquid as bank current accounts, although not always quite so convenient to use as a means of payment (the advent of the Post Office Giro has, of course, changed this). Trustee Savings Banks and building societies have for long provided the possibility of more remunerative employment of surplus cash and to some extent they can also offer means by which payments can be made out of depositor's accounts, although this not so highly developed as to equal the banks or the P.O. Giro. Even the interest the banks offer on deposit accounts has not been as good as that which can be obtained from the 'near banks'.

7

The Bank of England

It has already been seen in describing the commercial banking system how this is subject to regulation by the monetary authorities, notably the central bank. Every developed country has its central bank occupying a key position in the financial structure; in America, it is the Federal Reserve; in France, the Banque de France, in Germany, the Deutsche Bundesbank; and in Britain, the Bank of England. Although it is usually a public institution, the central bank has traditionally had a certain degree of independence of the government, greater in some countries than in others. A basic function of a central bank is to act as banker both to the government and to the commercial banking system. Increasingly, however, central banks have been called upon to fulfil other roles and while we here examine those performed by the Bank of England, many of these are common to the majority of central banks.

The Bank of England is one of the oldest central banks, being founded in 1694. Just over 250 years later, in 1946, it was nationalised and thus became formally part of the public sector. However, the Bank had for long been an agent of government, so that the act of nationalisation did not make much difference in practice, although it did make more explicit the power of the government over the commercial banks and indeed over the Bank of England itself. At the head of the Bank of England is its Court, composed of a Governor, Deputy Governor, and sixteen Directors, all appointed by the Crown on the recommendation of the government of the day. Four of the Directors are full-time officials and they, led by the Governor and Deputy Governor, control the day-to-day running of the Bank. The major functions performed by the Bank of England will now be described. These may be divided into internal and external ones, the former being naturally more numerous.

INTERNAL FUNCTIONS

First, the Bank of England acts as banker to the Government, the latter's account in the Banking Department being termed 'public deposits'. Into this account flow taxation receipts and out of it government spending, including National Debt redemption. The credit balance in 'public deposits' is never very large, for it would not be economic for the Government to have it so, and in any case there is a statutory obligation to apply automatically any surplus of revenue over expenditure to reducing the National Debt. The Bank of England also holds the accounts of certain commonwealth and foreign central banks and through these some international official settlements may be made.

BANKERS' BANK

By far the largest depositors with the Banking Department are the commercial banks, whose accounts are termed 'bankers' deposits'. As we have seen already, this represents part of the cash reserve base of the commercial banks and is also used as a means of inter-bank settlement. Payment for new notes and coins issued to the commercial banks is made by debiting 'bankers' deposits'. Net indebtedness between the public and the private sectors is settled through these 'public' and 'bankers' deposits' in the Banking Department of the Bank of England: a relative increase in the flow of taxation receipts over current government spending will result in a debiting of 'bankers' deposits' and a crediting of 'public deposits'. Conversely, if government spending rises faster than taxation and other revenue, then 'public deposits' will be debited and 'bankers' deposits' credited. It should be noted that sales and purchases by the Government of its own securities (Treasury bills and gilt-edged stocks) have similar implications: when net sales are made the flow is from 'bankers' ' to 'public deposits'; net purchases reverse this. It will be realised that since these fiscal (taxation and government spending) and monetary factors (sales and purchases of government bills and stocks) affect 'bankers' deposits' they also, therefore, determine the cash base for money supply creation.

NOTE ISSUE

The right to issue money is one which the state has always taken unto itself. Today the Bank of England is the only issuer of bank notes in England and Wales; while coins are supplied as required by the Royal Mint. The Bank of England, therefore, supplies notes and coins to the commercial banks, who in turn meet the demands of the ordinary public for cash. Bank notes are still issued by individual Scottish and Northern Ireland banks, but these must be backed, pound for pound, by holdings of Bank of England notes.

As the name suggests, it is the Issue Department of the Bank of England that performs the note issue function: 'notes issued' make up the liabilities side of its balance sheet. The Issue Department supplies notes only to the Banking Department, which in turn issues them as required to the commercial banks. Formerly, on the assets side, as a backing for the note issue the Bank had to hold gold, when this country was on the Gold Standard; the amount of notes allowed beyond this was known as the 'fiduciary issue'—that is, unbacked by gold.

The note issue today is backed by another form of paper, namely government stocks and Treasury bills. Any increase in the 'fiduciary issue' by the Bank requires Treasury permission, the giving of which has to be notified to Parliament. The issuing of notes and coins is primarily suited to meet the cash holding habits of the public and a good illustration of this is the large increase that takes place each year in the note issue around Christmas. It is not the note issue that is significant nowadays in the total money supply, but rather the reserve base of the commercial banking system. It must also be remembered that the note issue is a method of government financing—that part of the National Debt upon which the Government pays no interest. To the extent that government spending is not financed by taxation or borrowing, then it must be financed by an increase in the note issue.

NATIONAL DEBT

As another of its internal functions the Bank of England manages, on behalf of the Government, the National Debt. This Debt represents the extent by which Governments have, over the years, financed part of their spending by borrowing from the citizens of this country, as well as from those abroad. Currently, the size of the National Debt is in the region of £33,000 million, roughly the equivalent of one year's output of goods and services in this country. A small part of this total National Debt is owed externally, mainly the American and Canadian long-term loans extended to Britain immediately after the war, but sometimes also any outstanding medium term borrowing from the International Monetary Fund. The largest part of the National Debt, nearly two-thirds, consists of marketable securities (government 'gilt-edged' stocks) divided according to maturity into shorts (under 5 years), mediums (5 to 15 years), longs (over 15 years) and undated. The other parts of the internal debt are National Savings and the Floating Debt, the latter consisting of Treasury bills and Ways and Means Advances (short-term lending of surplus funds to the Exchequer by government departments). Part of the internal debt may, of course, be held by non-residents: sterling balances are, for example, usually invested in short-dated stocks and Treasury bills. Annual interest rate payments to holders of government debt total around £1,400 million, but the Government itself receives interest on the funds it on-lends to local authorities or nationalised industries, so that the net interest cost to the revenue of the National Debt is just over £500 million. And inflation over the years has further reduced the real burden of the debt.

The Government issues new debt either to raise cash (to cover the excess of spending over taxation) or to replace maturing issues—the latter can be created as the Treasury sees fit, but the former requires the approval of Parliament. The authority to raise funds by borrowing is given by Parliament to the Treasury, which in turn employs the Bank of England as its agent to manage the National Debt. (It should be noted that this is *not* done by the National Debt Commissioners, who are in fact Commissioners for the *Reduction* of the National Debt, and in this capacity they administer the sinking funds.) The Bank of England gives advice to the Treasury as to the appropriate terms of new issues (the coupon rate of interest, the price, the maturity, any conversion offer, etc.) and when the terms have been decided upon the Bank draws up and sends out a prospectus advertising the issue to the public, whose applications are received at the Loans Office of the Bank. Since government stocks are created in large blocks of several hundred million, they are usually initially taken into the portfolios of those government departments with funds to invest and then fed out gradually to the public through the Government Broker (the stockbrokers, Mullens and Co.) who also buys in maturing issues. In this way the authorities can exert an influence on the gilt-edged market and so-called 'tap' stocks are often created for this very purpose. The Bank maintains a Register of the names of those holding government stocks and pays out interest, and eventually the principal, on the due dates.

There are certain principles of debt management that the Bank attempts to follow, although these may have to give way to changing circumstances and policies. Traditionally, in those sales and purchases of gilt-edged stocks through the Government Broker, the Bank has attempted to preserve an 'orderly market', moderating the rate of change in the level of interest rates, as well as at times the upper level itself. More recently, this objective has had to give way to the needs of money supply control, with the result that market interest rates have moved to much higher levels, in the absence of official support at these times by way of net purchases of gilt-edged stocks. It was also a principle of management that the average redemption date of the National Debt should be kept as far distant in the future as possible by a policy of 'funding'—the replacement of floating debt by stocks, as well as of maturing stocks by longer dated ones. In former times, before high rates of inflation reduced the real burden of the National Debt, there was continuing concern to reduce the 'dead-weight of debt' (with coupon rates of 3 to 5 per cent!) by the establishment of sinking funds to gradually retire the debt or by conversions to a lower interest charge.

LENDER OF LAST RESORT

In the early history of banking there were many failures because of 'runs on the bank', that is, sudden demands for cash that the banks could not immediately meet, although if given time could probably have done so. In modern times this ready availability of cash is ensured by the much greater sophistication and development of deposit banking and by the central bank always standing ready to act as a 'lender of last resort' to the banking system, so that it in turn may meet the public's demands upon it and thus stave off financial panics.

In Britain, this 'last resort lending' by the central bank is not extended directly to the commercial banks themselves, but indirectly through the medium of the discount houses. It is they who may obtain cash, at a price and for a stipulated period, from the Bank of England, either by way of re-discounting bills or by loans on the basis of acceptable security. The commercial banks can therefore solve their own cash problems by immediate recall of their day-to-day loans to the discount market, in the knowledge that the latter can then resort to the Bank. If the monetary authorities wish to see some upward movement in short-term interest rates, the Bank will give assistance only at the 'front door' —that is, by charging Bank rate (or even perhaps up to 1 per cent above it—but this is rare). Bank rate lending has traditionally been for 7 days, although in recent years the period has often been shorter than this. When forced to seek assistance at the 'front door', it is said that the market is 'in the Bank' and has obtained assistance on penal terms. The market reacts by subsequently endeavouring to increase the yield obtainable from Treasury bills by lowering its bid for them at the next tender. If, however, there is no desire on the part of the monetary authorities to see interest rates go higher, than the Bank may 'at the back door' buy bills at prevailing market rates from the discount houses or even at times from the banks direct, if the banks hold the maturities which the authorities particularly wish to purchase. The Bank's agent for these 'back door' operations is its 'special buyer', Seccombe, Marshall and Campion, Ltd., the smallest of the discount houses. Bill purchases and sales by the 'special buyer'may often be for 'smoothing operations'—that is, evening out flows of cash between the public and private sectors.

Although now part of the public sector, the Bank has traditionally performed a liaison function between the Government (more specifically the Treasury) and private financial institutions, like the many different kinds of banks and other financial intermediaries. The greater part of official monetary policy is conducted by the Bank of England, thus involving a regulatory role in relation to the private financial sector. Any representations to the Government which that sector wishes to make are generally made through the Governor of the Bank of England. We have already so far touched upon some of the instruments of monetary policy, but these will be described in greater detail in a later section when dealing with the various means of economic regulation at the disposal of the government.

EXTERNAL FUNCTIONS

GOLD RESERVES

The Bank of England is the custodian of Britain's reserves of gold and convertible currencies for use in the settlement of international payments. (As already noted, this gold used to provide the backing for the internal money supply.) Nowadays the Bank's holdings are fairly evenly divided between gold and convertible currencies, but in the mid-sixties gold accounted for as much as 80 to 90 per cent. The reserves held in the Bank of England are also those for the whole of the Sterling Area; Overseas Sterling Area countries pass on to London their earnings of gold and convertible currencies from trade with the non-sterling world and receive in return credited sterling balances. Overseas Sterling Area countries therefore hold their reserve balances in sterling and settlement of inter-area indebtedness is made through these.

The Bank holds the country's reserves in what is called the 'Exchange Equalisation Account', which was set up in 1932 when Britain went off the Gold Standard. The E.E.A. has two components: gold/convertible currencies and sterling. When the commercial banks require gold or, more usually, foreign currencies, to enable their customers to make payment for imports, the banks obtain these from the E.E.A. in return for sterling. The sterling portion of the Account therefore increases; the gold and convertible currencies part reduces. Since the sterling part is invested in 'tap' Treasury bills (those issued direct and not through the weekly tender) the ability of the E.E.A. to finance the Exchequer is incidentally thereby increased.

EXCHANGE RATE

All member countries of the International Monetary Fund agree to keep the external value of their currency in the foreign exchange market within 1 per cent on either side of an adopted par value (which itself, however, may be changed through devaluation or revaluation). It is therefore the duty of a central bank to intervene in the foreign exchange market as a buyer or seller of its currency against other currencies in order to keep the 'spot' (immediate delivery) rate within these limits. Like all member countries, except of course America herself, Britain pegs the external value of the pound to the U.S. dollar, currently at a rate of $2·40 = £1. The Bank must therefore prevent this rate going above $2·42 by supplying pounds to the foreign exchange market in exchange for dollars. Conversely, to keep the rate from falling below $2·38, the Bank must use the gold and foreign currencies of the E.E.A. to buy pounds. This indeed is the mechanism whereby the E.E.A. supplies gold and foreign currencies to the banking system.

There is no obligation upon I.M.F. members to keep the forward exchange rate for their currency within any particular limits, although certain central banks have at times done so. The Bank of England did so for three years before devaluation in November 1967. The forward rate is an agreed future rate of exchange—a sort of 'futures' market in foreign exchange.

EXCHANGE CONTROL

In order to keep sterling strong in the foreign exchange markets, and thus ease the central bank's intervention task, a system of exchange control operates in this country. This is designed to restrict the supply of sterling going to non-residents and to ensure that U.K. residents pass on the foreign currencies they receive through trade, and in other ways, to the E.E.A. Exchange control operates, for example, by restricting remittance of sterling funds abroad and allowing only 'authorised dealers' to hold foreign currencies. The Exchange Control Act of 1947 provided the Treasury with authority to impose our system of exchange control regulations, but it is in fact administered on the Treasury's behalf by the Bank of England.

INTERNATIONAL MONETARY AFFAIRS

The Governor of the Bank represents Britain in international monetary affairs, either in joint activities with other central banks or at international monetary gatherings, such as the International Monetary Fund and the World Bank in Washington, or the Bank for International Settlements at Basle. These meetings concern the operation of the world's monetary system for settling international transactions or making loans. As the recipient, particularly during the sixties, of sizeable short- to medium-term assistance, Britain has figured prominently at monetary gatherings held to devise international borrowing arrangements to lend support to sterling. The Sterling Area itself is an international monetary system that came into being during the inter-war period, with the Bank of England holding a natural position of chairmanship.

This concludes our description of the Bank of England as Britain's central bank. We now turn to a particularly British institution, the London discount market, which, as we have already seen, occupies a unique position between the central bank and the commercial banking system.

8

Other Financial Institutions

DISCOUNT MARKET

The London discount market is composed of eleven discount houses, many of whom evolved from the early bill brokers. Broadly, the discount houses make their living by borrowing very short term funds from the banking system and investing them in longer term assets that give a return higher than the cost of the borrowed funds. The margin between the two is sometimes not very great, so that for their profitability the houses are dependent upon a large turnover. The total resources borrowed by the houses are nowadays in the region of £1,600 million, although this amount fluctuates. In their employment these resources are spread, on average fairly equally, over four main asset categories: Treasury bills, commercial bills, short-dated British government securities and other assets, including sterling and dollar certificates of deposit.

The discount houses obtain their funds from a wide range of banking institutions, but chiefly from the London Clearing banks. These loans are on a day-to-day basis, known as 'call money' lending since the loans are virtually repayable on demand. Lending to the discount market thus gives the banks an opportunity to employ funds in a very liquid form, while still earning a significant rate of interest. As security for call money, the discount houses deposit with the banks some of their bill and bond holdings. The minimum charged by the banks for loans to the discount houses is known as the 'call money rate', traditionally fixed at ⅜ per cent above the rate that the banks pay on deposit account. Other rates charged for loans to the discount market are higher than this, particularly when they come from the non-clearing banks, the overseas banks being the next largest lenders after the Clearers.

One of the chief ways in which the discount houses employ these borrowed funds is in the holding of bills, notably government Treasury bills. These are a form of short-term government borrowing, usually for three months, bills of a minimum denomination of £5,000 being sold at a discount and redeemed at par. At the weekly Treasury bill tender, conducted by the Bank of England, the discount market submits a syndicated bid for the whole of the tender on offer, thereby in effect underwriting it. The price bid is below the ultimate redemption value of three-month bills and this difference provides the rate of interest earned by holding the bills. A discount house rarely in practice holds bills to maturity, but instead sells them to the Clearing banks for their liquid assets portfolio. These banks agree not to bid on their own account at the tender and are thus never holders of bills less than two weeks old. But there are other bidders for bills, so that often the discount market receives only a small allocation—the bills being allotted by the Bank to the highest bidders, that is those willing to lend to the government at the lowest rate of interest.

The discount houses also hold commercial bills, on which they earn a higher rate of interest. A commercial bill is a form of bridging finance for trade and industry to cover the period between dispatch of goods and receipt of payment, or between expenditure on the factors of production and ultimate sales of the finished product. The majority of commercial bills are bank bills, that is, they have been 'accepted' by a recognised bank or acceptance house (a merchant bank) who stands surety against default by the firm upon whom the bill is drawn. Trade bills are those that have not been accepted by a bank and thus carry a higher rate of interest. There is also finance house paper, which is accepted by banks, but which is not in respect of actual goods. Some discount houses hold foreign currency bills, being permitted to finance the holding of these by borrowing in the euro-currency markets.

The third of the discount houses' major asset categories is 'bonds', British government securities maturing within five years. (These may originally have been issued in this category as a short 'tap' or have reached it through the passage of time.) The houses trade actively in these 'bonds', turnover in them during a year often being ten times their holdings at any particular time. 'Bonds' have special attractions for the discount market when interest rates are falling, and therefore bond prices rising. Conversely, when interest rates are rising, the houses endeavour to run their bond portfolios down to a very low level. Being major operators in the bond market, the discount houses provide a convenient collecting point for the maturing issues which the authorities generally like to buy up in the market in advance of the redemption date in order to smooth cash flows.

The fourth category is termed 'other assets' and is one which has shown considerable growth in recent years, at certain times becoming the second largest of the four. This growth reflects the development of newer money market instruments like sterling and dollar certificates of time deposit, issued by the non-Clearing banks, the discount houses providing a secondary market in which the depositor can sell his C.D. and thus go liquid again. Also in the 'other assets' category are short-dated securities other than those of the British Government, namely dominion and colonial and U.K. local authority stocks, including 'yearling' (one-year) bonds.

Since the discount houses' borrowing costs reduce immediately upon a cut in Bank rate, while their previously purchased assets continue to earn the higher yield, periods of falling Bank rate are advantageous to discount houses' profitability, just as they are generally disadvantageous to banks' profitability. At such times, as well as dealing actively in bonds, discount houses will be aggressive bidders for Treasury bills, thus assisting the downward movement in short-term market rates.

When describing the functions of the Bank of England, we mentioned the special relationship it has with the discount market as its 'lender of last resort'. Borrowing at Bank rate generally means that the market is paying more for that portion of its funds than it will earn in their employment, since Treasury bill yields, for example, are below Bank rate. The discount houses normally react to being put into the Bank by lowering their bid at the next Treasury bill tender in order to raise the yield. This in any case is what the authorities wish them to do. When Bank rate itself is raised, the discount houses naturally adjust their bid by the fullest extent, since their total borrowing costs immediately increase, while a large part of their assets are on the previous lower yield basis.

We have now looked in some detail at the three major institutions of the U.K. financial system: the Bank of England, the Clearing banks and the discount market, with the inter-relationships between them being specially highlighted. As agent of the Government, the Bank's general monetary policy and particular instruments exercise a strong governing influence upon the operations of the Clearing banks, who have traditionally linked their interest rates structure fairly rigidly to the Bank of England's discount rate. The Clearing banks provide the major element in the national money supply and are substantial lenders to the public sector through their holdings of Treasury bills, government stocks, lodgement of special deposits and advances to nationalised industries and local authorities. The discount market is heavily dependent upon the Clearing banks for its resources, but in return provides them with an opportunity for profitable, but still highly liquid, employment of part of their deposits. The Clearing banks and the discount market trade with one another in Treasury and commercial bills, as well as government bonds. The discount market is the medium in this country through which the central bank alleviates cash shortage in the banking system. A substantial part of the discount market's resources is invested in public sector debt. Like the Clearing banks, the discount houses are affected by the Bank of England's conduct of monetary policy and are indeed themselves an instrument of it.

MONEY MARKET

In concluding this section, it will be appropriate to explain a term frequently used in financial journalism, namely, the 'money market'. When employed in this context 'money' refers to very short-term borrowing and lending—such as lending at call by the Clearing banks to the discount market (indeed originally the term referred almost exclusively to these two institutions). The cost of 'money' is therefore the interest rates charged for short-term loans for periods ranging from overnight, through the range of 7 days, 1 month, etc., up to 3 months.

With the move in recent times to much higher interest rates it became more and more obviously worthwhile to employ short-term funds to the fullest; while at such interest rate levels borrowers were disinclined to do so on too long term a basis. Thus, there was a very marked expansion in the volume of short-term lending and borrowing, in particular by local government authorities, but also by hire purchase finance companies. The growth of the non-Clearing banks has increased their participation in money market activities and they have, in addition, developed their own 'inter-bank market', in which they lend their surplus cash balances to one another (as also now do companies participating in the 'inter-company market'). In many of these newer money market activities borrowers and lenders are brought together either by specialist brokers, or by discount houses and a few stockbrokers acting in this capacity. At times the funds available in these money markets have been greatly enlarged by the acceptance and switching into sterling of foreign currency deposits, the availability of these being greatly facilitated by the development of euro-currency markets, and notably the euro-dollar.

MERCHANT BANKS

Merchant banks derive their name from the fact that originally they were very much concerned with foreign trade and its financing. This is still true, although these banks have in addition developed many other activities. More formally, they are known either as Accepting Houses or as Issuing Houses, although the larger merchant banks combine these aspects. The words 'Accepting' and 'Issuing' indicate the two major functions of merchant banks. The first of these relates to the traditional activity of helping to finance trade by the 'acceptance' of bills of exchange. The second, 'Issuing', refers to the newer activity of providing capital for companies through the issue of stocks and shares. Among leading merchant banks are some very well-known names: Barings, Hambros, Hill Samuel, Lazards, Morgan Grenfell, Rothschilds, Samuel Montagu, Schroder Wagg and Warburg.

When looking at the ways in which the discount market employs its resources, we have already touched upon bills of exchange, or 'commercial bills' as they are more usually called today. It will be appropriate here to describe them in greater detail, in order to understand better the role played by the merchant banks, and indeed the discount houses. A bill of exchange is designed to overcome certain difficulties, due to time-lags, in making payment for goods. A manufacturer exporting goods would like to be paid as soon as he parts with them; the foreign importer is equally naturally reluctant to pay until he has actually received the goods and some months may elapse before this happens. What takes place, therefore, is that a bill of exchange is drawn up on the basis of the importer paying in, say, three months time. The exporter can get his money immediately by selling his bill at a discount to someone, like a discount house, prepared to hold it and collect payment from the importer at the end of the period. The difference between the discounted value and the face value on maturity is generally expressed as a rate of interest earned by the holder of the bill. Willingness to discount a bill (and at a lower rate of interest) is greatly enhanced if an acceptance house guarantees payment on the bill should the importer default, and for this the merchant bank charges an acceptance commission. In addition to helping to finance trade in this way, a merchant bank will arrange shipping, insurance, etc. Commercial bills may also be used for financing domestic trade and industry, being in this case known as 'inland bills'.

The second major activity of a merchant bank is assisting companies to raise new long-term capital for expanding their business, either by installing additional fixed assets or by acquiring other firms: it is in this latter respect that merchant banks get involved in takeover bids and counter-bids. After discussing with its client the amount and terms upon which new capital is to be raised, the issuing house undertakes to find the funds, acting as sponsor and underwriter to the issue. The broker to the issue is called in and large institutional investors are sounded out as to the acceptability of the issue, these usually also being offered sub-underwriting. More, however, will be said about the new issue procedure at a later stage (see page 266).

As well as being financial advisers to companies, merchant banks also act as their bankers in the normal way. It is from business organisations that merchant banks accept deposits, not from the ordinary members of the public. On deposit account merchant banks pay a higher interest than the Clearing banks do directly, but also charge more on their advances.

Dealing in foreign exchange is a notable merchant bank activity and associated with this is the leading part they play in the euro-currency markets, particularly the euro-dollar. Two of the banks, Rothschilds and Samuel Montagu, are members of the London Gold Market, Rothschilds acting as Chairman.

Investment management has been one of the newer and rapidly growing activities of merchant banks. This includes acting as advisers to other bodies in the investment of their funds, in stocks and shares, property, etc; as well as running their own unit and investment trusts, about which more will be said later (see page 87).

The merchant banks, unlike the Clearers, have not in the past been subject to any formal reserve or liquidity requirements laid down by the monetary authorities: in fact they keep only a small cash reserve, but their liquid assets are proportionately larger. Like other non-clearing banks they were subject to the cash deposits scheme, although this was never used. But the new reserve requirement will be applied to the merchant banks. The Bank of England has always kept a check that each merchant bank has the resources necessary to back up its acceptances. The power of the Bank over the merchant banks lies partly in its ability to dictate which acceptances it is prepared to take as 'eligible security' when extending loans to the discount market. In addition, merchant banks have been subject to the same sort of lending ceilings imposed on the Clearing banks, those ceilings applying to their acceptances as well as their advances.

OVERSEAS AND FOREIGN BANKS

The remaining category of banks is overseas and foreign. British overseas banks are those having their head offices in London, but their branch network abroad, often in a Commonwealth country, although also in areas like South America. Many of these overseas banks are wholly or partly-owned subsidiaries of London Clearing banks. Foreign banks are those whose branches are in London and their head office in another country; notable in this category are the London branches of American banks.

The original development of British overseas banks was naturally associated with Britain's colonising activities, economic as well as political. They are still largely concerned with the financing of trade between the United Kingdom and the areas in which they operate, as well as acting as local banks to the overseas subsidiaries of British companies. Similarly, foreign banks in London service the British subsidiaries of foreign parent companies, their deposits mainly coming from these sources, rather than from U.K. residents and companies.

Both overseas and foreign banks naturally transact a good deal of foreign exchange business and in more recent years have been especially active in the euro-dollar market, this being an inducement to many U.S. banks to set up branches in London, particularly at times when the parent banks were anxious to recruit such funds to ease credit scarcity in the United States. Foreign and overseas banks provide call money to the discount market and are also substantial holders of British government bonds.

OTHER FINANCIAL INTERMEDIARIES

We have now dealt with Britain's various banking institutions. There are, however, other types of financial intermediaries that are not banks, but which nevertheless play an important part in the transfer of funds from savers to active users. This middleman activity is what is meant by the term 'financial intermediary'.

HIRE PURCHASE

Finance houses are suppliers of hire purchase credit, in this way channelling savings back into consumption. Hire purchase enables the immediate acquisition of a consumer durable (especially a motor car) on the basis of an initial deposit of only a percentage of the price and payment by instalment of the remainder over a stipulated period of years, together with an interest charge. Hire purchase is also available for business and industrial equipment and in this way goes for investment rather than consumption.

As already seen, most of the Clearing banks have a part or controlling interest in finance houses. For the personal borrower hire purchase is an alternative to a bank advance, although generally a more costly one. About half the funds the finance houses lend out come from deposit and current accounts held with them by industrial and commercial firms, since the interest paid is a good deal higher than that given by the banks. The rest of their funds the finance houses obtain from Clearing and merchant banks, the latter often employing in this way foreign currency deposits swapped into sterling. The finance companies themselves also directly recruit deposits from overseas residents. In recent years the finance houses have been brought within the same sort of lending ceilings to which the banks are subject. In addition, the Department of Trade and Industry can from time to time regulate the amount of initial deposit and length of repayment period in hire purchase contracts, in order to restrict, or relax, credit availability. This is known as 'terms control' and in the Crowther Report on Consumer Credit (March 1971) the government was urged to abandon this method of credit regulation. The Bank of England, in its paper on 'Competition and Credit Control' (May 1971), did indicate that hire purchase companies are in future to be subject to some sort of overall monetary regulation, similar to that outlined for the banks, and as part of this the imposition of ceilings on hire purchase lending is likely to be ended.

BUILDING SOCIETIES

For the largest consumer durable purchase of all, namely a house, building societies supply long-term credit in the form of a mortgage. These societies recruit a good deal of their resources for house purchase loans from ordinary members of the public, paying a competitive rate of interest on all money placed with them. Building societies must conduct their affairs on a non-profit-making basis, the difference between their borrowing and lending rates being only such as to cover operating expenses, pay tax on interest to depositors and shareholders and maintain reserve ratios. For deposits placed with it to have trustee investment status, a society must have reserves of around $2\frac{1}{2}$ per cent of total liabilities (this percentage is reduced for the larger societies, but most keep about 1 per cent above the minimum). On the assets side at least $7\frac{1}{2}$ per cent must be held as liquid assets, that is investments and other non-mortgage forms. Up to $92\frac{1}{2}$ per cent of their funds could therefore be used to grant mortgages for house purchase, but in practice the societies keep to a lower level of around 85 per cent. House purchasers usually obtain a mortgage of at least 80 per cent of the price (normally up to a maximum of £10,000), with a repayment period of 25 years, although the average mortgage life is considerably shorter than this.

Other Financial Institutions

We come now to a group of financial intermediaries that are major suppliers of long-term capital to business and government through their investment in stocks and shares. Insurance companies and pension funds harness the ordinary man's savings on a contractual basis, through his regular payment of insurance premiums and pension fund contributions. The annual flow of new investment funds available in this way is very considerable.

There are two major categories of insurance company business. The 'Life' side deals with life assurance and pensions, both of which are long-term affairs, so that life funds can, until they are required, be placed in suitably longer term investments to match liabilities. Life funds are substantially invested in Government stocks and ordinary shares, but increasingly in recent years there has also been direct investment in property development. Insurance companies do make loans to their policy holders for house purchase. General insurance, concerned with fire, accident and marine insurance, is dealing in much more uncertain areas and therefore the investment of these premiums must be in short term, readily marketable forms.

A growing number of employees are covered by company pension schemes, these either being self-administered by the company itself or provided through an insurance company as a group scheme. Once again, these pension funds have substantial resources for investment, until they are required to be paid out as pensions. Interest and dividends may be received by pension funds free-of-tax and for this reason are known as 'gross funds'. The forms in which investments can be made are subject to the 1961 Trustee Investments Act.

INVESTMENT AND UNIT TRUSTS

Once more, these trusts are bodies that gather up savings and through the capital markets provide business firms with finance. For the small investor, unit and investment trusts enable the individual risks of investment to be spread over a large number of shares. Some trusts however are slanted towards investment in certain industry sectors or geographical areas or to obtaining a particular type of income.

An investment trust is a company formed for the purpose of

investing its shareholders' funds (together with any loan capital borrowed from outside) in a number of stocks and shares. The shareholder's dividend comes from the interest and dividends received in respect of the investments acquired, but as with any other company there is no obligation to pay out everything.

The participants in a unit trust are not shareholders, but purchasers of a unit representing the part-ownership of a general portfolio of stocks and shares held by the trust, each unit being a composite in miniature. The managers of the trust make the market in the units, selling and buying them back at prices reflecting the current market value of the stocks and shares held. The whole of the interest and dividends received from the portfolio, less management expenses, must be distributed to the unit holders.

THE STOCK EXCHANGE

The willingness of people to lend their savings (or, in the case of financial intermediaries, those of other people) is greatly enhanced if they know that, if needs be, they can liquidate their investment. If a person buys a fixed interest investment with a definite redemption date, he gets repayment of his loan when it matures. But should he want to disinvest before this, or if he had lent on a basis of no guaranteed repayment (such as an irredeemable stock or an equity share) then to get his money out he is dependent upon someone else being willing to take over his place as lender, in other words to buy his investment from him. The ability to liquidate depends therefore upon marketability.

The London and provincial stock exchanges provide this market in which existing stocks and shares can be bought and sold, and through which newly-created ones may be issued. Those wishing to buy or sell securities do so through a stockbroker, who in turn buys from or sells to a jobber. It is the jobber who holds the 'book' of stocks and shares; the stockbroker acts merely as agent for the ultimate buyer or seller, whether an institution or a private investor.

PART THREE

National Objectives and Government Policy

9

National Objectives

Since so much of what happens in the economy nowadays springs from conscious Government policy, it is as well to start by considering first of all the ends and means of Government policy, before dealing with, one might almost say, the resultant economic background. What then are the major objectives of Government policy? What is the Government aiming for?—in addition to winning the next general election, although this motive can have very real, and sometimes almost disastrous, economic consequences. We will, however, concern ourselves here with the economic objectives, leaving aside those in the realms of foreign policy, defence and politics. Broadly speaking, since the Second World War, Government economic policy in this country has been directed towards four major objectives—full employment, growth, and a strong and stable £. Although these are all desirable objectives, but not necessarily equally desirable, our post-war experience has indicated that some of them are antagonistic to one another. To understand why this should be so, it is necessary to look more closely at the nature of these objectives, and then at the policies which the Government adopts in pursuing them.

FULL EMPLOYMENT

The continuation of the state of full employment attained during the Second World War into the post-war period has been a prime objective of all Governments in power in this country since 1945. The tenacity with which this goal has been pursued represents in part a natural revulsion from the very high rates of unemployment which prevailed during the inter-war years. In the 'twenties the unemployment percentage kept just above 10 per cent, but in the first half of the 'thirties it was at the extremely high level of 20 per cent, which meant that one in every five workers was out of work. The outbreak of war changed this, although it was not until 1942 that unemployment fell to the sort of level to which we are more accustomed today. During the war itself it was felt that men would fight with better heart if they were given some indication of the kind of post-war world they were fighting for. Among the pledges made was the avoidance of any return to the mass unemployment of the 'thirties. The level of unemployment to be tolerated was probably put most concretely by Lord Beveridge, his target being a national average unemployment of no more than 3 per cent, which in the light of the inter-war experience seemed to be aiming low. Today, if unemployment does reach this level everybody begins to get very worried. In fact, since the end of the war the annual unemployment percentage in this country has for most of the time ranged between only $1\frac{1}{2}$ to $2\frac{1}{2}$ per cent.

It is often argued that this over-full employment in the post-war years has been the cause of failure to achieve some of our other objectives. Over-full employment gives rise to inflation and weakens the value of the £, both internally and externally. A move to a higher average level of unemployment is advocated on the grounds of discouraging labour hoarding, encouraging the mobility of labour, providing labour for those export industries which tend to be starved of it, and helping to contain any tendency towards excessive 'wages push' inflation.

It is possible to advocate a higher level of unemployment without being in any way inhuman, provided certain preconditions are present. First of all, regional development policies must have been successful in spreading employment opportunities more evenly throughout the country, so that a national average rate of unemployment of 3 per cent does not mean, as at present, a rate as high as 8 per cent in certain parts of the country. For those who are unemployed, there must be an adequate level of unemployment benefit; adequate, that is, to provide the basic necessities of food, clothing and housing; but not necessarily enough to cover the H.P. on the car, the 'tele', and the 'fridge. (In recent years the disadvantages of over-adequate provision of unemployment and other benefits have become apparent in the incidence of voluntary unemployment, including strike action.) Unemployment must also be temporary, with official encouragement of labour mobility and the provision of retraining and rehousing facilities. If all these conditions exist, then the economy can be operated on the basis of the existence of some spare labour capacity, without thereby imposing intolerable hardship. But whether a Goverment adopting such a policy can survive electorally is another matter.

There was considerable uproar throughout the country when the 'stop' policies of Selwyn Lloyd in mid-1961, combined with the exceptionally severe winter of 1962/63, resulted in a national unemployment percentage of 3·9 per cent. The economy had to be hurriedly pushed into another expansion phase to meet the approaching election. In mid-1966 the mere suggestion by Harold Wilson that unemployment in the coming winter might reach 2 per cent was greeted with considerable dismay, particularly by the trade union movement. With regular public opinion polls providing a continual indication of the Government's popularity, or otherwise, it requires strong nerves to hold the economy on a course that will result in rising unemployment.

GROWTH

The clamour for growth arose again in this country with the Selwyn Lloyd 'stop' of mid-1961. The stagnation into which the economy was plunged in 1962 caused a national reaction against the 'stop-go' cycle and there was a demand for continuous expansion. Growth became the thing for any self-respecting economy to exhibit. 'Growth' is defined in terms of the annual percentage rate of increase in gross national product on a constant price basis; in other words the rate at which the national output of goods and services increases in real, and not just money terms. Behind this universal clamour lay a mixture of motives. Since it is a trait of human nature, nowadays apparently to be indulged, for people always to want more, then a larger national cake is the only way of giving everyone a larger slice. Growth is also necessary if desirable social projects are to be undertaken without a large increase in taxation. Growth may also be required to provide the necessary export surplus to enable us to lend long-term capital abroad and make economic grants to the underdeveloped countries, as well as continue our overseas defence commitments. In our desire for growth there has, in addition, been an element of keeping up with the continental Joneses.

The setting up of the Common Market in 1958 gave a tremendous boost to the economic growth of the member countries, who had been in any case slower than Britain to recover from the effects of the Second World War and, in their case, the enemy occupation. Part of the explanation of why some of the Six were able to achieve higher growth rates was because they could draw on surplus labour from fellow member countries like Italy, as well as run-down their rural population. Another suggested reason for the disparity has been Britain's lower rate of investment in manufacturing industry at home. Whatever the cause, it is undeniable that the overall growth in this country has been much less: reflecting years in which there has been almost a complete absence of growth, as well as expansion years in which our rate of growth has still been below that of other countries.

ACHIEVEMENT OF GROWTH

There are various ways by which economic growth may be achieved. If there is slack in the economy, with labour and machines lying idle, the bringing of these into production should increase the total output of goods and services. With the economy already at the full employment level, any further growth in real G.N.P. can only come from expansion in the labour force or increased productivity, that is greater output per worker. The first of these depends on such factors as the underlying population growth rate, hours worked, immigration, etc. Improving productivity is a matter of management, technological development and increased investment: all these with the object of raising the output of the individual worker.

THE GROWTH OBJECTIVE

'Growth' is not, of course, something to be sought after for its own sake, it is what we do with the fruits of the growth that is more important. Our real objectives are not growth itself but the raising of the standard of living of the poorer sections of the population; the building of more houses, schools, hospitals, and roads; and paying our way internationally by balancing our payments. If we were to look at how our national factors of production are employed, at the nature and distribution of the £42,000 million of goods and services produced each year, we would probably find that a significant proportion of the factors, and the total product, went into activities which we would be no worse off without, and indeed might be better off. The ending of such activities would automatically release resources to help satisfy our national objectives, without any additional growth, or at least not as much growth as we were seeking in our National Plans. After all, we do produce *new* goods and services each year to the extent of £42,000 million or £750 per head of population; and some of the goods produced in the previous year will still give us service for many years ahead; so that even by just producing the same total GNP each year we should still be able to do new things with it. If therefore we examined more closely how we used our existing GNP capacity, and decided to use it better, we should not be forced to set ourselves targets that fail to be reached, and thus tend to discredit the whole planning exercise. A more rational allocation of existing resources is just as important as achieving faster growth. The existence of physical limitations may in any case enforce this approach.

CONFLICT OF OBJECTIONS

Of the four broad economic objectives, the two which we have so far looked at are undoubtedly 'good for business': the pursuit of full employment and growth usually ensuring a high level of industrial activity and rising profits. But what is good for business is unfortunately not always conducive to the internal and external stability of the £; and so when the prime objectives of Government policy become for the moment a strong and stable £, this is apt to be at the expense of full employment and growth. The advocates of growth would argue that this need not be so. Nor need it, if the overall growth is reflected just as much in the export sphere and if the growth attempted is not in excess of our available resources. But, the experience of the past twenty years has shown that in practice these conditions are not adhered to, and thus there is inevitably a conflict of objective between growth on the one hand and a strong and stable £ on the other.

The objectives of the internal stability and external strength of our currency are, however, in accord with one another: indeed the latter is often dependent upon the former. An absence of internal stability in the value of the £, that is the presence of 'inflation', tends to discourage exports and encourage imports, and thereby weakens the £ in the foreign exchange markets. It is, of course, also possible to have external weakness, without there being any internal instability, due to speculation regarding a possible change in the £ = $ parity, following a revaluation or devaluation of some other currency. However, it is still true to say that if there is an absence of internal stability in its value, then the £ is also very likely to be weak in the foreign exchange markets. Because this is so, it is logical to start by considering first of all the objective of stability in the internal value of the £.

STABLE £

The value of the £ is what it will buy in terms of goods and services. If the prices of these goods and services are rising, then obviously each £ buys less of them and we say, therefore, that the value of money is falling. Conversely, if prices are falling then the value of the £ is rising; but we have not enjoyed this state of affairs since the mid-1930s. For this reason we will here be almost exclusively concerned with the problem of inflation. When we talk about stability in the value of money today, we really mean seeing that our monetary unit does not lose its value too rapidly. A fall in the value of money, or a rise in the general price level, is what is covered by the one word 'inflation'; the opposite of inflation is 'deflation', and when we are trying to move out of a deflationary state, this is known as 'reflation'.

PRICE CHANGE MEASUREMENT

The rate of inflation or deflation is measured in terms of the Index of Retail Prices (the 'cost of living index') prepared by the Government statisticians. There is also an Index of Wholesale Prices showing how industrial prices have risen, as well as the cost of industry's materials. However neither retail nor wholesale price indices give an adequate measure of the general price level: what is called the 'GNP deflator' tries to do this. It attempts to pull out that GNP growth which is purely due to price increase. It measures price changes in respect of goods and services currently produced, that is the Gross National Product, but does not measure price changes of existing assets, like houses for example. The GNP deflator is an amalgam of parts of the retail and wholesale price indices, certain earnings indices and other measures of cost increase in the construction industries and transport, etc. The method of calculating the deflator is to break GNP down over time into its major components and then to apply to the yearly values of these the appropriate price change index to bring them down to a constant price basis. These are then aggregated again to give real GNP value for each year and this can be compared with the current price GNP value to show the rate of inflation.

DEMAND-PULL INFLATION

The causes of inflation are indicated by the names given to the two main types that are customarily distinguished; namely, 'demand-pull' inflation and 'cost-push' inflation. With 'demand-pull' inflation the rise in prices is caused by the pressure of excess demand on a strictly limited supply of goods and services; or put more colloquially 'too much money chasing too few goods'. The resultant higher prices are a means of rationing by the purse the limited supply of goods and services, and thus bringing into equality supply and demand. Demand inflation arises when purchasing power is enlarged by an expansion of bank personal loans and hire purchase facilities, and when industrial earnings rise faster than the output of goods and services. It may result from the willingness of employers in such a situation to bid against one another. It may also result from Government action that increases money supply, either in the crude form of just turning on the printing presses and producing more money, or more subtly by reducing taxation and/or increasing Government expenditure. If the volume of goods and services does not expand to match this additional money put into the hands of the public prices will rise. Monetarists, like Milton Friedman, indeed argue that inflation is only a monetary phenomena and solely due to a faster rise in the quantity of money relative to growth in output.

In all that has been said above, the level of saving is assumed not to rise; if it falls, this adds to the inflationary pressure. Another basic assumption of course is that the economy is already fully employed, so that further growth in aggregate demand cannot be matched by increase in aggregate supply and therefore prices will rise. In practice this will probably happen before the full employment level is reached.

COST-PUSH INFLATION

Cost-push inflation arises, as its name suggests, from cost increases having to be passed on to the consumer in the form of higher prices. Raw material costs may be higher because of a rise in world commodity prices. Wage costs may rise due to exploitation by the unions of a situation of labour scarcity. This latter form of 'cost' inflation is often labelled 'wages-push' inflation. It generally operates most strongly in the later stages of an economic expansion phase. Before that stage is reached productivity improves rapidly, reflecting a faster rise in output than in labour force; therefore this improvement can help absorb some of the wage increase. The experience of recent years in this country has revealed some newer sub-species of wage-push. There has, for example, been 'growth anticipation' inflation, where wage claims have been calculated on the assumption that a certain economic growth rate will be achieved: hence the constant pressure from the TUC that Government growth targets should be more ambitious. When anticipated growth is not achieved, the result of such claims is of course inflationary. There may also be an enlargement of labour's share of the national cake, at the expense of the other factors. This effect may be quite deliberately sought by the more socialistic of trade union leaders. But to the extent that not all labour's gain is at the expense of other factors, there will be a general price rise effect and hence we can talk about 'income claims' inflation.

Although these two types of inflation ('demand' and 'cost') may be distinguished, they normally co-exist; one feeding the other. In a situation of excessive pressure of demand the unemployment percentage will usually be very low and this will provide a favourable environment for wages-push inflation: this in turn will increase industrial earnings and so add to the demand inflation. A rising cost of living is also an incitement to the workers to make wage demands and so there develops the wages-prices spiral.

There can however sometimes be conditions of pure cost inflation, with no contribution from excess demand. It is argued that such a situation exists when employment and output are falling, but prices and wages rising fast—a situation that has been referred to as 'stagflation', a stagnant economy, but nevertheless inflation. In such a paradoxical situation a lot may be due to the unions' monopoly power and indeed inflation in general may often be due at least in part to aspects of imperfect competition or market power.

GAINERS AND LOSERS

In an inflationary climate there are gainers and losers, as an inevitable consequence of the distinction between real assets and money assets. The former can perhaps keep up with inflation, the latter usually cannot. Also of significance in this context is the ratio of a person's monetary assets to his monetary liabilities. Broadly speaking, the gainer from inflation is the person who owes more money than is owed to him. As inflation erodes money values, so also will it erode the real burden of a net liability position. But usually rather than try to be gainers from it, people are quite happy if they can manage to avoid suffering under inflation. The ability to avoid suffering during an inflationary climate depends really on the extent to which one can do something about it. Usually bygones are bygones; but in making present economic decisions about matters that will extend over time one can build into calculations some allowance for a future rate of inflation. Planning on this basis is part of 'inflationary psychology'. In trying thus to anticipate future inflation one has to do so in terms of duration as well as degree, and this may not always be easy. When an inflationary psychology becomes widespread and entrenched, it not only itself adds to the price rise but it also makes less effective Government anti-inflationary monetary and fiscal policy: for example, high interest rates are no longer a deterrent to borrowing and spending.

There are some groups that cannot allow for inflation, or at least can do so only to a very limited extent, and when this is the case they experience a loss of real income. Overall there is a redistribution of wealth to those who can keep pace with inflation from those who cannot. In this way inflation may be just as lacking in social conscience as deflation. The chief sufferers under inflation are naturally those whose incomes do not vary: the recipients of pensions, fixed interest income and those whose salaries are only infrequently reviewed. Sufferers who have invested in fixed interest securities can do nothing to safeguard their past savings: those that borrowed from them on this basis enjoy the benefit. In the case of holders of Government debt, they are merely regarded as having been subject to an 'inflation tax', that usefully helps to reduce the real burden of the National Debt. Traditionally, savers who wished to safeguard their savings against inflation put their money into equities to give them ownership of real assets; but with the severe wages-push squeeze on profits this protection has appeared at times rather thin.

Wage earners are better able to keep pace with inflation, and even keep ahead of it, through strong trade union bargaining power. Indeed, in framing their wage claims they build in an allowance for future inflation. Employers can attempt to protect their profit margins against increases in wages and material costs by prompt pricing action. This is not always possible, however, due to competitive pressures or in some cases through orders being obtained on a fixed price basis. With the real value of items expressed in monetary terms being eroded by inflation, companies with net monetary assets lose; while those with net monetary liabilities gain. Those companies that have in the past raised a large proportion of their capital on a fixed interest basis, and at a lower interest rate level, are clear gainers. Even where profits do not get squeezed by rising costs they are usually not so good as they appear. Since company balance sheets rarely show real values of capital assets, depreciation charges are on the basis of historical rather than true replacement cost. With pre-tax profits larger companies are encouraged to pay out more in dividends than they ought to do, if they are to make adequate provision for preservation of fixed assets.

In seeking stability in the value of the £ the Government is not aiming at absolute stability, indeed in some circles a mild degree of inflation is held to be a necessary stimulant for a healthy economy: a rate of inflation of up to 2 to 3 per cent being regarded as quite tolerable. But in the post-war period the rate of inflation in this country has averaged nearly 4 per cent. In some years it has been as high as 5 to 6 per cent and this has given rise, not only to concern, but also to an unfavourable balance of trade. In 1970 it reached the high level of 8½ per cent and by the middle of the following year was running at a rate of nearly 10 per cent. Such rates, are still, of course, moderate by South American standards, where inflation is endemic and currencies may be devalued two or three times in the course of a year.

Britain's rate of inflation in the post-war period has, however, been historically high and certainly the highest experienced so far in the twentieth century. Up to the First World War, we enjoyed comparative price stability and during the inter-war years the cost of living actually fell at an average rate of nearly 2 per cent a year. The essential feature distinguishing these periods from the past twenty years was, of course, the degree of unemployment. It has been the overfull employment of the post-war years which has more than anything else contributed to the high rate of inflation experienced during this time. This can be seen when the degree of, or absence of, inflation is related to the unemployment percentage prevailing in this country during three periods of this century, leaving out the wartime years.

UNITED KINGDOM

Period	Average Unemployment %	Average Annual Rate of inflation %
1900–1913	4·3	+0·8
1920–1939	13·3	−1·8
1946–1970	1·9	+4·0

STRONG £

The phrase 'a strong £' is thought by some people to have a jingoistic ring about it and to denote a willingness to sacrifice economic welfare and human happiness to some arbitrarily chosen exchange rate parity.

FOREIGN EXCHANGE MARKET

What do we really mean by wanting 'a strong £', as opposed to 'a weak £'? This can be quite simply explained by the law of supply and demand, operating in the market. In the case of the £, the 'market' is the foreign exchange market and to this people come (but not literally, for it is generally all done by telephone) who want to buy a particular currency in order to pay for goods which they have bought from the country of that currency. There will also in the market be exporters who have earned that country's currency and who wish to exchange it into their own or some other currency. Thus, to take the £ as an example, there will in the foreign exchange market be people wishing to sell £s, as well as those wishing to buy £s. The 'price' of the £ is the rate at which it exchanges for other currencies, and particularly the U.S. $. It is movements of this price, or exchange rate, which like any other price brings into equilibrium the supply of, and demand for, any particular currency. If there are more people trying to sell £s in exchange for U.S. $s than there are people wishing to buy £s with U.S. $s, then the price of the £ will fall in relation to the U.S. $: instead of being $2·40 = £1, it may fall to $2·39 = £1. This fall in price will tend to bring about equality in the demand for, and supply of, £s by encouraging some holders of U.S. $s to buy £s, since they are now cheaper in terms of U.S. $s; while some holders of £s will be discouraged from selling them, because they are getting less U.S. $ for each £. This falling tendency of the price of the £ in terms of other currencies is what is meant when the £ is said to be 'weak'.

CONSEQUENCES OF WEAKNESS

Does it matter if one's currency is 'weak' in the foreign exchange markets? Obviously it does, or the Treasury and the Bank of England would not get so worried every time the £ comes under pressure and the rate falls. The main reason it matters nowadays is that, to achieve some sort of stability in exchange rates for trading convenience, the member nations of the International Monetary Fund have agreed to adopt a certain rate of exchange (or par value) of their currency against either gold, or more usually against the U.S. $, which itself is held against gold at $35 to the fine ounce. Exchange rates are allowed to fluctuate only to the extent of 1 per cent on each side of this adopted par value. To keep its exchange rate within this range, the central bank of the country concerned has, as we have already seen, to be prepared to buy and sell its own currency in the foreign exchange market. When its currency is weak, due to over-supply in the foreign exchange markets, then the exchange rate has to be 'supported' (i.e. stopped from falling any further) by mopping up the surplus; that is, the central bank concerned has to buy up its own currency with gold or other foreign currencies which are more in demand. This means that weakness in the external value of one's currency gives rise to a continuous drain on the gold and convertible currency reserves, and if the weakness continues there is a danger of the reserves being completely exhausted. This is rarely allowed to happen: instead supplementary reserves are borrowed from other countries and international bodies, and steps are taken to correct the cause of weakness. But, if the reserves were allowed to be run down completely, the country would quite simply no longer be in the position to support its exchange rate and it would therefore sink below the IMF par value. Such a depreciation would mean that the country's imports would cost more and it would also earn less in foreign currencies by its exports. IMF obligations apart, these together with possible domestic inflation effects are the real underlying disadvantages of a continuing weakness in the external value of a currency.

BALANCE OF PAYMENTS

To understand how this weakness may be avoided, or corrected, it is necessary to consider how the excess supply position of a currency in the foreign exchange markets arises. Basically, it may result from a country's balance of trade; that is, the relationship between its exports and imports, although capital flows also have to be taken into account. If a country's imports exceed its exports, then in the foreign exchange market its currency will tend to be plentiful in relation to foreign currencies. The amount of sterling earned by foreigners selling goods to this country will be greater than the sterling required by foreigners to pay for British goods. As regards foreign currencies, the requirements of British importers will exceed the foreign currency earnings of British exporters.

Apart from visible trade, there are what are termed the 'invisible' items; that is, payments received for services rendered by us to foreigners, as well as payments made for foreign services used by British nationals. Among such service items are banking, insurance, shipping, etc.; but in addition, receipts of interest and profits from British owned assets overseas are included as 'invisible' credits; while in respect of the British subsidiaries of foreign companies remitted profits count as debit items, as also do interest payments to foreign holders of British Government debt. In the 'invisible' debit category is also included Britain's overseas military expenditure and economic grants to members of the Commonwealth.

The combined flow of payments and receipts in respect of visible and invisible items makes up the balance of payments on current account. The other major component in the balance of payments is, as might be guessed, the capital account. This is largely made up of private investment capital flows, although there are also some much smaller inter-government loan items. In the long-term capital account, debits are outflows of capital, either in the form of direct investment by companies in their overseas subsidiaries (including profits retained by these subsidiaries) or in the form of portfolio investment, that is purchases of shares in overseas companies. Credit items are capital inflows, representing foreigners' acquisitions of assets in this country, again either by direct or portfolio investments.

Short-term capital flows are nowadays also included in the calculation of the balance of payments, being grouped with long-term capital in the second part, entitled 'Investment and other capital flows'. (Under the previously employed 'basic' method, balance was derived from the current and long-term capital accounts; short-term capital flows were outside this, as part of monetary movements or accommodating items like international borrowing and changes in the reserves.) Short-term capital flows reflect changes in those of Britain's external assets and liabilities having maturities of less than one year. Notable among these are, of course, the sterling balances held in London by the Overseas Sterling Area and Non-Sterling Area countries, representing the external liabilities in sterling of the U.K. banking system. In the main, sterling balances are a fairly passive form of short-term capital movement, their changes largely reflecting shifts in the balance of payments position between the United Kingdom on the one hand and the O.S.A. and N.S.A. on the other, as well as also between the O.S.A. and the N.S.A. themselves.

When Britain is in trading deficit, if the rest of the world is prepared to accept payment in sterling balances this takes pressure off the reserves and to encourage this the authorities may increase U.K. short-term interest rates to improve the return on these balances. Britain's banks also accept foreign currency deposits from overseas (especially euro-dollars) and when these are swapped into sterling there is a benefit to the official reserves. The extent to which trade credit is given and received from abroad is another item in the short-term capital category.

The overall balance deriving from current and long and short-term capital accounts should be reflected in what has happened to the gold and convertible currency reserves, after taking into account any international borrowing or repayment by this country. This is the last item in the balance of payments table, being entitled 'Official financing' and made up of changes in official reserves and official borrowing. In practice the two sides of the balance of payments table do not exactly correspond. Since the official financing figures are accurate, the error must lie somewhere in the vast complex of trade and capital flows. To take account of this error a 'balancing item' is added to the current balance and investment and other capital flows to make the total 'currency flow' correspond to the known official financing position. The balancing item is composed of unrecorded elements of trade and unidentified capital movements, and in recent years has been discovered to contain a substantial amount of under-recording of exports.

10

National Income Determination

To achieve its objectives the Government employs a wide variety of techniques, but most of these fall conveniently into one of three categories: fiscal measures, monetary policy and direct controls. The manner in which policies in these three groups work towards the attainment of the four major objectives will be better understood if some simple explanation is first given of the theory of national income determination, the development of which was largely the work of Lord Keynes.

National income is simply the flow of new goods and services produced during a period of time (such as a year) by a country's factors of production (including its stock of capital assets). Probably, to the businessman, the term 'national output' would be more readily understood than national *income*. 'Income' is however the word traditionally used in economics to describe a flow of wealth produced or benefit enjoyed from the ownership of wealth. This latter is of course also the normal everyday use of the word: we readily talk about our 'income' from investments. The total value of the national output of goods and services can in fact be computed by adding up everyone's income; that is, the incomes of the factors of production received as wages, rent, interest or profit. For the purposes of this chapter we may also think of national income as the 'demand' side: the total incomes of the factors of production available for spending, either directly or indirectly, on consumer or capital goods. In the same way national output can be thought of as the 'supply' of goods and services.

As in the case of a factory, the economy can operate at various levels of output of goods and services, and consequently at various levels of employment, The fact that demand and supply are in equilibrium is no guarantee of full employment, for overall demand and supply can be equal to one another at almost any level of national income. At a low level of income there will be a high degree of unemployment of the factor labour. To raise employment it is necessary to raise the level of income. Ideally, the level of activity in the economy should be that which provides full employment. When this stage is reached, any further rise in money incomes cannot be matched by additional output due to lack of available labour and in the absence of any improvement in productivity. In such circumstances, the only result of further incomes increase, beyond the point of full employment, will be to raise prices.

To appreciate how the Government may go about raising the national income up to a condition of full employment, or alternatively restraining income rises from going beyond this point, it is necessary to look at the major components of total income and total output. As was seen earlier, income and output must necessarily be equal, since the total sales value of output eventually finds its way back to the factors of production as their various forms of income: rent, wages, interest and profits. The income received by these factors will either be spent or saved. Those on a low income will tend to spend rather than save; while those on a high income will save a major part of it. The tendency to save more or spend more, at high or low income levels respectively, is known as the propensity to save or to consume. The allocation of the additional increments of income as between saving and spending differs of course from the division of the total income: thus we have the concepts of 'marginal' propensity to consume or save. When the national income level is rising, or falling, these marginal propensities are of greater significance than the overall division of income as between consumption and saving.

Into all this must of course be introduced the activities of the Government. Total factor incomes are reduced by taxation, so that what is left is personal disposable income and it is this which is available for private consumption or saving. But the money taken in taxation may be regarded quite simply as spending or saving carried out by the Government on behalf of its citizens. The way in which the Government allocates tax receipts will have the same importance as the public's propensity to save or to consume. In addition, the relationship of taxation to Government expenditure has an important bearing on the level of national income and employment.

SAVING EQUALS INVESTMENT

On the supply side, national output consists in the main of consumer goods and services and capital goods, the latter representing investment. Output of consumer goods and services will tend to be adjusted to consumption spending. Since national output must be the same as national income and since the output of consumer goods will be geared to consumption, savings must tend towards equality with investment. We say 'tend' because the activities of saving and investment are often the independently arrived at decisions of entirely different groups of people. Not surprisingly, therefore, saving and investment often from time to time get out of line. They will eventually become equal again, but only through a variation in the level of national income, and therefore of employment.

If saving exceeds investment, this means that less is spent on consumption and therefore stocks of consumer goods tend to pile up. This represents a form of investment: in stocks. Thus, investment comes into line with saving. Eventually, manufacturers will cut back their production schedules because of the pile-up in stocks, and by doing so will create unemployment. This in turn brings about a reduction in incomes and people's ability to save. In this way also, savings and investment are brought into equality; but, it should be noted, at a lower level of income and employment.

When investment rises above saving, the process works in reverse and these two are brought into equality at a higher level of income and employment. Investment in excess of saving means that spending on consumer goods is greater than the production of them; stocks are therefore run down, this representing a form of disinvestment. To replenish these stocks, production schedules are increased and this raises incomes and employment. At this higher level of incomes, there is greater saving, bringing it into line with investment.

ECONOMIC FLUCTUATIONS

The theory of income determination as propounded by Keynes was largely developed to explain the chronic unemployment of the 1930s. In the pre-war economy, with Government intervention at a minimum, economic fluctuations could be largely attributed to the discrepancies between saving and investment, and particularly to variations in the level of investment.

By its nature investment tends to be lumpy. This can be most readily appreciated by considering the case where a manufacturer of consumer goods plans to increase his sales by 50 per cent. This means that he must increase his present capacity from, say, 10 machines to 15. Normally, assuming 10 per cent per annum depreciation, his investment demand would be for only one new machine a year. But, with the decision to expand his capacity, he will suddenly require six machines from the engineering firm supplying them. The latter thus experiences a sixfold increase in the level of his business, purely on the basis of his customer's planned 50 per cent increase in capacity. This fact that a given increase in national income (that is, rise in sales of goods and services) sets off a much greater increase in investment has been labelled by economists as the 'acceleration principle' or simply the 'accelerator'.

The accelerator can also work in reverse. As soon as the growth rate in sales of consumer goods slackens, investment falls back to an even greater extent. And if consumer expenditure ceases to grow altogether, then the drop in investment is very steep. To return to our example: once the consumer goods manufacturer has achieved his desired capacity, his demand will fall back to the normal 10 per cent replacement level. If, however, there is a drop in consumption, with the result that some of his machines are now lying idle, then he may during this time make no provision at all for replacement. As a result the enginering firm will be faced with a zero level of demand.

A particularly prominent example of this in recent years has been the experience of steel plant producers like Davy-Ashmore and Wellman Engineering Corporation. The demand for their products comes of course from the steel industry, but this in turn is partly based on the needs of consumer durable manufacturers in the motors and domestic appliances sectors. Towards the end of the 1950s, to meet the anticipated future requirements of its customers, the steel industry planned to increase its capacity half as much again by 1962. As will be appreciated from the hypothetical example already given, this inevitably meant a much greater increase in activity by producers of steel-plant, as their profit experience between 1960–62 shows.

Pre-tax Profits £m.	1958	1959	1960	1961	1962	1963	1964
Davy Ashmore	1·93	2·82	4·08	4·27	4·11	1·45	−0·59
Wellman Engineering Corporation	0·85	1·32	1·63	1·92	1·74	1·18	0·69

However, just at the time the new steelmaking capacity was coming on stream, the economy moved into a 'stop' phase and steel production dropped from 24 million tons in 1960 to $20\frac{1}{2}$ million tons in 1962. Even when production picked up again in 1964, with a new peak of 27 million tons being reached in 1965, the capacity of the industry by that time was in the region of 32 million tons. As a result, from 1963 onwards there was for a time almost a nil demand on the plant suppliers from the U.K. steel industry.

Although expansion in consumer goods sales inevitably brings about a much greater upturn in the level of activity on the part of capital goods producers, the suddenness and magnitude of this could be moderated if only consumer goods producers were prepared to phase their expansion or if they all did not attempt to expand at the same time. But in practice this is usually just what happens. When the economy is in an expansion period consumer goods producers will all experience at the same time a higher level of sales and many of them will as a consequence decide to expand their capacity as quickly as possible, in order to take full advantage of the current boom conditions.

THE MULTIPLIER

But the effect on the economy and the national income is not restricted simply to the increase in investment expenditure causing a higher level of activity in the capital goods sector. This greater activity means an increase in employment and in the incomes of those employed by engineering firms. The engineering workers will spend much of their income on consumer items and this in turn generates activity and incomes in other areas. Thus, there is what is known as a 'multiplier' effect on total national income, following an upturn in investment. The greater the propensity to consume of those whose earnings are enlarged by the upturn in investment, the greater will be this multiplier effect. Put another way, the multiplier is the inverse of the marginal propensity to save. If the marginal propensity to consume among say the engineering workers is four-fifths of their income and the marginal propensity to save one-fifth, then the multiplier will be five. For every £100 million of increased investment there will eventually be a £500 million increase in national income. It should not of course be forgotten that part of the increased income gets taken in taxation, so that the ratio of Government spending to taxation also determines the magnitude of the multiplier.

Both the accelerator and the multiplier can work in reverse and in doing so also interact. Although consumption is usually quick to turn down after severe restrictive measures, the two year upturn in investment may not yet have been completed, so that for a time capital expenditure remains high. However the downturn in consumption does cause future investment intentions to be considerably revised; so that when current capital expenditure projects are ended the continuing demand on the capital goods sector is for replacement only, and perhaps not even that. Thus, there is a dramatic drop in the level of operation of the engineering sector, with the corresponding contraction in employment adding to the unemployment already existing in the consumer goods industries. This explains why the greatest degree of unemployment is not usually experienced until some twelve to eighteen months after the imposition of severe 'stop' measures, when the existing programme of capital commitments has been completed. This was what happened after the mid-1961 'stop': the peak level of unemployment of 3·9 per cent not being attained until February 1963. On that occasion of course the situation was considerably aggravated by the exceptionally severe winter of 1962/63, but even after the winter had passed, unemployment was greater throughout 1963 than it was during 1962. The same was true after the September 1957 crisis: the unemployment percentage not reaching its peak of 2·8 per cent until the opening months of 1959. More recently, although a restrictive period began towards the end of 1968, the high point in unemployment did not come until 1970/71.

In the post-war period it has not been the investment cycle which has been the primary cause of fluctuation in the level of economic activity and national income, although variation in the level of investment is still a factor in such fluctuations. If they had been allowed to do so, the post-war consumer spending booms would probably have worked themselves out; but they were in fact brought to an end by restrictive Government action. However, although the triggering mechanism may be different today, nevertheless, the income determination principles enunciated in the 1930s are still useful. Government action to curb inflation halts the growth rate of consumption and inevitably sets in train a reduction in investment and therefore further contraction in demand. When there is a desire for expansion, because national income has come down well below its full employment level, reflation will be accelerated by both private and public sector investment expenditure. This will generate income to a greater extent than say taxation reduction, because some of the increased disposable income could be saved rather than spent.

On the basis of income determination theory, Government policy must therefore aim to encourage, or restrict, the overall level of demand in the economy in order to raise employment, or curb inflationary rises in income beyond the point of full employment. Total demand is composed of consumption, investment and the Government's own expenditure. Any one, or all, of these three may be operated upon; but the resulting national income increase, or decrease, effect achieved will vary considerably, depending upon which is operated upon. The actual techniques of encouragement or restraint lie in the spheres of fiscal and monetary measures or methods of direct control.

II

Government Policy

FISCAL POLICY

In recent years there has been a good deal of controversy among economists as to the relative merits of fiscal and monetary policy in the management of the economy: Keynsians have naturally favoured the former; while Monetarists, like Milton Friedman in America, pin their faith in regulating money supply (keeping it at an average constant growth rate of around 5 per cent) and do not much believe in attempting to fine-tune the economy, which they argue can itself have a destabilising effect. It is not our purpose here to enter into the controversy, but simply to give as objective a description as possible of what is meant by fiscal and monetary policy.

Fiscal measures are those which alter the level, not only of taxation, but also of Government expenditure. Such variations are usually introduced by the annual April budget; but in recent times fiscal elements have also been part of 'little budgets' and other packages of special measures brought in at varying times of the year. Broadly, the operation of fiscal policy is by the Government, when it wishes to expand the economy, spending proportionately more than it takes in taxation. Conversely, by increasing taxation proportionately to expenditure, the Government can pursue a policy of restriction. Put another way, when expansion is desired the Chancellor of the Exchequer will budget in the direction of deficit; while a policy of restraint involves budgeting for a surplus, or at least a smaller deficit. Higher Government expenditure may be in the form of increased social benefits or more capital expenditure in social areas such as housing, hospitals, roads, etc., either directly or by making loans more freely available to local authorities or nationalised industries. Reduced Government spending, to restrict the economy, is usually brought about by cuts in, or by re-phasing of, capital projects; or by making charges for social services.

DIRECT TAXATION

Taxation may similarly be reduced or increased in order to expand or contract the economy. Such changes may be in either direct (on persons or companies) or indirect (mainly on goods) taxation. The distinction between direct and indirect taxation used to be on the basis of incidence: whether the burden of the tax stayed at the point at which it was first levied. This usually happened in the case of direct taxes, but indirect taxes were normally passed on to the consumer in the form of higher prices. Nowadays, however, it is not always possible to determine which taxes will be passed on and which will be borne where they are levied. The Selective Employment Tax, for example, although levied on companies was intended to be passed on to the consumer by the charging of higher prices for services.

Variation in direct taxation may take the form of changes in income tax or surtax rates, or in tax-free allowances; both of which will bring about an increase or decrease in personal disposable income. But not all of an increase in disposable income due to tax reduction will necessarily go on consumption: some of it will be saved. The allocation between consumption and saving will depend on the marginal propensity to save or to consume on the part of the social groups affected by the taxation reduction. Groups with the greatest propensity to consume will obviously be those with low incomes and large families. Thus, the greatest consumption expansion effect from the lowering of direct taxation would come from a reduction in the lower rates of income tax and from increased allowances for wife and children.

An increase in direct taxation might result in a cut in saving, as well as in consumption. However, the greatest consumption reduction effect would be achieved by higher taxation of the lower income groups, since they have the greatest propensity to consume. This could be done by curtailing allowances and raising reduced rates of income tax. Social and political considerations often stand in the way of such an approach and more often than not it is the standard rate of income tax, and even surtax, which is increased; although this may little affect those who are the greatest spenders, that is proportionately to their income.

Fiscal policy is in fact purposely used as a means of redistributing wealth. Direct taxation is designed to take proportionately more from high income earners; while much of Government expenditure on social services goes only to those in need. Taxes on incomes are usually 'progressive', with the average tax rate increasing up the income scale. A 'regressive' tax would be one where the average rate went down as income rose. Nowadays, the word 'regressive' tends to be applied more widely to those taxes that do not take sufficiently more from the rich than from the poor: such as most taxes on goods (except those on luxuries), as well as our system of local rating. The condition of those so poor that they pay no direct taxation is obviously left untouched by any reduction in taxes. This has given rise to the suggestion that there should be a 'negative income tax', in the form of a direct payment by the Government to those who are below a certain income level. In 1971 something like this was introduced: a Family Income Supplement, giving a cash benefit for poor families with children.

INDIRECT TAXATION

The greater part of indirect taxation is found by duties on drink and tobacco, and from purchase tax, levied mainly on consumer durable goods. In addition, there is the regulator, whereby all main customs and excise revenue duties and purchase tax rates may be increased, or decreased, by 10 per cent of the duty. Excluded from the scope of the regulator are the protective and anti-dumping duties, as well as vehicle excise and TV licence duties.

VALUE-ADDED TAX

The type of indirect taxation employed in the Common Market is the value-added tax. This is a form of turnover tax and like purchase tax is borne by the final consumer. V.A.T. is however a multi-, rather than a single-stage tax, levied at each stage of the production/distribution process. When selling goods and services, suppliers must include on their invoice an additional amount in respect of V.A.T., calculated on, and over and above, the basic selling price. Each person adding value pays the tax to the authorities but reimburses himself by passing it on, so that in effect it ultimately falls on the consumer. V.A.T. is levied on the difference between sales revenue and what has been spent on materials, components and semi-manufactures from other firms and from abroad. In practice, the manner of calculating liability is to apply the V.A.T. percentage to the value of sales and then subtract from this the total of all the separate amounts of V.A.T. on materials, etc., invoiced to the manufacturer or distributor. The 'value-added' on which V.A.T. is levied is therefore broadly the wages and salaries bill, plus profits. It is intended that V.A.T. will be introduced into Britain in April 1973 and will replace purchase tax and S.E.T.

The new tax will be spread over a wider range of goods than purchase tax and will also embrace services; but relieved from V.A.T. will be those food items that have not been subject to purchase tax and also exempt will be newspapers, periodicals and books. The most important relief from V.A.T. will be on exports, where a zero rate will apply. The significance of the distinction between exemption and a zero rate is that in the former case, being outside the system, no refund can be claimed for any V.A.T. paid on materials, etc., whereas with a zero rate it can. An exporter therefore gets a refund of any tax paid on goods invoiced to him (but only because he is unable on his export sales to pass the tax on). It should be stressed that V.A.T. is a *neutral* tax. It is not borne by the producers and distributors of goods and services, but passed on to the consumer. Therefore it does not give any special advantage to exporters nor any particular incentive to investment (on grounds, say, of low labour input implying less value-added). Of course, if this new form of indirect taxation brings in a greater revenue, it may be possible to reduce somewhat the burden of direct taxation: this is what is meant by some of the critics of V.A.T. when they say that it is *not* neutral but regressive. If company taxation is reduced as part of this, then by improving after-tax profits there could be greater encouragement to efficiency, investment, export growth, etc. But this is not a feature of V.A.T. as such, merely a consequence of re-allocating the burden of taxation.

COMPANY TAXATION

With the introduction of the Corporation Tax the system of company taxation in this country was radically altered. Previously, company profits had been subject to two taxes: a flat rate profits tax of 15 per cent and income tax at the standard rate. Dividends paid out were subject to further taxation only if the recipient's personal rate of tax was higher than the standard rate. The change to the Corporation Tax was foreshadowed by the Chancellor in his emergency Budget of 1964, shortly after the Labour Party assumed office. Full details of the new system of company taxation were not however given until April 1965, and even then the actual rate of tax was still undisclosed. After the May 1966 Budget the Corporation Tax was put into operation, the rate being announced as 40 per cent. Company profits are taxed at the Corporation Tax rate, and on earnings distributed to shareholders income tax is paid at the standard rate, the company acting as the collecting agent for the Inland Revenue. Thus, to the extent that company earnings are distributed the total tax revenue coming from profits is higher. The Corporation Tax gives therefore an incentive to retention rather than distribution of earnings. This in itself furthers certain policy objectives: such as increased self-financed investment by industry and some moderation in the rate of dividend growth as part of an incomes policy. Recently, however, the Conservative Government has announced an intended reform of this tax that will reverse these tendencies.

The announcement of the rate of Corporation Tax was not the only element of company taxation contained in the May 1966 Budget. A surprise item was the Selective Employment Tax, although the possibility of some form of payroll tax was mentioned as far back as 1961, at the same time as the 10 per cent surcharge regulator. The Selective Employment Tax is levied on employers' National Insurance contributions. In the case of central and local government service, nationalised industries and transport undertakings, S.E.T. is refunded or offset. At first manufacturing industries not only received a refund but in addition a premium; the latter was withdrawn in 1965, except for development areas where it continued until 1970. The object of the S.E.T. was to extend the burden of indirect taxation to services; hitherto the bulk of indirect taxation had been purchase tax on goods. It was also hoped that the S.E.T. would halt the tendency for any additions to the work force to find their way largely to service activities rather than to manufacturing. The Conservative Government is pledged to abolish S.E.T. and towards this end reduced the tax by half in 1971.

117

BORROWING REQUIREMENT

The central Government's taxation receipts and other current revenue are usually greater than its current expenditure, there being what used to be termed an 'above the line' surplus. There is invariably a deficit on capital account ('below the line'), since new loans to local government and state enterprises exceed repayments of previous loans. The current surplus covers part of this capital account deficit, the remainder is termed the 'borrowing requirement', being that part of Government capital expenditure that has to be financed by borrowing. This entails issuing Government stocks and bills, which are taken up by the public and by the banking sector, although there may also at times be substantial borrowing from overseas residents and central monetary institutions.

MONETARY POLICY

When we talk about raising or lowering the level of demand in the economy in order to cure unemployment or curb inflation, what basically we are talking about is purchasing power—either having the money to buy the things we want or being able to borrow it readily and cheaply. The latter is what we term 'credit'; as we have seen, the extending of credit itself enlarges the money supply. The supply of money also has a bearing on the rate of interest (which is the cost of credit, or, in the longer term investment sense, capital) and therefore on the level of investment and credit financed consumer durable demand. Because of the unavoidable inter-relationships between money, credit and interest rates, many of the weapons of monetary policy tend to influence all three (or sometimes only two), rather than any particular one.

Demand embraces investment as well as consumption; the former being to some extent more dependent than the latter upon the cost and availability of credit or capital. In the case of investment projects where the pay-back period is long, total interest payments may be as much as, if not more than, the capital cost; so that the prevailing level of long term interest rates may be decisive in determining whether the project is to be undertaken. The cost and availability of bank overdrafts will similarly influence stock levels in industry and during credit squeezes there may be substantial disinvestment in the form of running down stocks.

Consumption is influenced more by the supply of money: although much of consumer expenditure nowadays increasingly relies on consumer credit, notably hire purchase; this being particularly so in the case of expenditure on consumer durables. Variation in hire purchase terms regarding initial deposits and the repayment period is a usual feature of a credit squeeze.

When looking at the objective of internal stability in the value of the £, we saw how a major cause of inflation was the excessive pressure of demand upon a limited physical supply of goods and services. One way of attempting to control this is to cut back purchasing power by reducing money supply and credit. If, on the other hand, the economic problem is one of stagnation and high unemployment, then to get national income growing again and bring down the level of unemployment, demand must be helped to expand by making credit and capital easy and cheap to obtain.

WEAPONS OF MONETARY POLICY

Consideration will now be given to the techniques of monetary policy employed by the 'authorities' (this term denoting the Treasury and the Bank of England). We will first of all describe those techniques that have been in use over recent years (and at the moment of writing still are) and which in the main have been applied to the London Clearing and Scottish banks. A knowledge of these monetary instruments is, in any case, essential to a full understanding of the economic policies pursued during the sixties. Many of these traditional weapons of monetary policy, are however, soon to be replaced. The proposed new arrangements have been outlined in a Bank of England paper so that it is possible to give here some general description of them, although neither their exact details nor date of implementation are as yet known.

Like fiscal policy, and some direct controls, monetary policy can be used to expand or contract the economy. It does so by increasing or decreasing the supply of money and credit and by lowering or raising the price of credit, which is the rate of interest. Controlling the money supply means essentially controlling the level of bank deposits. Since, as we have seen earlier, these are built upon a cash reserve base, which in recent years has been 8 per cent of deposits, the potential for growth in bank deposits can be regulated by increasing or diminishing the amount of cash inside the banking system. While this may be brought about by fiscal policy, in the monetary sphere it is achieved by 'open market operations', by the Government buying or selling its own securities: selling if it wishes to reduce cash, or buying if it wishes to increase it. The securities bought and sold may be either Treasury bills or government stocks. Open market sales only force a contraction in deposits when the banks are unable to replenish their tills by encashing their liquid assets. At present the banks must hold a minimum of 28 per cent in liquid assets, including the 8 per cent cash, but if they are comfortably above this, loss of cash can be made good by reducing liquid assets, either by selling bills or calling in loans from the discount market. If the actual liquidity ratio prevailing is however near to the minimum, then, following a loss of cash due to open market operations, the banks must bring down their total deposits into line with their reduced cash reserve by selling investments or reducing loans: the authorities usually preferring them to do the latter. To ensure that their open market operations really bite, the authorities may even go as far as bringing down liquid assets near to the minimum ratio by the use of the 'special deposits' technique, whereby the banks are required to place a certain percentage (usually in 1 per cent stages) of their gross deposits with the Bank of England, this not to be included when calculating the liquidity ratio.

It used to be thought that by restricting the available supply of liquid assets the banks would be kept near the minimum liquidity ratio and that in addition the potential for growth in deposits would be limited. However, the considerable growth of commercial bills in the mid-sixties, which defeated attempts to restrict the supply of liquid assets to the banking system, showed up a major weakness in this form of monetary control. The creation of commercial bills was eventually brought under restriction and their eligibility as security against Bank of England lending to the discount market was curtailed.

Apart from seeking to limit the potential for growth by restricting the cash and liquid assets base, one of the other major factors in the creation of bank deposits is the extent of bank lending by way of advances, itself a major element in total credit supply. Since it is not in the self-interest of the banks to restrain their lending, this being the most profitable employment of depositors' funds, the authorities usually require to issue instructions to the banks on this subject. Official directives from the Governor of the Bank of England to the banks relate to the type of lending to be encouraged or discouraged or to the amount by which advances may grow over a period of time. Freer lending generally requires very little official encouragement, other than an intimation that bank lending is no longer to be regarded as being under restraint; although in 1963 it was facilitated by a reduction in the minimum liquidity ratio from 30 to 28 per cent.

Control over credit also extends to commercial bill financing, since in the case of merchant banks particularly it is often quite immaterial whether financial assistance is given by overdraft or by commercial bill. Quantitative restriction of lending has also applied to the hire purchase finance houses. Thus, directives from the Bank of England have in recent years been addressed, not solely to the Clearing banks, but also to many of the other financial institutions, including the discount market, merchant banks and finance houses.

Most of the other instruments of monetary policy have been applied only to the London Clearing and Scottish banks. In the middle of 1968 a special weapon for control over the merchant, overseas and foreign banks was announced (although never used except perhaps as a threat). This was the 'cash deposits scheme', under which the non-clearing banks could be called upon to place a certain percentage of their deposits (resident and non-resident sterling and foreign currency switched into sterling) with the Bank of England. The percentage called for could vary as between resident and non-resident deposits, and in special circumstances as between individual banks and types of banks. The instrument was obviously intended to give the authorities more control over inflows of funds from abroad, although it was not resorted to, even when these built up to very large proportions again during 1970.

INTEREST RATES

Official monetary policy may also be directed at raising or lowering the level of interest rates. By so doing, the authorities can increase or reduce the cost of borrowing and thus discourage or encourage investment; this having repercussions on the level of national income and employment. In addition, the authorities may wish to have higher short term interest rates for external reasons, to stem any possible outflow of foreign funds or encourage an inflow at times when sterling is weak in the foreign exchange markets.

Probably the best known method of influencing the level of interest rates in this country is by the raising or lowering of Bank rate. Bank rate is the rate of interest charged when the discount market is forced to borrow from the Bank of England. When the banking system is short of cash, and is calling in loans rather than lending more to the discount market, the latter may be forced to borrow from the Bank of England. If the authorities wish to see a rise in interest rates, lending to the discount market will only be at Bank rate, rather than at the lower prevailing market rate on Treasury bills. Borrowing at Bank rate means inevitably that the discount market is paying more for the funds it obtains than it will earn in their employment, in holding bills or bonds. The discount market may therefore seek to earn more on Treasury bills by lowering its bid for them. Thus, Treasury bill rates will tend to rise when the discount market is frequently forced to borrow from the Bank of England at Bank rate.

Bill rates rise even more, of course, when Bank rate itself is increased. When this happens there are in addition many other rates which have by tradition been formally linked to Bank rate and these automatically rise, including the Clearing banks' lending and deposit rates. The link between Bank rate and many of the other short term interest rates is less formal. Nevertheless, they also tend to follow the direction of Bank rate movements, although to varying degrees. There are certain managed rates where the Government itself fixes the level, such as on National Savings, as well as the rates charged to local authorities for loans from the Public Works Loans Board.

'Open market operations' influence the level of interest rates in two ways. Net sales of Government securities reduce cash in the banking system and thus cause the discount market to have recourse to the Bank of England. When this effect is deliberately contrived by the authorities it is referred to as 'making Bank rate effective'. As well as driving the market into the Bank, open market sales may also, according to the state of demand in the stock market, influence the price of Government securities and thus the yield expressed as a rate of interest.

DOMESTIC CREDIT EXPANSION

Towards the close of the sixties, the British Government, at the instigation of the I.M.F., adopted for the management of the economy the concept of 'domestic credit expansion'. This is merely the normal money supply measure (coins, notes and bank deposits) adjusted to take account of credit drawn from, or extended, abroad. Since money supply alone is defined solely in terms of bank liabilities it includes only that part of credit which appears on the assets side of the banks' balance sheets. But in years when Britain has a balance of payments deficit, credit also accrues to the Government through its borrowing from abroad and run-down in the reserves (it will be remembered that loss of gold and convertible currencies increases the sterling portion of the E.E.A. and therefore its ability to lend to the Government by holding 'tap' Treasury bills). In such years the full pressure of demand in the economy, and therefore of inflationary forces, is not revealed by the money supply alone, since the latter does not cover that part of demand made possible by external credit and which has to be satisfied by imports (in the absence of this additional supply of goods the revealed inflation would be greater).

Broadly, therefore, D.C.E. is money supply, plus external deficit, or minus external surplus. When Britain is in balance of payments deficit D.C.E. will be greater than money supply; when in surplus it will be less. Two methods of calculation are employed. Under the first of these D.C.E. is: bank lending to both the public and private sectors, together with increase in the public's holdings of notes and coins, and lastly borrowing by the public sector from overseas and through reduction in the reserves. This method shows only the resulting major credit flows: it does not fully reveal what made them possible. This is more clearly done in the second method of calculating D.C.E. on the basis of: the public sector's borrowing requirement, less any sales of public sector debt made to the non-bank private sector; and bank lending to the private sector. The advantage of this second method is that it highlights the expansive effect of Government expenditure (in excess of taxation) on the economy, and also on D.C.E., which can only be counteracted by domestic borrowing from the ordinary public. If the required volume of net sales of public sector debt seems or proves unattainable, then emphasis in official policy has to return to the fiscal factor, namely to reducing the public sector borrowing requirement by cutting Government spending or increasing taxation.

Adoption of the D.C.E. concept marked a change of emphasis in monetary policy that ultimately led to reforms being proposed. Before 1969 monetary policy in Britain had been conducted mainly in terms of interest rates and physical controls over bank lending. Interest rate policy was intended more for external than for internal effect and there was in any case a certain reluctance to see rates go too high. The liquidity ratio, with ancillary special deposits, was generally regarded as being more important than the cash ratio as a means of controlling growth in the banking system's deposits. With the Government Broker always ready to support the gilt-edged market at times of weakness (in part a desire to prevent interest rates from going too high) the banking system could always acquire cash by unloading its gilt-edged stocks. Cash could also be obtained through the discount market's right of recourse to the Bank of England (unlimited by the absence of the sort of borrowing quotas that prevail in other countries).

From 1969 onwards monetary policy got so much identified with money supply control that there was a general impression that it was being tried for the first time, in the postwar period at any rate. Under the 'new monetary policy' managing the economy boiled down to the simple matter of regulating the money supply through operating on the cash base of the banking system. This was done by open market operations in the gilt-edged market, when necessary being prepared to push the required net sales on to the market regardless of the effect this had on the price of stocks and the level to which interest rates were raised. Hence the saying: you cannot control the money supply *and* the rate of interest. In popular presentations of the new concept of monetary policy the crucial role of the government borrowing requirement in money supply growth was purposely played down, the whole painful burden of adjustment being conveniently put on the gilt-edged market, thereby avoiding unpopular taxation increase or Government spending cuts. The authorities did in fact from then onwards impose a pretty strict curb on the extent to which the Government Broker was allowed to support the market.

The concept of D.C.E. began to appear less apt during 1970 with Britain in massive external surplus coupled however with galloping inflation (a higher rate of money supply growth was being tolerated since external surplus was deducted to arrive at the D.C.E. figure). The new monetary policy did not appear in any case to be having much success in coping with wage-push inflation. Just when this latest fashion in economic thinking seemed therefore to be on the wane, it was a little surprising that the Bank of England should in mid-May 1971 put forward certain proposed structural reforms in monetary policy as a practical backing for the money supply concept.

THE NEW MONETARY POLICY

The Bank's 'consultative document' was entitled 'Competition and credit control' (reproduced in the Bank of England Quarterly Bulletin, June 1971). The Clearing banks had long complained that the traditional weapons of monetary policy tended to bear more on them and to handicap their ability to compete, particularly with other financial institutions that had developed considerably as a result. The Bank was now prepared to re-model its monetary instruments to make them less discriminatory, but the Clearing banks themselves had to contribute to this freer environment by abandoning their cartel agreement as to common rates of interest paid on deposits and charged for advances. The authorities in any case now wished to see credit rationed more by price than by official ceilings, even if this meant that working capital for British industry was to become at times more expensive. The comparative cheapness of bank loans in Britain had always made excessive credit expansion difficult to curb and also explained why our economy seemed so much less responsive than those of other nations to the discount rate weapon.

The changes proposed in the instruments of monetary regulation were not only intended to promote greater freedom in the private financial sector but were also expressly designed in terms of the new policy of control through money supply. The cash and liquidity ratios (and also the unused cash deposits scheme for the non-clearing banks) are replaced by a reserve requirement, of possibly around 12½ per cent and made variable by the call for special deposits. Ceilings will be abolished but bank lending still subject to qualitative guidance from the authorities. The reserve requirement applies to *all* banks (Clearing, merchant, overseas and foreign) with the non-clearing banks also being brought within the scope of special deposits. Parallel arrangements are to be worked out for the hire purchase finance companies; while care will be taken that the activities of the discount houses do not conflict with the new arrangements for the banks. The reserve requirement will apply to all sterling deposits received from outside the banking system, including resources obtained from switching foreign currency deposits into sterling, with the possibility of discrimination between resident and non-resident deposits. Those bank assets officially acceptable for reserve requirement will be: bankers' deposits at the Bank of England (but *not* till money); Treasury bills; call money (but *not* with inter-bank or local authority temporary money markets); British Government securities within one year of maturity; those local authority and commercial bills eligible for rediscount at the Bank of England.

It will be seen that the new arrangements give extra dimension to money supply control in that the reserve requirement applies to a much wider range of bank deposits and can readily be made variable, thus reducing or increasing the multiple by which bank deposits can be created on the reserve base. The reserve base itself is to be much more vigorously operated upon by the Government's open market operations in its own securities, with the possibility of official purchases of stock being more strictly limited, thus helping to discourage unloading by the banks. This aspect of the new policy was put into immediate effect; indeed it was in large measure merely a confirmation of what had been happening in practice over the past few years.

EXTERNAL ASPECTS OF MONETARY POLICY

So far, we have been concerned primarily with the internal aspects of monetary policy, apart from a reference in passing to the need sometimes for high short term interest rates to retain foreign funds. In this area the U.K. authorities during the three years up to devaluation supplemented their interest rate policy by intervening in the foreign exchange market as forward buyers of sterling. By thus supporting the forward rate they attempted to keep down the cost of covering foreign funds swapped into sterling and so prevent this cost absorbing the whole of the interest rate differential, which would have caused foreign funds to flow out. More recently, towards the end of 1970 and in the opening months of 1971, it was believed that the Bank of England intervened as a forward *seller* of sterling, expressly to increase the cost of cover and thus discourage inflows of foreign funds that threatened to undermine control over money supply and credit. At that time the alternative of reducing Bank rate was inappropriate to the continuing need for a restrictive domestic monetary policy.

The external side of monetary policy is also concerned with exchange control and the broader aspects of exchange rate changes. In this area of monetary techniques the primary objective is of course to improve the balance of payments position and safeguard our reserves; although exchange rate flexibility and even devaluation are sometimes advocated, not just to permit growth, but also to stimulate it. Exchange control could have been included in our third category of 'direct controls' but it is perhaps more convenient to consider it here. Exchange control is chiefly concerned to limit the outflow of sterling funds from this country and in so doing help to restrict the supply of £s in the foreign exchange markets, thereby strengthening the £. Restrictions on outflows of sterling may relate to private capital investment abroad, either in the form of portfolio investment by individuals or direct investment by British companies in overseas areas. Foreign travel currency allowances may also be strictly limited for the same reason.

DEVALUATION

Adjustment of a country's rate of exchange is most frequently in a downward direction and represents a fall in the external value of the currency; in other words a reduction in the number of units of foreign currencies exchanging for it. When exchange rates are left free to find their own relationship with one another, this is known as a policy of 'flexible' or 'floating' exchange rates.

But when the downward adjustment is by official decree, and is sudden and sizeable, then this is termed 'devaluation'. Since devaluation is forced upon a country by the weakness of its currency in the foreign exchange markets it can hardly at first sight be recognised as a policy ensuring a strong £. Devaluation can however be expected to improve the balance of payments position and in so doing therefore prevent any further weakening in the external value of the currency. The way in which devaluation makes the balance of trade more favourable is that it tends to discourage imports by making them more expensive; while at the same time improving the competitiveness of exports because their price in terms of foreign currencies may be reduced. Furthermore, exporting becomes more profitable since foreign currency earnings are worth more when translated into the domestic currency; provided, that is, export prices have not been reduced to the full extent allowed by the devaluation. An example will probably best explain this: a devaluation of the £ from an exchange rate of $5 = £1 to $3 = £1 means that British goods can now be sold in America at $3 instead of $5 and yet still give our exporters the same sales receipts in terms of sterling. By the same token, an American article costing $5, which could previously have been imported into Britain for £1, will now cost £1 13s. 4d. But British exporters might still be competitive without reducing their prices fully in foreign currency terms; if, in our example, the British exporter only reduced his price to $4, this would mean that his sales receipts in terms of sterling would be higher: £1 6s. 8d. per article, instead of £1.

Devaluation greatly improves the 'invisibles' part of the current account, since dividend, interest and profit income received from abroad in foreign currency is automatically worth more in the devalued currency; while such outward payments remain the same in terms of the devalued currency, although obviously worth less to non-residents in foreign currency terms. Capital account is likely also to benefit from devaluation. With the event having taken place, speculative 'leads and lags' will be unwound and therefore short-term capital movements will be more favourable. The long-term capital account improves because foreigners can now acquire assets in the devaluing country much more cheaply in terms of their own currency.

Internally, devaluation has an expansive effect on the country's economy, particularly for exporting industries, but also giving manufacturers a price advantage in the home market in relation to foreign imported goods. However in the medium-term devaluation, in itself and through the favourable external payments position it brings about, can build up powerful inflationary pressures that may eventually erode the competitive advantage in international trade originally gained from the devaluation.

REVALUATION

Revaluation is the opposite of devaluation: it is the adoption by a country of a higher rate of exchange, whereby its currency exchanges for a larger number of units of other currencies. A country is forced to revalue when its external payments position becomes so strong (as a result probably of having a lower rate of inflation than its trading competitors) that its central bank has to acquire large unwanted amounts of weaker currencies through obligatory intervention in the foreign exchange market and when the external surplus and speculative short-term capital inflows in anticipation of revaluation are greatly enlarging domestic credit supply and thus endangering price stability. Such a country has two choices open to it: acquiescence in the faster rate of inflation or revaluation. Revaluation has its painful internal effects. Exports are discouraged and imports encouraged, so that the level of activity in domestic industry is likely to be lower. Revaluation is deflationary, just as devaluation is inflationary. Income received from abroad by residents in the revaluing country (companies and private individuals) is now worth less to them in domestic currency terms, so their purchasing power is reduced. These deflationary forces set in train by the revaluation may in the long run give the country a favourable balance of trade once again, thus undoing the effect of revaluation.

The Government may also seek to achieve its objectives directly, without going through either fiscal or monetary techniques. A list of such direct control methods could be almost endless, but we will here concentrate on those policies which have been most used and talked about in recent years. Some of these have already been touched upon in earlier chapters, because it was relevant at the time to do so. But now, both by way of introduction and re-capitulation, these direct control methods will be briefly sum-marised in terms of the objectives they seek to achieve. Some of them will then be gone into in much fuller detail.

The *'growth'* objective is the major concern of the national planning activities of the National Economic Development Council (and also formerly of the Department of Economic Affairs), with emphasis being placed on productivity improvement in order to achieve real growth in national output. The pursuit of this and *full employment* is furthered by regional development plans and by all those measures tending to foster labour mobility, including redundancy payments and the Department of Employ-ment's placement and industrial training activities. Direct methods of government policy to combat *inflation* are numerous and wide-ranging. One obvious way of curbing excessive demand is to encourage saving, which the authorities are always ready to try to do through the National Savings programme. The Govern-ment may also seek to avoid excessive price rises by a policy of restraint, or even prohibition, through an incomes policy or a standstill on prices and wages. The natural market mechanism for restraining any tendency towards rising prices is of course to foster competition between producers, and this may be done in many ways. The whole purpose of monopolies and restrictive practices legislation is to break down artificially created obstacles to free competition. Competition is also nurtured by giving positive official encouragement to consumers' associations. Com-petitiveness may be improved by withdrawing some of the pro-tection enjoyed by home producers; this being done by reducing tariff barriers, either as part of G.A.T.T. negotiations (General Agreement on Tariffs and Trade) or membership of free trade areas such as E.F.T.A. and the E.E.C. Direct measures designed to improve our balance of trade and ensure external *stability of the £* include schemes providing export incentive or import dis-couragement.

NATIONAL PLANNING

One of the most prominent examples of the direct approach in government policy has been the attempt at indicative planning, which in a formalised manner can be dated from the setting-up of the N.E.D.C. in 1961. Although this method was primarily directed at achieving growth, ancillary to this it also concerned itself with productivity, import substitution, regional development and many other aspects which touch upon the other objectives.

To get the U.K. economy on to a higher growth rate trend it was decided in 1961 that a special body should be set up to study the problem, since the Treasury's attention tended to be concentrated internally on financing the exchequer and controlling expenditure, and externally on the strength of the £ on the foreign exchange market and the resultant state of our reserves. In other words, the Treasury it was suggested was too occupied with the achievement of the other major objectives to devote sufficient energy to the matter of 'growth'. It was Selwyn Lloyd who proposed setting up the National Economic Development Council, at the same time as he introduced his 'little budget' of July 1961, which stopped the economy with such sudden force.

The first meeting of the N.E.D.C. was not held until the early part of March in the following year. The Council was composed of representatives of government, management and the trade unions; and they were to assess the performance of the economy, identify possible obstacles to growth, and generally seek ways of achieving a faster growth rate. A staff, in the form of the N.E.D. Office, was also set up and this was organised into two divisions, the economic and the industrial. This staff prepared the first National Plan for the period 1961 to 1966, which was published in February 1963 under the title of *Growth of the United Kingdom Economy to 1966*. The first plan took as the target growth rate the figure of 4 per cent and the implications of this, both in terms of national economic factors and individual industries, was indicated. For the first time there was a formal attempt to bring together objectives and the ability of industry sectors to contribute to these objectives. As a result of the industrial enquiry, which the preparation of the plan involved, many firms were probably encouraged to approach their own planning for growth in a more formal manner.

The next major report produced by the N.E.D. Office outlined what were believed to be the necessary conditions to be brought about if the United Kingdom was to achieve a higher growth rate. The 4 per cent growth target of the first plan was in fact not attained, the actual growth rate during that period being 3 per cent per annum, which was really no higher than that achieved in the years immediately preceding the plan period. The causes for this failure, the fact of which became obvious long before the end of planning period was reached, were analysed in a progress report entitled *The Growth of the Economy*. Shortage of skilled workers, combined with an insufficiency of private sector investment, held back productivity; while our imports exhibited greater tendency to grow than did exports. The second National Plan covered the period 1964/70 and this time was prepared by the newly-set-up Department of Economic Affairs, in consultation with the N.E.D.C. In the second plan, the growth rate sights were lowered a bit to $3\frac{3}{4}$ per cent, but even this, in the event of economic crisis which followed, soon proved to be impossibly high.

The third planning exercise, entitled 'The Task Ahead', was published at the beginning of 1969. It was expressly described as 'a planning document, not a plan', no growth rate target being set forth. Instead the document was intended to provide a basis for consultation between Government and industry about the economic prospects up to 1972, upon which decisions in both public and private sectors could be based. Certain priorities of government policy were set out, notable among these being a balance of payments surplus target of £500 million. 'The Task Ahead' was yet another indication of the extent to which growth ambitions were having to give way to balance of payments realities. Since the creation of the Department of Economic Affairs had been very much bound up with the growth objective, it was not surprising, in view of the change in official priorities, that it should be abolished in October 1969, its planning role reverting to the Treasury. A further irony was that the N.E.D.C. continued in existence.

When the D.E.A. had earlier taken over much of the N.E.D.C. national planning role, the latter was left to concentrate on the development of what might be called 'grass roots' planning, by the setting up of the 'little Neddies' or, to give them their official title, the Economic Development Committees. These Committees concern themselves with the growth of the major industries whose outputs make up the gross national product. About twenty Economic Development Committees were created, providing a valuable liaison between the level of the industry and the firms in it, and the overall national planning function. National objectives were passed down and practical difficulties passed up. The E.D.C.s enter into a working partnership with firms in planning their expansion in the context of the prospects for the industry, as well as national growth expectations. In addition, they attempt to help firms improve their efficiency, particularly where this will increase exports and save imports. As Sir Robert Shone wrote in an article in the *Board of Trade Journal* (11th February 1966): 'The committees serve as a means of securing the consultation and involvement of industry in the making and implementation of the National Plan'.

Thus, the National Economic Development Council and the former Department of Economic Affairs represented a different type of state intervention in the affairs of industry. This method has come to be called 'indicative planning' or 'planning by consent', the development of which in France took place somewhat earlier and the apparent success of which impressed many people on this side of the Channel. But national planning in Britain has rather tended to assume a continuation of existing habits in the use of national wealth; and therefore to do anything extra the GNP had to grow. As a result, unnecessarily and, as it turned out, impossibly high growth targets were set. Doing so may also of course have been motivated by a desire to keep up with the continental Joneses. There was perhaps too much 'think of a number' in the approach to national planning. This may have been indicative of a lack of realism in the planning and in the thinking of the personnel involved. It would be ironic if this were so, for among the reasons given for setting up the N.E.D.C. and the D.E.A. were not only that the Treasury had objectives other than growth to pursue, but also that it tended to be somewhat remote from industry. It may be true that Treasury administrators have little experience of or contact with the industrial environment. In the recruitment policy pursued by N.E.D.C. there was an honest attempt made to get nearer to industry by recruiting, on secondment for a period of 2–3 years, business economists—that is, economists who have actively participated in the management activity of their firm. But the later formed D.E.A. appears to have been staffed more by academic economists and economic journalists, whose contacts with industry may in fact have been very little closer than those of the Treasury administrators. Although in one sense it may be desirable to have national plans made by expansionist-minded economists, once growth has been accepted as almost an overriding objective, nevertheless a very real danger lies in the academic's lack of experience of the industrial behaviour of both labour and management. As a result, the whole planning exercise is always in danger of becoming utopian, and based on theoretically satisfying models which immediately fall to pieces under practical difficulties and human nature.

With the resort once more to severe 'stop' measures in July 1966, many industries and firms undoubtedly felt that they had been led up the garden path and encouraged to base their expansion plans on over-ambitious national targets, later finding themselves as a result in a chronic excess capacity position. It has since become obvious that the whole thing was at the outset approached from the wrong direction. The selection of a growth target was a pointless gesture—this was clearly recognised in the third of the planning exercises. More useful has been the work done by the 'little Neddies' at the grass roots of industry: trying to get rid of restrictive practices, avoiding unnecessary duplication, encouraging amalgamation of uneconomic small business units, improving the individual firm's export capability, ascertaining why certain imported items cannot be supplied from home production, encouraging import substitution as much as possible. This is more of a 'putting things right' activity and, where successful, will result in a higher growth rate without the selection of any magical figure.

There must still of course be an overall assessment of the position of the economy; of what could happen, what we want to happen and where the economy is going; in order to discover what needs attention at the level of the industry and the firm. As Samuel Brittan pointed out in the *Financial Times* of 6th April 1966 'The kind of planning that is really needed is what the military call "contingency planning"; in other words, recognising that the future may hold out a larger number of alternatives, and trying to prepare for as many of them as possible so as not to be caught unawares'. We will return to this theme later when we come to consider the economic cycle and how the firm can take its existence into account in its business planning.

EXPORT INCENTIVES AND IMPORTS CONTROLS

It is frequently argued, particularly in the face of a need for unpleasant deflationary policies, that more direct and effective ways of correcting an adverse balance of trade lie in giving inducements to exports, while imposing penalties or even embargoes on imports. Export incentives suggested are frequently in the form of tax rebates and in this country towards the end of 1964 some mild encouragement was in fact given by allowing a rebate of certain indirect taxes entering into the cost of production of exported goods. The value of this incentive was however small; equivalent to only about $1\frac{1}{4}$–$3\frac{1}{2}$ per cent of total export sales. At the same time, to discourage imports, a surcharge of 15 per cent was imposed, later reduced to 10 per cent and then abandoned altogether in November 1966. Other methods of limiting imports are to impose quotas and licencing regulations, either on the basis of the type of article or the country of origin. The entry of certain Japanese manufactures into this country is still subject to import quota, as also are textiles from Hong Kong.

Towards the end of 1968, when Britain's balance of payments still showed no signs of moving into surplus, despite devaluation, the Government was forced to introduce an import deposit scheme to try and bring down the volume of foreign goods still flooding into the country. The scheme applied almost entirely to manufactured goods, accounting for about a third of our total imports. Importers had to deposit with H.M. Customs half the value of the goods being brought in, the deposit being repaid six months later, but earning no interest in the meantime. The scheme remained in force for two years.

Many of these methods of export encouragement or import discouragement do contravene certain international trading agreements, principally those of G.A.T.T. In the Treaty of Rome, it was foreseen that within the area of the Common Market such artificial restraints to trade would eventually have to disappear. Apart from international disapproval, such direct methods of operating on the flow of exports and imports by national governments are always in danger of giving rise to retaliation by other countries, thus bringing about a reversal of the trend towards greater liberalisation of trade. From the domestic point of view such methods are also unsatisfactory, on the grounds that they add to inflationary pressures, unless steps are also taken to reduce the level of home demand, which is the very thing these measures are often thought to avoid. In the absence of any rise in total domestic production, greater export sales must inevitably mean fewer goods available for the home market, which is in any case further deprived by the curbing of imports. If purchasing power at home is allowed to remain the same, the prices of the reduced supply of goods available for home consumption must inevitably rise. This increased inflationary pressure will eventually, due to rising costs, weaken export competitiveness, as well as have undesirable domestic economic and social consequences.

INCOMES POLICY

The condition of full employment prevailing in this country throughout most of the post-war period has provided a congenial climate for that variety of cost inflation known as 'wages-push'. This 'push' is very strong towards the end of an expansion phase, when unemployment gets down near to 1 per cent. At such times, attempts are made by the Government to halt the excessive rise in industrial earnings by trying to persuade the unions not to exploit their monopolistic bargaining position to the full. These attempts start with the 'appeal', pass through the 'voluntary basis', and end with the 'freeze'. Although these policies have been tried many times in the past, and failed, they continue to be suggested. The milder attempts at incomes restraint invariably founder on the rocks of human nature; on the strongly held convictions of certain groups that they are a legitimate exception to the overall restraint. Nor is the essential basis of social justice present when eventually the strong are allowed to break through the policy of restraint, which the Government of the day is able to impose successfully only upon the weak—the most flagrant example of this being the treatment of the nurses in 1962. In the end, the forces of wages-push have been halted when deflationary policies have at last been adopted, and the bargaining strength of the unions weakened by a rise in unemployment.

The course of events, beginning with the change of Government in October 1964 and going right up to July 1966, well illustrates the whole range of policies which governments are driven to, in an attempt to curb inflationary rises in industrial earnings, before resorting to the ultimate deterrent, namely deflation. Controversy within the Labour Party on the subject of incomes policy began even before it took office. At the Party conference before the election, the debate between the leading trade unionists and members of the parliamentary Labour Party revealed the seeds of later difficulties and disagreements. Mr. Frank Cousins for one refused to consider any policy of 'wages restraint' and insisted instead on talking about 'planned growth of wages'. This was accepted by the party leadership; Mr. Callaghan stating 'by "incomes policy" we do not mean wage restraint, we mean the planned growth of wages . . .'.

A White Paper on the Economic Situation, issued on the 26th October 1964, contained many of the new Government's first measures to deal with the inherited balance of payments deficit. Among these was the Government's stated intention to consult with both sides of industry in drawing up a plan to achieve an increase in productivity and an effective incomes policy, the latter being related to productivity and covering all forms of income. To encourage co-operation on incomes, particularly on the part of the trade unions, a Prices Review Body was to be established to try and get greater price stability. Discussion with the trade unions and the employers duly took place and the conclusions reached embodied in 'A Joint Statement of Intent on Productivity, Prices and Incomes', a draft of which was submitted to the T.U.C. and the employers' organisations at the beginning of November. The Statement of Intent was eventually accepted by both groups and signed, as had been hoped, before Christmas. Signing the Statement put the parties concerned in the position of making a public declaration that they fully realised that any failure to raise productivity, keep incomes increases in line with productivity, or maintain general stability of prices would result in a slower rate of growth and lower level of employment. The T.U.C. and employers' organisations undertook to co-operate in establishing machinery to keep watch on general movements in prices and incomes, and examine particular cases of increase. The N.E.D.C. was to carry out the first of these functions, whilst a National Board for Prices and Incomes was to be set up to discharge the second.

The way in which the Prices and Incomes Board was to operate was revealed in a White Paper (Cmnd. 2577) on *Machinery of Prices and Incomes Policy*, published in February 1965. After the Board had examined particular price increases and wage claims, it was hoped that any resulting judgment delivered would be implemented by voluntary co-operation, although the Government was prepared to give the Board statutory authority if this later proved necessary. Price increases were to be referred to the Board by the Department of Economic Affairs. A guiding light for incomes increases was to be recommended for each year. The Board's reports on the cases examined by it were to be made available within two to three months, or more quickly in the case of wage claims. On the 17th March it was announced that Mr. Aubrey Jones was to be Chairman of the Board for the first five years.

The second White Paper (Cmnd. 2639) on *Prices and Incomes Policy* was published in April 1965, and this named the members of the Board, as well as setting out the criteria to be used in examining particular cases of prices and incomes increase. On the basis of the National Plan growth target of 25 per cent between 1964 and 1970, the 'norm' for incomes increase was set to 3 to $3\frac{1}{2}$ per cent. Rises in excess of this were allowable only where existing levels of income did not give a reasonable standard of living, or where there was a major improvement in productivity, or a need to secure a desirable change in the distribution of labour. These exceptional increases had however to be counterbalanced by below the norm increases in other areas. In considering wage claims, less emphasis was to be given to comparisons with levels or trends of income in other employments; instead more attention was to be paid to the national incomes 'norm'. A large majority at the T.U.C. voted in favour of the new prices and incomes policy, but the Transport and General Workers' Union stood out against it.

At the beginning of May 1965 the first three price cases (relating to bread and flour, soap and detergents, and road haulage charges) were referred to the Board, and in the middle of the month the first wage settlement (that of the printers). The Board produced its first report (on road haulage rates) towards the end of June.

Action by the Board after the event was soon recognised as presenting difficulties, particularly in the case of wages, and so in September 1965 the Minister of Economic Affairs warned the T.U.C. Conference at Brighton that the Government was considering introducing legislation to provide for a compulsory 'early warning' of impending wage claims and intended price increases. As a counter-proposal, the T.U.C. suggested that it should operate a voluntary 'early warning' system, itself vetting wage claims. In deference to this, the Government postponed introducing a compulsory system and instead published in November 1965 yet another White Paper (Cmnd. 2808) on *An Early Warning System* to give the National Board for Prices and Incomes time to consider increases before they were put into effect. To keep things within manageable proportions, a list of goods and services, either of 'particular economic significance' or 'important elements in the cost of living', was drawn up and firms were asked to inform the appropriate government department at least four weeks before the price increase was due to take effect, as well as justify the increase. In the case of pay and conditions of employment, impending claims were to be notified to the General Council of the T.U.C., a special committee of which was to examine the claims and keep the Government informed about them. The C.B.I. had a similar duty. With pay claims, the standstill period was to be two to three months.

In case this voluntary system failed, the Government proceeded with drafting a bill to give the prices and incomes policy statutory force, including provision for making it illegal to make price increases or wage claims without notification. Progress with this bill was delayed by the dissolution of Parliament in March 1966. It was eventually published on the 4th July, but did not become law until after the emergency July measures.

During the eighteen months' period from the Statement of Intent right up to the middle of 1966, despite all these many variations on an incomes policy theme, average weekly earnings went up by 13 per cent and prices by $7\frac{1}{2}$ per cent; while output hardly rose at all. It was not surprising, therefore, that the July package of severe deflationary measures included a voluntary six months' standstill on incomes and reductions in working hours, followed by six months of 'severe restraint' and a year's standstill on prices. The details of this were contained in a White Paper (Cmnd. 3073) entitled *Prices and Incomes Standstill*. The only allowable exceptions were increases in pay as a result of promotion, age, or regular increments within a scale. At the time of the imposition of the standstill, six million workers had been expecting pay increases, already agreed, but under the July measures these were deferred for six months. While pay negotiations could still be carried on during the standstill period, they were not to take effect before January 1967; nor in the following six months, unless they could be given strong justification. During the twelve months' period the incomes 'norm' was to be regarded as zero. Exceptions to the standstill on prices were allowable only when necessitated by a change in world prices of imported materials, seasonal fluctuations in supply, or increased taxation. Whilst the standstill operated, the National Board for Prices and Incomes was to occupy itself by considering 'matters of long term significance in the field of productivity, prices and incomes'.

It was hoped by the Government that the standstill would operate successfully on a voluntary basis, although just in case it did not a temporary provision to forbid increases in prices and incomes without ministerial consent was included in the Prices and Incomes Bill. This part of the Bill was capable of being brought into operation by an Order in Council, subject to confirmation by Parliament within twenty-eight days, to give employers protection against legal proceedings for withholding pay increases already negotiated.

The final form of the Prices and Incomes Bill became law in August 1966. It established the National Board for Prices and Incomes, originally set up under Royal Warrant on the 8th April 1965. The Act also gave authority to bring into force a compulsory early warning system for proposed increases in prices and incomes. Part IV of the Act dealt with the enforcement of a temporary standstill on prices and incomes and this part was invoked in October 1966, after the standstill had been successfully challenged in the courts by certain unions.

Government Policy

In November 1966 a White Paper (Cmnd. 3150) *Prices and Incomes Standstill: Period of Severe Restraint* defined additional criteria to apply to prices and incomes increases during the first half of 1967. Prices could be increased where a firm's receipts were not adequate to maintain efficiency and undertake investment. Regarding wages, the only further permitted exceptions to the zero norm were increases for the lowest paid workers and those associated with achieved improvements in productivity.

When the period of severe restraint ended in the middle of 1967, an appeal was made for moderation in price and income increases during the next twelve months. Although there was a return to a voluntary vetting system, the Government provided for a continuation of its power to delay any particular price or wage increase. Immediately upon the ending of the severe restraint period, wages rose sharply. The I.M.F.'s annual report, published in the autumn, urged the British Government to continue with a tight incomes policy. But it was not until the spring of the following year that another white paper appeared on the subject: 'Productivity, Prices and Incomes Policy in 1968 and 1969' (Cmnd. 3590). While existing criteria for increases continued to apply, a 3½ per cent maximum limit was set for increases in incomes (except as part of a genuine productivity deal) and dividends. There were additional powers to delay pay and price increases for twelve months by referring them to the National Board for Prices and Incomes; while dividend increases were not to be excessive and were to be notified. The N.B.P.I. had during this time a multitude of references made to it by the Department of Employment and in addition it produced reports on such general topics as productivity, salary structures, payment by results, job evaluation, etc.

The year 1968 saw the tensions created by the incomes policy give rise to a period of much greater industrial strife. This caused the Government to turn its attention to the problem of industrial relations as such. At the beginning of 1969 the Department of Employment and Productivity produced its white paper 'In Place of Strife: A Policy for Industrial Relations'. This proposed the setting up of a Commission on Industrial Relations and the introduction of 28-day cooling-off periods, strike ballots and an Industrial Board to enforce the Government's proposed legal powers by the imposition of financial penalties. Opposition from the Labour Party National Executive was encountered on many of these proposals; so that when the bill was introduced in April the aspects of strike ballots and imprisonment were omitted. Further opposition naturally came from the T.U.C., which put forward its own plan for dealing with unconstitutional and inter-union strikes, rejecting the Government's proposed penal powers. In the face of this, the Government abandoned its Industrial Relations Bill, accepting the offer of the T.U.C. to intervene in unconstitutional strikes. Emboldened by this success, the T.U.C. called for complete repeal of the Prices and Incomes Act and in particular the ending of the N.B.P.I. and all power to freeze wages. Towards the end of 1969 the D.E.P. produced a white paper on 'Productivity, Prices and Incomes Policy after 1969' which proposed the merger of the N.B.P.I. and the Monopolies Commission into a Commission on Manpower and Industry. The guiding light for wage increase was formulated in terms of a band of $2\frac{1}{2}$–$4\frac{1}{2}$ per cent. Once again, there was outright rejection by the T.U.C. The published bill retained the Commission, but statutory incomes control was dropped, although a continued watch was to be kept on prices. The change of government ended further progress of this particular bill. Its subject matter, namely industrial relations, was however developed much further by the new Conservative Government. But the Conservatives were firmly opposed to any resurrection of an incomes policy, preferring instead to encourage employers, in both the public and private sectors, to stand up to excessive wages demands and to create the right sort of economic backcloth for this to take place. The National Board for Prices and Incomes was brought to an end in 1971.

PART FOUR

Economic Background

12

Economic Fluctuations

The notoriety acquired by 'stop-go' in the post-war years has led people to believe that fluctuations in the level of activity in the economy are something new—another of the many legacies of the Second World War. This is not so. Just as life has always been full of ups and downs, so also has the level of economic activity oscillated. Expansion, followed by depression, has been the natural order of things. At no time in our history has there been a long period of uninterrupted expansion. Yet it is for this that we have been seeking in recent years.

In the good old days they had their 'stop-go', only then it was called the trade cycle. The trade cycle was a longer lasting affair and much more of a natural phenomenon, there being very little government interference with the working of the economy in those days. Indeed, it has been the greater ability of governments to influence the natural course of events, aided by Keynsian economics, that has caused the post-war cycle to be such a much more hectic affair. The old pre-war cycle was generally spread over a longer period of time, usually seven years: the transition from expansion to depression was therefore less sudden. Another reason it was not so much resented was that it appeared to result quite naturally from the free play of economic forces. Government action could therefore not be blamed for what followed, although sometimes government inaction was a target of criticism. Under the old trade cycle, when the economy turned down, it often stayed down for quite a long time.

THE ECONOMIC CYCLE

A clear understanding of the nature and causes of the post-war rhythm of the economy is essential for good business planning, for without this the manager is liable to time his decisions badly. The economic cycle is popularly supposed to be the result of government policies; or wrong government policies. Our modern cycle is not regarded as a natural phenomenon. Many of its underlying causes are however to be found in some basic facts of human nature; such as the workers always wanting more and manufacturers preferring to sell in the easy home market rather than abroad.

The post-war economic cycle has normally extended over five years, and it is no coincidence that this is also the customary interval between General Elections. The cycle itself is in two parts: two to three years of 'stop' or restriction, and two to three years of 'go' or expansion of the economy. The duration of the 'go' periods has usually depended upon how quickly the expansion gets us into a balance of payments deficit position and how long we could go on financing (or even masking) this deficit by borrowing or running down our reserves. Britain's reserves in the post-war period have been at an average level of around £800 million and since this country can very easily slide into an adverse payments balance running at £300 million a year, it will be seen that the deficit can usually only be allowed to run for about two years (although under Labour it went on for much longer). The length of the 'stop' and 'go' phases also reflects the sluggishness or slow response of the economy to changes in government policy. The economy unfortunately does not seem to react to a gentle touch of the brake or to only a light foot on the accelerator: we have to push hard right down to the floorboard, in the case of both brake and accelerator, before it does what we want it to. In other words, the economy appears to be like a car whose body is too heavy for the size of its engine. Because governments seem unwilling to accept this fact, there is inevitably a delay while milder methods are tried first; so that the expansion lasts longer than it ought to do, and the slump also drags on longer than we want.

STAGES IN THE CYCLE

In describing the various stages of the economic cycle, it is easiest to start with the economy in an expansion phase, to describe the features of this, and then to deal in the same way with the period of restriction. It should not be imagined that the line of division between expansion and restriction is at all clear-cut; the boundaries are in fact often distinctly blurred. The economy may still be expanding quite vigorously, while government policies are already being couched in restrictive terms. Conversely, when reflationary policies are the order of the day, the economy may continue to be very depressed, despite official attempts to encourage it. One has therefore to decide whether it is the tone of government policies or the actual state of the economy which should determine the application of the label 'stop' or 'go' to any particular period in the cycle. If there is such a thing as a distinct watershed, this probably occurs when the final severe 'stop' measures are put into operation, often in great haste: July 1961 and July 1966 are examples of such occasions. After these shock events, the resultant downturn in the economy rapidly brings it into line with the general tenor of government policy and in every respect the climate can quite unequivocably be designated 'stop'.

BEGINNING OF EXPANSION

The entry of the economy into an expansion phase, normally lasting two to three years, is brought about by active official encouragement. The Government of the time (with perhaps a two years' distant General Election in mind) becomes anxious about the effect upon its public image of the comparatively high level of unemployment created by its restrictive policies. Since these same policies will also have brought about the desired surplus in our balance of payments, the time will be ripe in any case for a relaxation of restraints and even for giving the economy positive encouragement to expand once more. The first steps in this direction usually take the form of some easing of credit. Bank rate will be cut to give a general lead in interest rate reduction, although there may already have been some anticipation of this with a fall in yields on Treasury bills and fixed interest stocks. Removal of official restraints on bank lending may also be accompanied by the first repayment of 'special deposits'. Lending restrictions on H.P. finance companies will also be relaxed, with possibly a reduction in initial downpayments and lengthening of repayment periods. Later, relaxation will extend to the fiscal sphere. Rates of income tax will be lowered and allowances increased, the use of the regulator abandoned, purchase tax and excise duties reduced. At the same time, to generate economic activity, government spending will be increased, so that there will probably be a larger budget deficit.

All this causes consumer demand to revive, creating employment, and in turn more purchasing power. The consumer goods industries are naturally the first to recover from stagnation, and in particular those durable sectors where a large proportion of sales are credit financed and where purchase tax is a sizeable element in the final selling price. Notable among such sectors is motors. With non-durable consumer goods, such as food and clothing, the level of the demand is less influenced by economic policy, so that in a reflation improvement is less dramatic.

As a result of all these measures of relaxation, the unemployment percentage moves down from the peak level of 3 to 4 per cent of the work force reached in the depths of the 'stop' period. But during the first year of the expansion, labour still remains in a relatively easy supply. Firms previously operating below capacity and with their workers on short-time can expand production, without requiring new capital and labour resources. There is therefore a productivity gain. They can also achieve reduction in unit costs by being able to spread their fixed costs over a larger production volume. The excess stocks accumulated during the restrictive period begin to be run down and stock to turnover ratios return to a more normal figure. In this way profitability improves rapidly and business confidence revives. In the second year of profits upturn, dividends begin to be markedly increased, but retained profits are also higher.

INCREASED INVESTMENT

After some twelve to eighteen months of rising sales of their products, in the expectation that this will continue, manufacturers make plans to expand their production capacity—also being encouraged to do so by a seemingly ample cash flow (i.e. depreciation plus retained profits). There is, what is termed in the language of the national income statisticians, an upturn in 'fixed capital formation'; in other words a higher level of investment in fixed assets. This causes increased activity in the capital goods industries. But although this activity may become intense,* it is

* For an explanation of the magnified effect on the capital goods sector of an expansion by the consumer industries see page 109.

short-lived; the upturn in fixed capital formation usually extends over no more than two years, the first year coinciding with the second year of the consumer goods expansion.

In the second year of reflation, towards what proves to be the end of the expansion phase, unemployment may be down to nearly 1 per cent. At this level there is great scarcity of labour, since those remaining officially unemployed will in the main be the unemployables; so that in reality 'situations vacant' greatly exceed the number of those genuinely seeking employment. Such a climate is favourable to labour and wage demands are naturally pressed strongly. The tangible evidence of profit and dividend increases makes the workers deaf to any appeals for restraint. Employers in any case tend to be ready enough to accede to wage demands, since they are anxious not to lose sales and markets through strikes. With profits rising during this time, the increased wage cost can be partly absorbed; or else it can be passed on to the consumer, for the general price level will also be rising. With industrial earnings increasing at rates of around 10 per cent, higher prices are no deterrent to consumers' demand. So, after twelve to eighteen months of expansion, there begins to operate in the economy a powerful inflationary spiral.

ADVERSE BALANCE OF TRADE

This inflationary situation at home draws goods away from the export effort, while also raising their cost, to the detriment of our competitive position in world markets. Export industries have great difficulty in getting resources, particularly labour. At the same time our rising internal price level makes us an attractive market for foreign suppliers and the abundant purchasing power in the home economy sucks in imports. The high level of domestic production itself necessitates a greater volume of imported raw materials and semi-manufactures. Thus our exports decline, while our imports rise and we experience an adverse balance of trade.

In the early stages of this adverse balance it may have no effect on our gold reserves, foreigners being prepared to accept payment in sterling balances (particularly since these are interest-earning) and may be induced to invest short term in Britain. It is to encourage both these methods of financing a deficit that among the first of the restrictive measures is an increase in Bank rate. Monetary measures are resorted to first, because it is felt that these provide that 'gentle touch of the brake', which is all that the economy requires. Monetary measures are also (fortunately) less understood by the ordinary public and are thus not resented in the same way as are fiscal measures, such as a 6*d.* on income tax or a 1*d.* on beer. But these initial mild monetary measures are usually not powerful enough to contain a really rampant boom. The level of industrial activity and profits remains high; while the adverse balance of payments starts being increasingly reflected by falling gold reserves and weakening of sterling in the foreign exchange markets. Gradually, the whole range of monetary weapons is called into service and applied with increasing severity. Interest rates rise further, bank advances are restricted and there is also a progressive, but still relatively mild, tightening of hire purchase credit. All this remains ineffectual in reducing the excess pressure of demand. But there are certain sectors, like building, which are handicapped by rising interest rates.

It is at this time of increasing difficulty and cost of obtaining money that industry's spending on fixed assets is at a high level. This, combined with pressure from bank managers to fund bank overdrafts, forces companies on to the market to raise new capital at a time when it is particularly expensive to do so.

SEVERE 'STOP' MEASURES

Eventually, after the General Election, unpopular tougher measures can be put into effect. Among these will be increases in taxation and a severe tightening up on the availability of credit. Spending on consumer goods will in this way be discouraged and it is in these areas that the level of employment will be the first to fall; particularly in motors and the other consumer durables where much of the effective demand depends on hire purchase and where indirect taxation is high. Since the motor industry and its component suppliers comprise, not only a large, but a 'high earnings' segment of the national work force, the general demand reduction and unemployment effect of a lower level of activity in this area can be quite substantial. It is for this reason that 'motors' is a key sector in any attempt to expand or contract the economy: indeed the crucial test of effectiveness of such government policies

often lies in whether there is any resulting change in the level of
activity in the motor industry.

Unemployment will therefore spread to other sectors as a consequence of the reduced spending power of the workers in
those industries first hit; so that the demand reduction effect
becomes cumulative. As a result, the unemployment percentage
will rise from the low level of just over 1 per cent to something
nearer 2½ to 3½ per cent. Labour shortage will disappear and this
will discourage any continued hoarding of labour, thus adding
further to the slackness in the labour market. In such a climate,
there is a diminished ability to press wage demands successfully
and there will probably in any case be an official wage restraint
policy in force during this time.

Since in the second year of the capital goods expansion consumer demand is already falling, the new capacity comes on stream
just when there is less need for it. This was indeed what happened
in 1962, particularly in the domestic appliance industry, where the
existence of over-capacity eventually gave rise to considerable
price-cutting.

The lower level of demand, brought on by government policies
to discourage consumption, causes a decline in company sales and
thus in trading profits. With slackening sales, stock to turnover
ratios are likely to be higher, and working capital needs greater.
At the same time, the increase in fixed assets means that greater
provision has to be made for depreciation, so that pre-tax profits
are much reduced. All this puts severe pressure on company
liquidity: in many cases dividends have to be cut, stock levels
reduced and redundant workers put on short-time working or
even dismissed.

And so the economy slumps into another restrictive phase,
which is inevitably 'bad for business', just as the expansion period
was manifestly good for business. Businessmen's buoyant
optimism gives way to despondent pessimism; just as they could
not believe that the boom was ever going to end, so they now
become unable to envisage any future return to prosperity. With
the completion of current capital commitments, industry's investment falls to a low level. To the already existing unemployment
and short-time working in the consumer goods industries is added
that in the capital goods sector, causing the national unemploy-

ment percentage to reach its highest point. There is thus a further general contraction in purchasing power and the economy moves into the lowest point in the 'stop' period.

Such a pause does however present an opportunity to put many things right and to lay plans for a better future. The way in which this can be done will be described when we later come to consider the strategy to be adopted by the firm in the light of the economic cycle.

13

Course of the Economy

STOP TO STOP: JULY 1961—JULY 1966

The salient features of the economic cycle, including government corrective measures, can be well illustrated by recounting the events of the period that began with Selwyn Lloyd's famous 'stop' in July 1961 (and included Harold Wilson's equally famous one in July 1966). For although, after the 1961 experience, it was avowed that there would never again be a return to 'stop-go', the familiar pattern did reappear, albeit with some variation in timing. This chastening example of history repeating itself serves to underline the worthwhileness of attempting to understand the nature and causes of the economic cycle, in order that in our business planning we may take it into account.

Selwyn Lloyd's emergency Budget of 25th July 1961 was the culmination of a series of restrictive measures, beginning with the raising of Bank rate from 4 to 5 per cent in January 1960. It was really during 1960 that Britain ran up a large balance of payments deficit. After all the fuss and bother, 1961 eventually turned out to be a year of small overall surplus. Because of this, the authorities were subsequently accused by some of being too trigger-happy in the measures they took in the summer of 1961. (But, even more subsequently, the ineffectiveness of, for example, the policies pursued from the end of 1964 right up to the middle of 1966 tended to prove that severe 'stop' was in practice the only approach that really worked.)

There were plenty of warning signs in the early part of 1961 amply justifying the action taken in July. A deficit condition in the balance of payments reappeared in the second quarter of 1961, the first quarter having been in surplus. This, combined with fears of sterling devaluation engendered by revaluation of the deutschemark and guilder in the spring of the year, put the £ under considerable pressure. Domestically, there were also plenty of

unhealthy signs. Unemployment was still at the very low level of
1·2 per cent; with the result that inflation was running at the rate
of 4 to 5 per cent, while the increase in industrial earnings in 1961
was nearly 7 per cent over 1960.

'LITTLE BUDGET': JULY 1961

To remove these undesirable inflationary symptoms, as well as
restore foreign confidence in sterling, Selwyn Lloyd introduced
on the 25th July 1961 a final package of restrictive measures, these
being christened by the commentators of the time a 'little Budget'.
Bank rate was increased from 5 per cent to 7 per cent, after having
been reduced from 6 per cent in two stages in the latter part of
1960. Earlier, in his April 1961 Budget, the concept of the
'regulator' had been introduced by the Chancellor. In July he
brought this into operation, with the imposition of a 10 per cent
surcharge on customs and excise revenue (but *not* protective and
anti-dumping) duties and purchase tax. In doing so the Chancellor
took away £200 million from the public's spending power. It
should be remembered that in those days purchase tax rates were
quite high, so that the uplifting of them by another 10 per cent
was of significant proportions: purchase tax on cars, for example,
went up from 50 to 55 per cent. The Bank rate increase by a full
2 per cent and the use of the regulator were probably the two most
potent elements in the July package; but it was also announced
that government spending was to be restrained, and there was to
be stricter control of overseas investment. At the beginning of the
following month, the Finance Houses Association put up interest
charges and increased down-payments for car hire purchase. The
tightening of hire purchase, combined with the increased rate of
purchase tax, caused a drop in consumer spending on cars; this
being on top of the normal seasonal decline in the final quarter of
the year.

The fall in car sales in the second half of 1961 was quick to
cause a downturn in the general level of activity in the economy.
In the summer months the unemployment percentage had been
at its lowest practicable level, namely 1·2 per cent; but in the last
two months of the year it rose to 1·7 per cent, representing the
addition of another 120,000 to those out of work. The July
measures had caused businessmen's expectations about the future

to change from optimism to pessimism. But the level of investment continued to hold up during 1961, since it was the second year of the customary two-year period of upturn in fixed capital formation begun in 1960. Fixed capital formation by manufacturing industry was in fact at a peak level in the second half of 1961; and this was the time when the raising of new share capital had to be made on the basis of long-term interest rates up in the region of 8 per cent.

BALANCE OF PAYMENTS IMPROVEMENT:
RELAXATION MEASURES

The July measures brought the balance of payments quickly into surplus; so that repayment of the £539 million IMF loan, raised in August 1961, was able to start fairly soon and spread over the ensuing twelve months. The authorities were also able to take the first steps in relaxing the restrictions imposed during the summer. On the 5th October, there was a first reduction in Bank rate from 7 to $6\frac{1}{2}$ per cent, with another $\frac{1}{2}$ per cent reduction a month later. A 2 to $2\frac{1}{2}$ per cent guiding light for incomes increase was postulated in February 1962, this representing an attempt to substitute voluntary restraint for deflation. However, application of the 2 to $2\frac{1}{2}$ per cent principle frequently gave rise to strikes, particularly among engineering and shipbuilding workers. March 1962 saw two further Bank rate reductions, taking it back to 5 per cent. The April 1961 Budget was mildly expansionist: the 10 per cent surcharge being removed and in addition some of the purchase tax rates were further reduced. Towards the end of the month there was another $\frac{1}{2}$ per cent reduction in Bank rate. At the end of May, 1 per cent of the 3 per cent level of special deposits was paid back to the commercial banks.

NEW CHANCELLOR: MR. REGINALD MAUDLING

Cabinet changes in July 1962 signalled a marked shift in government economic policy. By that time the IMF loan had been fully paid back, so that the Government could afford to give the economy its head once more. The new Chancellor of the Exchequer, Mr. Reginald Maudling, was given this popular duty. In October he announced further measures to stimulate the economy: the relaxation of restraint on bank lending, the repayment of

£42 million post-war credits and an increase of £175 million in public sector investment. At the end of October another 1 per cent special deposits was repaid by the Bank of England to the commercial banks. In November more expansionist measures were announced. Purchase tax on cars was cut from 45 to 25 per cent, and this was probably the most decisive step taken in re-expanding the economy. Consumer expenditure on motor vehicles shot up immediately, despite the fact that this was normally a seasonally slack period. At the same time the Chancellor announced increased investment allowances and quicker write-off for heavy capital equipment. At the end of November the final 1 per cent of special deposits was released by the Bank of England. On 3rd January 1963 Bank rate was brought down to 4 per cent. Also in January, those remaining high purchase tax rates were cut back to 25 per cent, on such items as radios, records and cosmetics.

Despite these relaxations, throughout 1962 unemployment stayed around 2 per cent, representing at that time around 460,000 workers unemployed, which at that time was considered high. During 1962 also, investment dropped from the peak level of the second half of 1961, but did not, however, reach its lowest point until the early part of 1963. Growth in consumers' expenditure in 1962 was at a low rate of around 2 per cent. In the second half of 1962 inflation disappeared almost entirely, and this happy state of affairs continued during 1963. Company gross trading profits ceased to grow in 1962.

SEVERE WINTER: PEAK UNEMPLOYMENT

The severe winter of 1962/63, coupled with the already existing downturn in the economy, caused the unemployment percentage to rise to 3·9 per cent in February 1962. This was the highest degree of unemployment experienced in the post-war years: it was indeed fairly near the normal level of the pre-1914 years, when in fact there had been, significantly, almost a complete absence of inflation. This high level of unemployment gave rise to considerable concern, particularly on the part of the Prime Minister, Mr. Harold Macmillan, upon whom the 1930s had made a profound and lasting impression.

The April 1963 Budget was 'billed' as being expansionist, giving tax concessions amounting to some £270 million. Income tax changes took the form of increased allowances and modification of the reduced rate bands. Assistance to the development districts was increased, in order that there might be avoided any further repetition of the very high levels of unemployment experienced in some of the regions during the winter of 1962/63.

Consumer spending responded to this stimulation and in 1963 increased by 5 per cent over the previous year. Despite the better level of activity in the economy, the unemployment percentage, although it moved down from the high winter level, still remained above 2 per cent throughout the whole of 1963. The extra output was thus obtained with very little increase in the labour force and the earnings of those in employment went up by only 3 per cent. The high stock to output ratio, that had prevailed during 1962, was reduced during 1963, and went down even more in 1964. Thus, the reviving level of industrial activity in 1963 was on a very profitable basis and this was reflected by an 11 per cent rise in company gross trading profits.

RETURN OF BALANCE OF PAYMENTS DEFICIT

This expansion of the economy had not, however, gone very far before Britain moved back into balance of payments deficit in the third quarter of 1963. In fact, after April 1963, very little was done officially to stimulate the economy any further, since it had clearly begun to generate its own steam. Indeed, on the last day of November 1963, the Chancellor of the Exchequer warned that no more would now be done to increase public investment and that any wage settlements which went above $3\frac{1}{2}$ per cent would require very special justification. On 27th February, Bank rate was raised from 4 to 5 per cent.

By the beginning of 1964, the balance of payments deficit was already assuming large proportions, although in the first half of the year this was not reflected by any run-down in reserves. Mr. Maudling's April 1964 Budget was quite expressly 'deflationary', being aimed at reducing the growth rate of the economy down to 4 per cent: it had been growing at 5 to 6 per cent during 1963. Indirect taxation was increased by £100 million, including a 10 per cent increase in the duties on drink and tobacco. Government expenditure was to be held at the existing level. Several proposals were made to encourage saving, this being a more popular way of trying to reduce consumption than by cutting back on disposable income by raising taxation. These were still fairly mild measures when viewed alongside the magnitude of our international payments deficit. And signs of over-heating in the economy were by this time widespread. Inflation had returned and the cost of living index rose by 4 per cent in 1964. Unemployment in the second quarter of 1964 was down to 1·6 per cent and by the end of the year it was 1·5 per cent. As a result of this labour scarcity situation, industrial earnings in 1964 moved up at a rate of 8 per cent, as against 3 per cent in the previous year.

But, there were also signs that consumers' expenditure had begun to slacken. This was expected to bring a halt to the growth in imports. Part of this was also thought to have been due to an initial rebuilding of industry's stocks of materials, after the slackness of 1962; so here again some relief was expected. In addition, it was the Government's hope that British industry was about to achieve a significant break-through to a new peak of efficiency, which would satisfy the requirements of home demand, as well as provide an increasing volume of goods for the export market. To ensure competitiveness in the export market, unit costs had to be held down by continued operation at full capacity, and for this reason the home market had to be kept buoyant.

HIGH INVESTMENT: HIGH INTEREST RATES

Certainly industry was operating profitably during this period because gross trading profits showed a 15 per cent rise over the previous year, which, as we have already noted, was itself a good one. The year 1964 was the second one of expansion for consumer goods industries, but the first of an upturn in fixed capital formation. This higher level of investment gave rise to an increased volume of new shares issues, largely taking the form of debentures. (Further incentive towards financing on a fixed interest basis was to be given by the Corporation Tax, which increased the cost of dividends on ordinary and preference shares.) Unfortunately, industry's greater need for new capital came at a time of rising interest rates. In the autumn of 1963 the rate of interest on long-dated British government stocks had been just under 5½ per cent, but during 1964, when fixed capital formation started to increase, it was up to 6 per cent; and for the next two years it oscillated between 6½ per cent and 7¼ per cent (in the third quarter of 1966). Fixed capital formation and new issues reached their peak towards the end of 1965 and the beginning of 1966, when the long-term rate of interest was around 6½ per cent on government stocks, so that new issues of first-class company debentures had to offer around 8 per cent to be attractive to investors.

CHANGE OF GOVERNMENT

Despite the alarming proportions reached by our international payments deficit at the beginning of 1964, a full-blooded policy of restriction was not embarked upon until the change of government towards the end of the year, when the parlous state of our balance of payments was then given full publicity. On the 26th October, within ten days of assuming office, the new Labour Government published a White Paper on the 'Economic Situation', in which were set out the first measures for dealing with the then estimated £700 to £800 million deficit in our balance of payments for 1964. A surcharge of 15 per cent was levied to discourage imports of manufactures and semi-manufactures: the 15 per cent being additional to, and not merely an increase on, the prevailing rates of import duty. To give some inducements to exporters, they were to be given a rebate of certain indirect taxes, including those on oil, petrol and vehicle licences. To provide interim financing for the payments deficit, the Government announced that it had begun discussions with the International Monetary Fund to activate the U.K.'s drawing rights. None of these measures did much to affect the internal economic situation. Indeed, the attempt to reduce the volume of imports coming into the British market, given the continuation of the high level of home demand, was bound to add further fuel to inflationary pressures, as would also any diversion of goods from the home market into the export sphere.

Only two weeks after the 'Economic Situation' White Paper the new Chancellor of the Exchequer presented a first emergency Budget, the broad aims of which were the reduction of the balance of payments deficit and the implementation of certain social reforms. Some of the measures contained in this Budget did affect purchasing power, but probably more that of the middle class, than of the ordinary man in the street. The duty on petrol was increased by 6*d*. a gallon and the standard rate of income tax went up from 7*s*. 9*d*. to 8*s*. 3*d*. in the £, to take effect in April 1965. Increased rates of National Insurance contribution were also announced, as were certain pension increases (to become operative at the end of March 1965). There was to be a new form of company taxation, namely the Corporation Tax, expected to come into operation in April 1965. The estimated net effect of all these measures in a full year was to reduce the public's spending power by about £200 million.

A flight from sterling towards the end of November enforced the taking of the long delayed further Bank rate action, the rate being pushed up from 5 to 7 per cent. A few days afterwards, the Bank of England was able to announce a massive support operation for sterling. Credits amounting to $3,000 million had been extended to Britain by the central banks of many countries, to provide short-term financing to support the £. At the beginning of December, Britain drew on her stand-by facility ($1,000 million) with the IMF.

CREDIT SQUEEZE

The first of the 'credit squeeze' measures came a few days later on the 8th December, when the Bank of England asked the Clearing banks to curb the giving of advances in the spheres of property development, hire purchase and personal loans. The end of January 1965 saw some further measures announced for stimulating exports: the establishment of export councils to cover the main geographical trading areas, increased support for trade missions and market research, and additional facilities under the Export Credits Guarantee arrangements. But on the 22nd February, in response to overseas pressure, it was announced that the surcharge on imports would be reduced on the 27th April, from 15 per cent to 10 per cent.

A further effort to reduce inflationary pressures within the economy was made by attempting to progress with an incomes policy, with which the previous Government had not been very successful. The 'statement of intent' on prices and incomes was signed in December. The first meeting of the National Board for Prices and Incomes took place in May 1965.

Mr. Callaghan's April 1965 Budget involved taxation increases of another £200 million a year, raised chiefly by higher duties on tobacco and alcoholic drinks; there was also to be a taxing of long-term capital gains. The allowance of business entertainment expenditure against income tax was abolished, except in the case of the entertainment of overseas buyers, and the initial allowance of 30 per cent was withdrawn on business cars. Stricter control of foreign investment and exchange was also announced. The new Corporation Tax was described in more detail, but it was not to become operative until 1966.

The first call for special deposits was made by the Bank of England on the 29th April 1965, and was for 1 per cent. Shortly afterwards the Bank of England advised Clearing banks that their loans should not be expanded by more than 5 per cent during the year 1965/66, and this was later extended to the merchant banks and finance companies. A second drawing from the International Monetary Fund was made by Britain on the 12th May.

PREMATURE BANK RATE REDUCTION

On the 3rd June 1965, Bank rate was prematurely reduced from 7 to 6 per cent, but at the same time hire purchase initial deposits were increased: the minimum deposits on cars going up from 20 to 25 per cent; on electrical goods, except cookers, from 10 to 15 per cent; on bedding, furniture, cookers and water heaters the 10 per cent minimum remained unchanged. A few days later the Government announced that up to 1969/70 it would attempt to hold its defence spending at £2,000 million, on the basis of 1964 prices.

During the first half of 1965 inflation had been running at an annual rate of 6 per cent; while by the middle of the year the unemployment percentage was down to 1·3 per cent. Growth in industrial earnings was still proceeding at the high annual rate of 8 per cent, or nearly four times growth in output. There was little sign therefore that the Government's restrictive policies were having any effect in cutting back the excess pressure of demand, the continuance of which was bound to impede balance of payments improvement, although there was a certain unwillingness to recognise this at the time.

On the 27th July 1965 further measures were announced by

the Chancellor to strengthen the balance of payments, mainly by cutting back on public and private expenditure at home. Local authority and government investment was to be reduced in total by about £200 million and there was further restriction of local authority lending on mortgage for house purchase. Also introduced were building licences for private projects over £100,000, excluding housing and industrial building. Credit was restricted further by the repayment period for hire purchase debts being reduced from 36 to 30 months in August; except for furniture, bedding, cookers and water heaters. Tighter exchange controls were imposed and there was to be a reduction in the finance available for imports. The Government recognised also that it would have to accept postponement of certain social reforms and cheaper mortgages until the balance of payments position improved.

In September 1965, the T.U.C. not only gave its support for a voluntary 'early warning system' for wage claims and price increases, but later that month set up the necessary machinery. Two months after this a White Paper outlining the 'early warning system' was presented to Parliament.

February 1966 saw a further, but still moderate, tightening up on hire purchase credit. The repayment period on most goods was reduced from 30 to 24 months, with the minimum initial down-payment going up from 15 to 25 per cent (on furniture the increase was from 10 to 15 per cent). In the case of cars and motor cycles, the repayment period only came down to 27 months and there was no alteration of the minimum deposit.

The delayed Budget of May 1966, after the March General Election, took another £400 million out of the economy. The rate of Corporation Tax was fixed at 40 per cent, but there was no change made in income tax. It was announced that the 10 per cent import surcharge would be abolished in November. A reduction in the balance of payments deficit on capital account was to be achieved by a voluntary programme of restriction with regard to the outflow of direct investment funds to the more advanced countries in the Sterling Area, and by economies in government spending overseas. A new and unexpected measure was a Selective Employment Tax, designed to discourage labour hoarding and halt the flow of too much of the work force towards service industries, as well as spread the burden of indirect taxation, which had hitherto rather been concentrated on consumer durable items. To encourage saving a new issue of National Development Bonds was announced. The Chancellor went so far as to indicate that he thought that his measures would be found to have exercised a sufficient check on home demand. However, as inflationary pressures continued, it became increasingly obvious that the whole series of measures taken from October 1964 to May 1966 had in fact done little to reduce the excess pressure of demand in the economy; and this was mainly because very few of them had adversely affected the purchasing power of the man in the street.

With the continuing excess pressure of demand in the economy, it was not surprising that the balance of payments position in the first part of 1966 did not exhibit any continuation of the improvement during 1965. On top of this, there was the seamen's strike in May and June. This had adverse international payments repercussions in the holding up of exports and in the loss of British shipping earnings, coupled with the need to use foreign ships.

SEVERE 'STOP': JULY 1966

These two factors necessitated the resort once more to crisis measures; again in the month of July.* This time these were severe enough to administer the required 'stop' to the economy, in the same way as Selwyn Lloyd had successfully done in July 1961. Bank rate was put back to 7 per cent on the 14th July. A second call was made for 1 per cent special deposits, the ceiling on bank advances of 5 per cent above the March 1965 level was extended until March 1967, and indeed until further notice thereafter. Although there had earlier appeared to be the possibility of some relief, the Chancellor now indicated that no special arrangements would be made to enable the banks to ease the severe pressures placed on company liquidity by the coming into operation of the Selective Employment Tax in September 1966, as well as by the payment of tax on dividend distributions. Hire purchase minimum deposits were raised from 25 to 40 per cent on cars, motor cycles and caravans, with the repayment period cut to

* This is when the Treasury presents each year its post-Budget assessment of the economy.

24 months; downpayments on furniture were raised from 15 to 20 per cent; and from 25 to 33⅓ per cent on domestic appliances. All this was expected to bring about a marked reduction in hire purchase borrowing. In the taxation field the regulator was resorted to again, with a 10 per cent surcharge on purchase tax and excise duties; but on this occasion it was not applied to duties on tobacco. A special surcharge of 10 per cent was to be placed on surtax due for payment in September 1967. A statutory six months' standstill was proposed for wages, to be followed by a further six months of severe restraint. Companies were expected to hold down dividends for twelve months, and there was to be a twelve months' standstill on prices. Government overseas expenditure was to be reduced by £100 million and private basic travel allowances brought down from £250 to £50. Central and local government expenditure was to be cut by £150 million. Private building controls were extended downwards to take in projects of between £50,000 and £100,000, but housing and building in the development areas remained exempt. It was expected that altogether the July measures would take £500 million of purchasing power out of the economy.

Thus, by July 1966 the five-year cycle was complete and we were indeed back to square one. The July measures had their effect; short-time working and redundancies followed very soon afterwards, particularly (and significantly) in the motor industry. The national unemployment percentage moved up from the very low level of 1·1 per cent at which it had been in July 1966, and by the end of the year it had risen to 2·6 per cent. In the final quarter of 1966 Britain had a substantial balance of payments surplus.

THE CHANGING CYCLE: 1967–70

During the second half of the sixties the economic cycle became less regular, in terms of timing and features. There was a very short 'stop' after the July 1966 measures. From 1967 to 1968 there was another 'go' period, during which, however, unemployment did not fall. The next two years (1969 and 1970) saw the economy once more in a restrictive phase, but inflation reached a high rate, so that this condition came to be termed 'stagflation'.

IRREGULARITY OF THE CYCLE

The change in the character of the economic cycle was due to certain new factors. The significance of these had not immediately been recognised: instead the commentators thought that some of the basic laws of economics were breaking down. The different nature of the cycle can be quite simply attributed to certain features of the Labour Government's economic policy. Right up until Roy Jenkins became the Chancellor, there was an unwillingness to embark on policies that really were deflationary in effect and to sustain them for the necessary period. The slender parliamentary majority of the Labour Government from October 1964 to March 1966 was undoubtedly a factor in this. In pursuit of social and economic objectives, under Labour the level of government expenditure mounted, providing a strong inflationary force in the economy that entirely offset the increases that were made in taxation. Under the previous Government the borrowing requirement had never been much more than £350 million; but in Labour's first three fiscal years it was £500, £700 and £1,300 million.

The Government was only able to put the economy into a two-year expansive phase after 1966 because it was prepared to allow the balance of payments deficit to continue for longer than ever before in the post-war period, incurring in the process enormous international indebtedness of the order of £3,000 million. Covering the deficit by external borrowing also financed the Government's excess of expenditure over taxation receipts. In consequence of domestic saving not being required to cover the Government's borrowing needs, the overall pressure of demand on the economy was that much greater and had to be satisfied by drawing in goods from abroad. In this way the problem became self-perpetuating and the Government had to resort to devaluation, as well as to massive international borrowing.

ECONOMIC MANAGEMENT UNDERMINED

On those occasions when an attempt was made to deflate there was found to be difficulty in doing so. Taxation increases took money out of the economy, but rapidly rising government spending put it back again. When there was eventually a preparedness to try to combat inflationary pressures by running the economy at a higher level of unemployment of around $2\frac{1}{2}$ per cent, there was found to be no longer any useful easing of pressures resulting therefrom. This was because the level of benefits paid to the unemployed had been greatly increased (with the introduction of redundancy payments in 1965 and earnings-related unemployment benefit in 1966) so that total demand did not fall much as the rate of unemployment rose. There was also not quite the same urgency to seek employment and this combined with trade union practices meant that the existence of a growing body of unemployed did little to reduce the wage bargaining power of those still in employment, further enhanced by more liberal giving of state subsidies that encouraged resort to the strike weapon. The upshot of all this was that $2\frac{1}{2}$ per cent unemployment during the years from 1967 onwards was not the same as it had been in 1962–63. The failure to recognise these aspects as causing profound changes in the nature of things in the economy, led to fiscal policy being (wrongly) rejected as no longer adequate and a call for greater use of monetary policy as a more effective instrument of regulation. For some people the appeal of this alternative also lay in the opportunity it appeared to offer of avoiding cuts in government spending or unpopular tax increases. But monetary policy too was found to be powerless to deal with rampant wages-push inflation, for some of the very same reasons that had caused fiscal policy to be ineffectual.

There were other prominent features of the second half of the sixties. One was the prolonged period of historically very high interest rates. This was initially a reflection of the weak state of Britain's balance of payments, but when this improved a rise in international rates, and later inflation, came along to keep up the level of long-term interest rates in Britain.

These general remarks explain why the character of economic fluctuations from 1967 onwards has been slightly different. Not because the basic laws of economics were no longer valid, but because certain aspects of government policy had effects that were only belatedly recognised and allowed for. Having by a preliminary assessment facilitated our understanding of them, a more detailed examination of the course of economic events from 1967–70 will now be undertaken.

DEVALUATION: 1967

What has been termed the 'international interest rate war' reached a peak of intensity in the autumn of 1966. A disarmament conference was called at 'Chequers' towards the end of the opening month of 1967, attended by finance ministers from several countries, the object of which was to achieve international co-operation to bring down the level of interest rates. A fairly swift reduction did take place during the first half of that year, until it was arrested by the Middle East crisis in the summer. Britain co-operated in the de-escalation with three reductions in Bank rate to bring it down from 7 to 5½ per cent, thus also forming the first stage of a reflationary policy.

During 1967 the brake was taken off the economy rather too quickly, as events were later to prove. There was no real political need for such haste, since the General Election was not due until 1970. Nevertheless, in February a £660 million increase in government spending was announced to stimulate the economy. The April Budget was presented as being broadly neutral, but there was some easing of hire purchase restrictions in the case of motor cycles. With demand for advances having fallen, the Chancellor removed the ceiling on bank lending and announced a more flexible use of special deposits in future for the control of advances growth when this again became necessary. Early in June there was a further easing of hire purchase regulations, this time on the important category of cars. There was also an increase in pensions and other National Insurance benefits. Towards the end of August there took place a more general relaxation of hire purchase restrictions, in which cars and motor cycles again benefited.

The middle of September saw the disastrous national dock strike. The disruptive effects of this on trade, causing greater loss of exports than imports, together with the premature reflation, put the country in severe balance of payments difficulties once again. There were two increases in Bank rate, but a more drastic measure was required and on 18th November the £ was devalued by 14·3 per cent. An accompanying package included putting up Bank rate to a new post-war peak of 8 per cent; a strict curb on bank advances; and a retightening of hire purchase regulations on cars. The Government set itself a target for balance of payments improvement of £500 million, involving a shift of £1,000 million of resources into exporting. To give support to sterling over the devaluation period, the I.M.F. and central banks provided further loans of $3,000 million. In return the British Government agreed to submit to 4-monthly reviews of the U.K. economy by the I.M.F. and to undertake that the borrowing requirement in 1968/69 would be no more than £1,000 million. Mr. Roy Jenkins succeeded Mr. Callaghan as Chancellor of the Exchequer.

GOLD CRISIS: 1968

As the level of consumer spending continued high, it became increasingly clear that if more resources were to be made available for exports something would have to be done to curb home demand. A major criticism of the Government's devaluation strategy was that it had been slow to take sufficient necessary accompanying deflationary measures. It should however be said that many of those who had previously advocated devaluation had tended to present it as an alternative to deflation. It was only afterwards that it became apparent that they had always intended devaluation to have with it a deflationary package.

In the middle of January 1968 the Prime Minister announced some cuts in government spending, but not all of these took immediate effect. At the same time he indicated that the Chancellor would be taking action in the forthcoming Budget to restrain demand. This announcement immediately set off a pre-Budget boom in consumer spending, in order to beat the tax increases that the Prime Minister had clearly indicated were coming. When Budget time came along in March, the Chancellor had therefore an even greater problem to deal with. As a result, he imposed a £900 million massive increase in taxes, including higher purchase tax and S.E.T. The effect of the Budget and the Government spending cuts announced earlier by the Prime Minister was to reduce drastically the borrowing requirement from the £1,335 million it had been in the previous fiscal year to a negative requirement in 1968/69 of £270 million. Although bank lending had been subjected to a standstill at the time of devaluation, in the early part of 1968 the banks continued to increase their advances, so that the Bank of England towards the end of May imposed a 104 per cent ceiling on their further growth.

On the international monetary scene the year 1968 was a very troubled one. Following devaluation of sterling the dollar had come under attack. There was considerable excitement in the gold market in the latter part of 1967 and the first quarter of 1968, culminating in the creation of a two-tier gold system. During the summer the foreign exchange markets were disturbed by riots in France. There was also during this period some movement out of sterling balances, since there was still no sign of improvement in the U.K. balance of payments and many overseas holders of sterling were still smarting over the losses they had suffered through devaluation. In July, Basle lending arrangements enabled the British Government to give an exchange value guarantee on reserve balances held in sterling. In the middle of November the foreign exchange markets were again in turmoil, due to speculation as to possible devaluation of the franc and revaluation of the deutschemark. The member countries of the Paris Club accordingly met at Bonn and agreed that, in order to restore calm, deficit and surplus countries would require to take further action to achieve external payments equilibrium.

It had now become obvious that devaluation and the belated accompanying measures had not brought about any transformation in Britain's balance of payments position. Indeed the deficit on current account for 1968 was even greater than in the previous devaluation year. Devaluation itself had brought about automatic improvement in the invisibles account, through raising the sterling value of income received in foreign currency, while leaving unaffected the sterling income of overseas residents. But devaluation had also involved an immediate substantial increase in the sterling value of imports and in the absence of any marked decline in their volume the trade account remained in large deficit, since our exports were slower to build on the competitive advantage that devaluation had given them. Consumer spending during 1968 remained much higher than expected and was a major factor in keeping up the level of imports, as well as depriving export markets. So when he returned from Bonn, the Chancellor announced yet another package of measures to curb home demand and bring our external payments into balance. Purchase tax and other duties were raised by 10 per cent by the reimposition of the 'regulator'; Clearing bank lending was to be brought down to 98 per cent of the level at the time of devaluation; a 50 per cent deposit was imposed on imports.

EXTERNAL PAYMENTS SURPLUS: 1969

To reinforce the restraint on bank advances, these were made more expensive through Bank rate being put back to 8 per cent in February. Government spending continued to be kept in check. The need for this had been emphasised in discussions that took place between the I.M.F. and, on Britain's side, the Treasury and the Bank of England in October of the previous year. Subsequently, in May 1969, a Letter of Intent from the British Chancellor to the I.M.F. reaffirmed the importance attached to the size of the borrowing requirement and to the newly-adopted concept of 'domestic credit expansion'. The April Budget increased taxes by a further £350 million and shortly afterwards the Chancellor revealed that his aim for 1969/70 was to ensure that D.C.E. growth would not exceed £400 million. The attainment of this objective was virtually assured by the huge projected Budget surplus for 1969/70, leading to an actual negative borrowing requirement of almost £1,120 million.

By the middle of 1969 there was firm evidence that Britain's balance of payments had at last been brought into sustained surplus, through exports rising strongly, while imports levelled off. A combination of devaluation, deflation, import deposits and tight curb on government spending had together achieved this result, but it was impossible to say which had been the most decisive of these. It was fortunate that Britain's external position was now satisfactory for this enabled sterling to weather the upheavals in the foreign exchange markets caused by devaluation of the franc in August and revaluation of the deutschemark in October.

All was not quiet on the industrial relations front. The unions had grown restive under the strict curb on consumer spending (it rose by only ½ per cent during 1969) and the increased cost of living effects of devaluation. The unions also felt that they had lost ground during the periods of incomes restraint of 1966/67 and they wished to catch up. Wage claims were pressed with greater militancy and from 1968 onwards there was a marked upturn in the number of strikes and working days lost through them. To deal with this the Government attempted to move during 1969 in the direction of reform of industrial relations. It met with severe opposition from the T.U.C. and gave way to it; thus encouraged, the T.U.C. went further and repudiated the whole concept of incomes policy. Industrial earnings during 1968/69 rose in each year by 8 per cent and in the final quarter of 1969 there was evidence of acceleration in this rise, thus sowing the seeds of what was to become the major problem of the next two years, namely runaway inflation.

THE GREAT INFLATION: 1970

The early part of 1970 saw two ½ per cent reductions in Bank rate, taking it back to the more normal peak level of 7 per cent. The second of these cuts was made in the Budget, which despite being the last before the Election was only very mildly giveaway, mainly reducing income tax by £200 million. Bank lending was allowed to grow by 5 per cent, but another ½ per cent special deposits was called, just to illustrate the new flexibility in the use of this monetary instrument.

The mid-June election saw the Labour Party removed from office. During the campaign there was a growing awareness of the strength of the inflationary forces and there were also some doubts about how firmly based was the balance of payments improvement (although these were later shown to have been unwarranted). The high rate of inflation did not have its usual effect of causing deterioration in Britain's trading position, because on this occasion other countries were also suffering from inflation, even although not to quite the same extent. Britain was therefore able to retain much of the advantage devaluation had given and indeed the rise of our export prices gave a terms of trade advantage, which in the short run at any rate was favourable in value terms to our visible trade balance.

The new Conservative Government gave no appearance of great activity in its early summer months of office. In view of its Election promises and the growing evidence of severe cost-push inflation (with wage claims being couched in 20 to 30 per cent terms) some surprise was expressed at this apparent inactivity. The tragic death, so soon after taking office, of the Chancellor of the Exchequer, Mr. Iain Macleod, was a set-back in the formulation of the new Government's policy measures. Towards the end of October, Mr. Macleod's successor, Anthony Barber introduced a Mini-Budget, the character of which seemed, however, more to satisfy the early redemption of election pledges, than to combat inflation. It was announced that in the following April there would be a 6*d.* reduction in the standard rate of income tax and that corporation tax would be brought down from 45 to 42½ per cent. More immediately the system of investment grants was ended, with a return to investment allowances. A programme of cuts in growth of government spending was announced that would extend over several years, but there were more immediate increases in charges for social services. Two days later, the banks, having as usual exceeded their lending ceiling, were asked to place another 1 per cent special deposits with the Bank of England, this being done to discipline them.

In 1969 Britain had earned a large balance of payments surplus and that in 1970 was even larger. This enabled repayment of a substantial part of the outstanding international indebtedness much earlier and to a greater extent than had originally been thought possible at the time the debts were incurred. But as one problem had been solved another had taken its place. The year 1970 ended with inflation reaching 8½ per cent, wage-push being still the major factor in this, with earnings rising at 13 per cent. The policy stance adopted by the Government was to encourage resistance to excessive wage claims by its example in the public sector, even at the expense of great public inconvenience, not being too ready to settle in order to avoid this. Money supply control, which had eased in the first half of the year, was tightened again. The Government made it clear that it would not attempt to alleviate the effects of this on companies' liquidity, since this might weaken their resistance to wage demands. A mounting toll of bankruptcies and rising unemployment was the way in which monetary policy had to do its job. The Government refused to countenance any attempt to return to an incomes policy or freeze. It did however pursue a longer term solution through reform of industrial relations.

STAGFLATION 1971

The resistance of private sector employers (particularly in the motor industry) to excessive wage demands was not as firm as the

Government would have wished. It was perhaps unrealistic, however, to expect salaried management to put their own jobs at risk through a prolonged strike that might ruin the company, when this could be avoided by simply acceding to the wage claim and passing on the cost to either the customer or the shareholder, management itself incurring no financial penalty. In any case by being slow (not till April 1971) to reduce the state support going to the striker and his family, the Government continued to bolster the staying power of the workers in their stand against the employer.

By the middle of 1971 evidence of de-escalation of wages growth was quite meagre (despite over 3 per cent unemployment) and, with employers taking compensating pricing action to safe-guard their profit margins, inflation moved up to just under 10 per cent. The additional elements of the April Budget contained little of direct relevance to the inflation problem and the total effect was in fact reflationary to the extent of £600 million. Corporation tax was brought down further, to 40 per cent; S.E.T. cut in half; pensions and other social security benefits increased (including that for unemployment and those going to strikers' families). For the future, reform of company taxation and introduction of V.A.T. were announced.

A second Mini-Budget in July 1971 indicated a pronounced shift in Government economic policy. There was no longer to be reliance upon rising unemployment to curb excessive wages growth. Instead, the economy would be vigorously expanded to bring supply into better balance with demand, as well as enable companies through increased turnover and trading profits to absorb cost increases rather than pass them on in higher prices. Just before the Chancellor announced his package, the CBI had appealed to its major company members to restrict their price increases to 5 per cent within the next twelve months. The Chancellor was able to respond with a 'double-the-regulator' reduction in purchase tax rates; the complete lifting of hire purchase terms control; and further investment allowances. It was hoped that, with this promise of faster economic growth and the offer of voluntary prices restraint from the CBI, the trade unions would also feel able to make some contribution to slowing inflation.

THE CHANGED SITUATION

We conclude with some general explanation of the apparent paradoxes in Britain's economic situation right at the end of the sixties and beginning of the seventies. For the unsophisticated these paradoxes seemed to necessitate throwing over completely and permanently what has become established doctrine regarding economic relationships, thus leaving us with no principles upon which to forecast likely future developments and policies. This view derives from a failure to realise that the differences of the 1969/70 situation were largely due to man-made elements (and mistakes) that could therefore be man-unmade and put right again, as well as undone by the passage of time. Eventually, therefore, previous generalisations and indicators would become true once more.

For most of the post-war period it had been possible to anticipate restrictive or expansive periods largely according to how Britain's balance of payments was going and therefore any system of advance warning indicators naturally centred upon this aspect of the economy's health. Although, as indicated earlier, the Government's principal economic objectives were often in conflict with one another, nevertheless the condition of these factors exhibited a certain reciprocating relationship during the various stages of the economic cycle. Thus attainment of a favourable balance of payments also normally meant that inflationary pressures had been brought under control; so that government policy could then be concerned with reducing the level of unemployment and stimulating growth in the economy. Higher unemployment also normally meant that inflationary pressures had eased, particularly those of the cost-push variety.

In most recent years, and especially during 1970/71, things have rather changed. Most unusually, a condition of massive balance of payments surplus has coexisted with an extremely high rate of inflation, the latter despite a rising level of unemployment. A favourable external payments position might have signalled a return to expansionist policies, although there was some need to prolong this surplus for debt repayment purposes. Rising unemployment should have indicated the appropriateness of expansion, but what stood in the way of doing so of course was the incredibly high rate of inflation. All this seemed to require a revision of our ideas about the relationship of economic objectives, as well as our advance indicators.

There are, however, several explanations for the changed situation in 1969/70 and a proper understanding of these makes it possible to envisage that at some time there will be a return to normal relationships and therefore to our customary method of assessing the economy. There were two principal reasons why we were able to have a substantial balance of payments surplus, although suffering from run-away inflation. The first was that many of our trading competitors had the same problem. Secondly, although in some cases they had a lesser degree of inflation, this difference was compensated for by the price advantage that devaluation had given us. (Devaluation had itself been an inflationary influence, but it also enabled us, from an external payments aspect, to tolerate this inflation for some time. An excessively favourable balance of trade can also engender inflationary pressures, since the supply of goods to the home market is diminished by the rise in exports and curb on imports.)

The existence of inflation during 1969/70 was largely due to severe wage-push pressures, despite rising unemployment. Wage claims were strongly backed by a readiness to take strike action, since through a variety of social benefits the state in fact subsidised the strikers—or at any rate their families. With the possibility of hardship removed, the strike weapon was readily threatened and therefore wage claims successfully pressed. Unemployment benefits had been greatly increased in themselves and also through the introduction of redundancy payments and earnings-related benefits. This kept up the basic level of purchasing power of those workers who became unemployed, as well as perhaps reducing their sense of urgency in the search for another job. The existence of the growing body of unemployed did little to restrain the bargaining power of those still in employment and union practices in any case kept the employed and unemployed as two separate classes.

These factors that created the unusual situation of 1969/70 could of course change and therefore in doing so make valid once more traditional cause and effect relationships and interpretations. To the extent that other nations, as seems likely, get their inflation under control before we do, then the consequences of this will

ECONOMIC FLUCTUATIONS: 1960–70

		1960	1961	1962	1963	1964	1965	1966	1967	1968	1969	1970
		←— Go —→		Stop	←—— Go ——→		←— Stop —→		←—— Go ——→		←— Stop —→	
Current Balance of Payments	£m	−265	−4	+112	+114	−395	−77	+43	−297	−306	+437	+631
Gross Domestic Product[1] % inc.		5	3½	½	4½	6	2½	2	2	3½	2	2
Unemployment[2] %		1·6	1·5	2·0	2·5	1·6	1·4	1·5	2·4	2·4	2·4	2·6
Industrial Earnings[3] % inc.		8	6½	4½	3½	8	8	7	3	8½	8	14
Inflation[4] % rate		1	5	4	2	4	5	4	2½	5	5½	7
Consumers' Expenditure % inc.		4	2	2	4½	4	2	2	1½	2½	1½	3
COMPANY FINANCE												
Gross Trading Profits	£m	3,760	3,665	3,620	4,070	4,591	4,758	4,442	4,620	5,024	4,948	5,029
Fixed Investment[5]	£m	1,021	1,239	1,168	1,044	1,236	1,420	1,521	1,485	1,615	1,813	2,072
New Capital Issues[6]	£m	212	310	183	173	234	264	430	313	313	277	122
Long-Term Interest Rates[7]	%	5·42	6·20	5·98	5·58	6·03	6·42	6·80	6·69	7·39	8·88	9·16
Stocks/Output Ratio (mid year)[6]		94	100	100	95	94	96	97	98	90	90	93

[1] 1958 prices.
[2] Monthly average as % of total employees.
[3] Hourly earnings in manufacturing.
[4] Index of retail prices.
[5] Manufacturing industry, at current prices
[6] Manufacturing industry.
[7] Average gross flat yield on 2½ per cent Consols.

Sources: Monthly Digest, Financial Statistics, Economic Trends—H.M.S.O.

increasingly show up in a deterioration of our trading balance, as our original devaluation advantage gets used up. We will then be back in a situation when government has to be concerned about inflation *and* the balance of payments. As to the relationship between unemployment and inflation, here again there is likely to be a shift back to normality. Action has to some extent been taken to reduce elements of the subsidy enjoyed by strikers. In the absence of any substantial increase in their amount, continued inflation will rapidly erode the real value of the various unemployment reliefs. As wages rise too, the alternatives of unemployment or strike will become more unattractive by comparison with remaining in employment. As all this happens the Phillips curve relationship should begin to be exhibited more clearly than has been the case in recent years and a given unemployment percentage begin to mean what it used to earlier in the sixties.

14

International Trade and Common Market

The competition being faced by businessmen today is not solely that from other domestic producers but is increasingly of an international character. World trade in the sixties rose at a rate of nearly 9 per cent per annum; very much faster than the average rate of GNP growth in most countries. This increased trade between nations resulted from many factors. It has, of course, been made possible by easier and faster communications. A growing internationalisation of consumer tastes, such as the adoption of western ways of life in the East (and indeed the American way of life by many Europeans), has provided producers with world markets and satisfied industry's growing need for greater volume to reap the economies of large-scale production and recoup research and development costs, particularly in the highly technological industries. It has therefore become imperative that goods should be allowed to flow more freely between nations and this has created a pressure of opinion for tariff reduction, coupled with the elimination of quotas and other restrictions on trade.

In the main, governments have encouraged this growth in trade, hoping that it would improve international relations, as well as provide enlarged opportunities for their domestic producers. Governments have also seen international trade as a way of keeping home industry competitive, counterbalancing the power of national monopoly groups and thus protecting the consumer from exploitation. Since the Second World War, the development of international organisations has not only fostered the desire for freer economic relationships, but has provided the driving force and co-ordinating mechanisms to attack the many obstacles to free trade between nations. There has been a concerted international effort to break down the protectionism of the depressed thirties, which had reversed the free trade movement begun in the mid-nineteenth century.

LAW OF COMPARATIVE COSTS

Free trade is desirable on economic as well as political grounds. The economic justification for free trade was formulated into the theory of comparative advantage or comparative cost, developed as far back as the eighteenth century by English classical economists like Richard and Mill. They argued that international trade brought about the most efficient employment of the world's productive resources by enabling specialisation, or division of labour, between nations, just as between people. As a result of countries concentrating on what they were most favourably placed to produce, the greater efficiency thereby achieved enabled the world's citizens to enjoy a much higher standard of living, consuming more wealth than they could produce solely by their own efforts. Not only were they able to consume a greater quantity, but also a greater variety of goods.

From earliest times, nations traded with one another on the basis of importing what they could not produce themselves and exporting those goods in whose production they had an absolute advantage over their neighbours. Temperate lands had of necessity to import tropical foods, but in turn exported to these areas final products of their own mineral wealth, coal and iron. The determining factors in this were the very obvious ones of climate and natural resources; and the basis of such specialisation was absolute advantage.

The theory of comparative advantage represents a further degree of sophistication: it states that it pays a country to concentrate its productive activity in those areas where it enjoys the greatest advantage over its neighbours; importing things where it may still have an absolute advantage, but not such a marked one. That such a basis maximises the wealth enjoyed in a country can be proved by a simplified example. The case taken will be that of two countries producing two major products. Their relative efficiencies in the production of these will be represented in terms of real labour cost: the time taken to produce the product. It will be assumed that other items of cost are insignificant.

Labour time (*in minutes*) required for production of:	Country A	Country B
Product X	10	30
Product Y	20	40

It will be seen that country A has an absolute advantage over country B in the production of both products; but its advantage is greater in the case of product X. The most efficient utilisation of economic resources in country A would therefore be to concentrate on product X and to satisfy all its requirements for Y by importation from country B. Conversely, country B should concentrate on the production of Y, satisfying its need for product X by importation from country A. This, it should be noted, is so despite the fact that B's absolute efficiency in X is greater than in Y.

The truth of all this becomes readily apparent when a comparison is made of the output of each product resulting from one hour's labour in each country: in country A it is 6 units of X, or 3 units of Y; whereas in country B it is 2 units of X or $1\frac{1}{2}$ units of Y. Taking labour cost as a basis for exchange value or price: in country A, 6 units of X will exchange for 3 units of Y; while in country B, 2 units of X will exchange for $1\frac{1}{2}$ units of Y. But, if country A were to sell 6 units of X in country B (where $2 X = 1\frac{1}{2}$ Y) it would receive $4\frac{1}{2}$ Y, instead of only 3 Y. Similarly, if country B sells $1\frac{1}{2}$ Y in country A (where $3 Y = 6 X$) it can obtain 3 X in exchange, instead of just 2 X.

MECHANISM OF INTERNATIONAL PAYMENTS

Settlement of foreign trade transactions may be achieved either by transferring bank accounts or by physically shifting gold and foreign currencies, although nowadays it is more by the former than by the latter method. Indeed, much of the world's trade is still settled through sterling accounts kept by non-residents with banks in London, through which payments can be made and received, even for trade that does not touch Britain's shores at all.

We now look in more detail at how payment is made in respect of trade between this country and abroad. A British exporter of goods, say to America, will receive dollars for them. What he really wants of course is sterling, so through the foreign exchange market his bank may sell dollars for him, crediting him with an addition to his sterling account. But a British importer of goods from America, may very well want U.S. dollars at this time, so the bank will in practice be able to match the two foreign exchange deals, debiting the British importer's balance. Of course, the British importer has to make payment in the United States, so that his bank will have the dollar funds, originally earned by the British exporter, transferred to its correspondent bank in America and then instruct it to transfer the funds to the credit of the American exporter. This may be done within the same bank or may involve transfer of deposits to another U.S. bank. Furthermore, the dollars earned by the British exporter and owed by the British importer may indeed have simply involved transfer of a balance from the U.S. importer's account to that of the U.S. exporter. Thus it will be seen that foreign trade settlement between countries involves mainly net movements of bank balances, rather than a multiplicity of individual movements (as in the case of domestic cheque clearing, described earlier).

The hazards in international trade are inevitably greater than in domestic. To cover these risks the Government Export Credits Guarantee Department insures exporters against bankruptcy or default on the part of foreign buyers, sudden imposition of import and exchange control restrictions in the importing country and war risks. Having obtained this insurance cover, the exporter is then eligible for medium to long term credit from his bank in cases where the foreign buyer is only prepared to buy if given favourable credit terms.

INTERNATIONAL CO-OPERATION TOWARDS FREER TRADE

Throughout the post-war period there has been a gradual dismantling of the wartime exchange controls and quota restrictions hindering the free movement of goods. But, in addition, there has also been a concerted international movement to bring about a reduction in tariff barriers. Among the stated purposes of the International Monetary Fund can be found such phrases as '... To facilitate the expansion and balanced growth of international trade ... To assist ... in the elimination of foreign exchange restrictions which hamper the growth of world trade ...'.

G.A.T.T.

More specifically dedicated to the task of removing the obstacles to trade was the General Agreement on Tariffs and Trade, signed at Geneva in 1947 by about twenty nations throughout the world.

There are today in the region of eighty member countries of G.A.T.T. The G.A.T.T. agreement sought to bring to an end discrimination in trade and negotiate reductions in tariffs together with the elimination of other barriers to trade. Since 1947 there have been six series of G.A.T.T. tariff negotiations. Most of these were conducted on a product by product bilateral basis between major nations trading in the product concerned; agreed reductions being extended on a Most Favoured Nation Clause basis to the other signatories of G.A.T.T.

The most recent of these tariff reduction agreements was the Kennedy Round, conducted this time on a multilateral basis, and concluded in 1967. Of all the G.A.T.T. series of negotiations, this has achieved the greatest reduction in tariffs, to the extent of just over a third, as against only 7 per cent in the previous Dillon Round. The process of reduction under the Kennedy Round was spread over four years. In July 1968, 40 per cent of the agreed cut in tariffs was implemented, with three 20 per cent instalments at the beginning of each of the three years 1970–72. As a result, in the case of Britain, by 1972 the average level of her custom duties on industrial products came down to 11 per cent.

E.F.T.A.

In addition to the world-wide concerted effort at tariff reduction under G.A.T.T., there have been certain regional free trade areas created. Notable among these have been the European Economic Community and the European Free Trade Association. Unlike the E.E.C., E.F.T.A. has been solely concerned with the reduction of tariff barriers between its members. Talks leading to the setting up of E.F.T.A. began in 1958, after the failure to establish a wider free trade area covering the whole of western Europe. E.F.T.A. was finally set up in 1960 under the Stockholm Convention, the seven member countries being: Austria, Denmark, Norway, Portugal, Sweden, Switzerland and the U.K. Since the end of 1966, tariffs on trade in industrial goods between these countries have been completely eliminated. Never regarded as being entirely satisfying in itself, E.F.T.A. has rather been seen as a bridge towards the eventual unification of the 'Six' and 'Seven'; in the meantime providing a means of keeping pace with the freeing of trade within the European Economic Community.

THE COMMON MARKET

The European Economic Community ('Common Market' or 'Six') was set up under the Treaty of Rome, signed in 1957. The member nations are France, Western Germany, Italy and the Benelux countries (Belgium, Netherlands and Luxemburg). The Community has a total population of 187 million and a combined GNP of £125,000 million. Supra-national authorities associated with the E.E.C. are the European Coal and Steel Community and the European Atomic Energy Community.

The broad aim of the E.E.C., as set up by the Treaty of Rome, has been economic union, perhaps leading eventually to political union. The economic goal was the merging of the six nations into a 'common market', within which goods and services and the factors of production flow freely from one country to another. A prominent feature of this was the eventual elimination of tariff barriers between the member countries and adherence by them to a Common External Tariff on their imports from the outside world. Originally, this state of affairs was to have been reached by 1970, allowing a twelve-year transition period: but in fact it was attained eighteen months ahead of schedule in July 1968.

In the sphere of agriculture there is also a common E.E.C. policy. Prices of agricultural produce are fixed to ensure an adequate income for the farming population. This level is maintained in the face of cheaper imports by placing a levy on the latter, to bring their prices up to the 'managed' level. Practice in the U.K. has been to allow the market price of agricultural produce to be determined freely, with a little or no restriction on imports, but to give British farmers a subsidy making up the difference between the actual market price and that guaranteed by the Government. Under the E.E.C. system the money raised by levies on imports goes into a central fund. This fund is used for market intervention to keep up prices: either through official purchase of surpluses or by subsidising exports. The fund is also employed in providing financial assistance to smooth the way for structural changes in the agricultural sector: by helping to mechanise farming or moving excessive agrarian populations to other centres and activities.

The Common Market has many other aspects apart from tariffs on industrial goods and agricultural policies. Among its major objectives are: the free movement of labour and capital within the community; the harmonisation of taxation and company law; and common legislation with regard to monopolies and restrictive practices. The member nations also consult with one another on economic policy and planning and, as part of this, intend to move towards monetary union. All these aspects are in fact inevitably intertwined and obviously action limited to any one of these spheres would frequently by itself not be completely effective.

EFFECT ON INDUSTRY OF BRITAIN'S ENTRY INTO THE COMMON MARKET

Even after the Kennedy Round tariff reductions, British manufacturers are still at a 10 per cent disadvantage in relation to their competitors producing and selling within the Community. It is this which makes it desirable that Britain and some of her E.F.T.A. partners should become full members of the Common Market. But expectations of what it will be like, once we are in, tend to be heavily tinged with optimism. It seems to be a general assumption that entry into the Common Market must necessarily be beneficial to British industry. While this could be a correct long-term assessment, once the weak have gone to the wall, in the short to medium term the adverse effects on British industry could be as great as, if not greater than, the hoped-for benefits.

Membership of the European Economic Community has for British industry two major aspects: the opportunity of a larger market and the intensification of competition. On the first of these it would seem that in broad terms British industry must necessarily benefit from our entry into the Common Market, since we gain access into a market of 187 million people; whereas for the Community the addition of Britain would add only fifty-six million, admittedly with an above-average level of GNP per capita. But, allied to this overall advantage, would be a further intensification of competitive pressures on British manufacturers; for within the Common Market the degree of competition is greater. British producers will face competition from continental counterparts who have had many years' experience of operating in more competitive conditions and who are already set up on the large-scale production basis made possible by the market. While beneficial to consumers, this intensification of competition has not been particularly good for profitability. For many years continental firms were subject to squeeze on their profit margins and this found reflection in a declining trend from 1961 of share prices in the majority of Common Market countries. In certain areas the pressure of competition may be eased for British producers by our membership of the E.E.C. In cotton textiles our manufacturers have hitherto had to bear the whole weight of Asiatic competition. Similarly, British paper manufacturers have suffered from the duty-free entry within E.F.T.A. of the products of Scandinavian mills. As a member of the Common Market Britain would share out these competitive burdens. Finally, on this aspect of competition, it should be noted that the provisions of the Treaty of Rome are stricter than existing British legislation on monopolies and restrictive practices.

As we have already noted, two major features of the Common Market are the abolition of tariffs between member nations and the adherence to the Common External Tariff as regards trade with the outside world. The first of these means that there would be a withdrawal of protection for British industry against the products of Common Market producers; but at the same time, an opportunity for our exporters in product categories where continental duties have been high. The opening up of the continental market may be most readily exploited by those British industry sectors which already export a high percentage of their total output: prospects are even better for manufacturers who are at the moment successful exporters to Europe. It may be said in general that our entry into the Common Market will provide a great opportunity for British products which are either recognised as being the best in the world or which have a (snob) appeal because they are traditionally associated with this country.

Regarding the adoption of the C.E.T., where this differs from the existing level of British import duties, certain industry sectors will experience an increased or reduced degree of protection against products from outside the Common Market. In addition, although the C.E.T. is fairly low on raw materials, many of those imported into this country come from Commonwealth sources and have hitherto enjoyed preferential entry. Certain British manufacturers may therefore find that, with the adoption of the C.E.T., duty on their imported materials is slightly increased. With regard to manufactured products, the present British tariff is in general higher than the C.E.T. and thus overall there would be a reduction in the degree of protection enjoyed by U.K. manufacturers against the rest of the world.

Apart from these tariff and trade aspects the possible effects of entry into the Common Market on British industry may also be analysed in terms of certain broad economic principles. Among the industry sectors likely to benefit would be those whose products readily enter into world trade because, with a high value to weight ratio, transport costs are proportionately very small—examples in this category are jewellery and scientific instruments. Another aspect of the transportation factor is the advantage which will obviously be enjoyed by those companies whose manufacturing facilities have a geographical location advantage in relation to the Continent, for example, in the south near a channel port, or near the proposed 'chunnel'.

The industries which will be most anxious to seize the opportunities presented by the larger market will be those where average unit cost falls markedly with extension of output, because of heavy fixed overheads due to capital intensiveness or large research and development expenditures. Industries where research and development expenditure is very large are electronics and aircraft. Also acutely alive to the opportunities arising from our membership will be those industries where production can nowadays only be economically undertaken on a mass-production basis, where there are economies of large-scale production to be reaped: the best examples of these being the motor and chemical industries.

There will, of course, be many industry sectors that will remain relatively unaffected by Britain's entry into the Common Market. Such cases will be where labour and raw materials represent a high percentage of cost, with manufacture not being carried out on a mass-production basis; or where the economies of scale can in any case be reaped at a relatively low level of output; or where production tends unavoidably to be on a one-off basis, because of a rapid pace of technical obsolescence, as with atomic power stations. Products with comparatively heavy transport costs (because of low value to weight ratio) do not in any case enter much into international trade, examples being building materials like cement and bricks. Producers whose products primarily serve the local British market, either because of the character of the product (perishability) or because of fashion and taste, will also be relatively unaffected. There are also some products subject to barriers other than tariff, such as national regulations and specifications, language, etc.

15

International Finance

Unless it is to be conducted on a barter basis, foreign trade inevitably raises the problem of how international payments are to be made. If there were a universally acceptable world currency used within and between nations, then, of course, there would be no problem. But in reality countries have different currencies and therefore there arises questions of acceptability and equivalence when it comes to making payments for goods traded.

FOREIGN EXCHANGE RATES

The price of goods to be exported will initially be expressed in terms of the manufacturing country's currency. A foreign importer may be prepared to pay in that currency or he may wish to pay in his own currency. In the second case there arises the problem of expressing the price of the article in the importer's currency, which can only be done on the basis of how many units of each currency is regarded as being equivalent to the other. This is what is known as the external value of a currency, as distinct from its internal value, although as we have seen these two aspects are related. We are talking, in fact, about the rate of exchange. If the price of a British article is £100, then a buyer in America must pay $240, on the basis of the current rate of exchange of £1 = $2·40. With a known rate of exchange we can therefore express the price of our goods in foreign currencies and trade can take place. We are, of course, still left with the problem of how a rate of exchange gets established in the first place.

In describing earlier the evolution of money, we saw how the precious metals like gold and silver were coined and used as money. These metals in fact provided a world currency, since they were universally acceptable. The rate of exchange between the coins of foreign countries could be determined by their gold or silver content, allowing for differences in fineness as well as in weight, this being known as the mint par value of exchange. Even when paper money was used, provided it was backed by gold or silver, the rate of exchange between bank notes of different currencies could easily be worked out on the basis of the gold or silver they represented.

PURCHASING POWER PARITY

This, of course, does not solve the problem of fixing the rate of exchange where currencies are not based on gold and where their internal values can change at different rates, thereby obviously necessarily affecting their external value. What is known as the 'purchasing power parity' theory provides in such cases a basis for determining exchange rates. What the same basket of groceries would cost in each country's currency provides a rate of exchange between these currencies: if the basket of goods costs £2 in this country and $4·80 in America, then the rate of exchange would be £1 = $2·40. If subsequently prices rise in Britain, while remaining stable in America, then the same contents of the basket in Britain might cost £3, but still $4·80 in America: in such circumstances the correct rate of exchange would become £1 = $1·60, that is the external value of the pound would have fallen, its exchange rate would have depreciated.

In practice, exchange rates are generally legacies of the past, rather than the result of any formal exercise in purchasing power parity. Nevertheless, differences in countries' inflation experience do tend to get reflected in the external values of their currencies through the resultant shifts in supply and demand in the foreign exchange markets. If the general level of prices is rising faster in one country, then its exports will become less competitive in world markets. On the other hand, with their prices remaining the same, imported goods will capture a larger share of the country's domestic market and therefore their volume will swell. Thus the country will experience an increasingly adverse balance of trade: exports falling off, imports rising. This will mean that the foreigner will be earning more of the country's currency, while requiring less of it; its supply in the foreign exchange markets will thus exceed demand. In such circumstances, the external value of that currency will tend to fall: the exchange rate will depreciate. This depreciation would itself ultimately restore equilibrium:

acting as an encouragement to exports, since they become progressively cheaper in foreign currency terms; while imports become dearer in the domestic currency and thus tend to fall off. With trade coming into better balance, depreciation in the exchange rate would be arrested.

It will be obvious that constantly fluctuating exchange rates would create a good deal of uncertainty and risk of loss, and might therefore cause a breakdown of trade. For example, an exporter in a country whose exchange rate was appreciating would get less in domestic currency terms when he exchanged his foreign currency receipts and this might wipe out his profit if he was tied by previous agreement to a fixed foreign currency price. An importer in a country whose exchange rate rapidly fell would be in a similar predicament: it would cost him more than he originally allowed for to purchase foreign currency to pay for the goods. In such a climate there is also the danger of trade wars being triggered off by competitive exchange rate depreciation in order to gain a stimulus to exporting. All this was very much the experience of the inter-war years, when nations were off the Gold Standard.

GOLD STANDARD

The Gold Standard itself ensured exchange rate stability by providing an automatic corrective to trade imbalance and through gold flows that kept within limits short-term exchange rate fluctuations. With internal money supply being gold-backed, any loss of gold through excess of import payments over export receipts meant that internal money supply contracted. This had a deflationary effect that not only reduced imports but also encouraged manufacturers to seek outlets for their goods abroad.

Since, under the Gold Standard, gold could be freely bought and sold, and also imported and exported, this also limited the extent of any exchange fluctuations around the rate determined by the gold content of national currencies. The extent of fluctuation was set by the cost of shipping gold. If a country's exchange rate appreciated above the mint parity by more than this cost, then foreigners would prefer to buy and ship gold to that country rather than settle payments by buying the currency at the higher exchange rate. Thus demand for its currency in the foreign exchange market would be reduced and its exchange rate would fall back again. The end of the range at which this took place was known as the 'upper-gold point' or 'gold-import point'. Ultimately, the effect of this inflow of gold would be to expand internal money supply and reduce the favourable balance of trade and hence put downward pressure on the exchange rate. Conversely, if the currency's external value fell below the mint par of exchange by more than the cost of shipping gold, then gold would flow out, for it would be cheaper for its importers to pay in gold, or buy foreign currencies with gold, rather than buy foreign currencies with their own currency at the poorer exchange rate. In thus reducing their purchases of foreign currencies, that is also reducing sales of their own, this strengthened the latter's exchange rate. The point at which this occurred was known as the 'lower-gold point' or 'gold-export point'. This loss of gold would contract the domestic money supply and ultimately correct trading imbalance and strengthen the exchange rate.

This operation of the Gold Standard is now, of course, largely of historical interest. The full Gold Standard has not operated in Britain (and many other countries) since before the First World War. From 1914 to 1925 the Gold Standard was suspended and when we returned in 1925 it was to a Gold Bullion Standard, with no internal circulation of gold coins and the Bank of England only prepared to buy and sell gold in large quantities. In 1931 Britain left the Gold Standard and exchange rates were left fairly free to fluctuate, although at times there was official intervention, using reserves, to prevent the fluctuations from being too violent.

STERLING AREA

It was at this time that the Sterling Area came into being, when certain countries that had close trading links with Britain decided that it was obviously more important to preserve exchange rate stability in relation to sterling, rather than to remain linked to gold. The Sterling Area is still in existence, consisting mainly of all independent Commonwealth countries (except Canada), South Africa, Britain's remaining colonial territories, the protected states in the Persian Gulf, Kuwait, Southern Yemen, Jordan, Libya, Iceland and Eire. Britain herself is, of course, a member of the Sterling Area; the other member countries combined make up the Overseas Sterling Area. Members of the Sterling Area hold their reserves as sterling balances in London, agreeing to settle their inter-area indebtedness through them and passing on to the Exchange Equalisation Account in London any gold and convertible currencies earned through surplus with the non-sterling world, receiving in return a credited sterling balance. This is what is meant by sterling's reserve currency role, which as a member of the E.E.C. Britain will try to phase out. Non-Sterling Area countries also hold a certain amount of sterling balances in London, so that frequently indebtedness between the Sterling and Non-Sterling Areas is settled through them, rather than in gold and convertible currencies.

The existence of the Sterling Area secures the continued widespread acceptance of sterling, thereby helping to strengthen it in foreign exchange markets, this also at times deriving support from the Overseas Sterling Area's external payments surpluses with the rest of the world. For the Area as a whole there is an economy in the use of gold and convertible currencies, since these are required only for external payments settlement with the non-sterling world. With the greater part of the Sterling Area's foreign trade payments being settled through London, this has helped to preserve the City's position as an international financial centre. During the Second World War, sterling balances were greatly increased as a means of payment of debts incurred by Britain in waging the war. In the immediate post-war years some of these were paid off in the form of unrequited exports from Britain; but their total rose again as a result of Britain's external payment deficits of the post-war period.

Sterling balances in London are interest-earning; when not held on deposit with a bank they are generally invested in U.K. Treasury bills and short-dated government stocks. These balances represent, of course, part of Britain's external liabilities and since during the post-war years their average relationship to our reserves has been of the order of 4 to 1, the possibility of their withdrawal has always given the U.K. monetary authorities very real grounds for concern. To discourage run-down of balances, U.K. interest rates have been kept relatively high throughout the post-war period. In the middle of the sixties, the authorities sought to supplement this by keeping down to reasonable proportions the cost of covering these balances in the forward exchange market against depreciation of the £'s exchange rate.

In recent times, particularly during sterling's difficulties in the sixties, there has been some loosening of Sterling Area ties. Some of the Overseas Sterling Area countries increasingly retained their gold and convertible currency earnings from trade with the non-sterling world, thereby building up local reserves, rather than passing them on to London. Long term investment capital from Britain was traditionally one of the benefits O.S.A. countries derived from membership, but in the mid-sixties, Britain put voluntary restraints on this flow, as part of a general tightening of exchange control regulations to try and strengthen sterling. Devaluation of the pound in November 1967 inevitably involved some non-resident holders of sterling in exchange value loss. To safeguard them in future, as well as discourage the trend towards local reserve holding, Britain, with the help of the Basle countries, was able to offer in July 1968 to O.S.A. countries a U.S. dollar value guarantee on the bulk of their minimum reserves that they undertook to keep in sterling.

POST-WAR MONETARY SYSTEM

In the years since the Second World War, we have been on a Gold Exchange Standard, the pound being pegged not to gold but to the U.S. dollar, with the latter being linked to gold at a price of £35 to the fine ounce. In recent years America has considerably limited its preparedness to buy and sell gold at this price, so that we now seem to have moved on to a Dollar Standard. For the greater part of the sixties the central banks of the West operated a 'Gold Pool', through which syndicated buying and selling operations sought to keep the free market price of gold near to the official American price of $35 to the fine ounce. In the latter part of the sixties a reduced supply of gold, coupled with an increased speculative demand for it, meant that the Gold Pool countries, and notably America, were forced to make substantial releases from their gold stocks in an attempt to hold down the free market price. The magnitude of this drain eventually caused the Gold Pool to be disbanded and the parties to it henceforth agreed to preserve a rigid separation between 'official' and 'free' gold markets. The central monetary authorities concerned were to continue to trade gold between themselves at $35 to the ounce, but neither to supply gold to the private market nor even perhaps to buy gold from it. Thus a two-tiered gold system was brought into being.

In many countries there is still a certain amount of reverence for gold, it being used as a store of value. It has frequently been suggested that the official price of gold should be increased, this being put forward not only by those advocating a return to the Gold Standard but also by those wishing to see an increase in the supply of international liquidity. Since a rise in the price of gold would be tantamount to a devaluation of the U.S. dollar in relation to gold, America has not been in sympathy with such suggestions. A general objection to any return to the Gold Standard itself is the absence of any logical relationship between the rate at which new gold is mined, and finds its way to official reserves, and the rate at which international trade grows, and hence the need for international liquidity. The problem of maintaining an adequate supply of international liquidity to match growth in world trade has instead, as we shall see, been tackled by the conscious creation of international credit. For much of the sixties, however, the addition to international liquidity came largely from the growth in non-resident holdings of reserve currencies like sterling and in particular the U.S. dollar, such growth being dependent upon Britain and America remaining in balance of payments deficit.

Although no longer on the Gold Standard, we returned after the Second World War to exchange rate stability, in the form of an administered fixed rate system. There has, however, been no return to any automatic corrective to trading imbalance which the Gold Standard offered. The link between the external position and internal money and credit supply remained severed; active government economic management instead being required. The impact of trade imbalance was taken on the reserves rather than on the exchange rate, so that correction of this imbalance depended largely upon domestic deflationary policies.

INTERNATIONAL MONETARY FUND

Exchange rate stability in the post-war years has been achieved through the creation in 1947 of the International Monetary Fund, which along with the World Bank resulted from the Bretton

Woods Agreement of 1944. Exchange rate stability was a prime objective in setting up the Fund, in a desire to avoid the international trade and payments disorderliness of the pre-war years. Each member country of the I.M.F. had to adopt a par value of exchange for its currency, expressed either in terms of gold or the U.S. dollar, and obliged to intervene in the foreign exchange market to keep its exchange rate within 1 per cent on either side of this adopted par value. As explained in our section on the Bank of England, a central bank does this by using its reserves to buy up its currency when it is weak in the foreign exchange market, but when it is strong supplying it freely in exchange for gold and convertible currencies. For those countries pegging their exchange rate to the U.S. dollar (that is the majority) this means buying and selling their currencies in the foreign exchange market against the U.S. dollar.

It will be realised that the ability of a country with a weak currency to keep its exchange rate from going below the lower support point depends upon the state of its reserves. For this reason a second major function of the I.M.F. is to provide medium term loans (3–5 years) to member countries whose currencies have been made weak by temporary international payments imbalance. Such loans give the country concerned time to take remedial action, without having to resort to savage deflationary policies that would not only be politically unpopular at home but would also have repercussions on other nations' balance of trade.

The amount a member can borrow from the I.M.F. is related to its quota, this being the same as its subscription to the Fund. The size of a country's quota or subscription was originally worked out on the basis of its pre-war share of international trade, but there have been periodic revisions to individual members' quotas, as well as to the overall total. Subscriptions are made 25 per cent in gold and the rest in the member's own currency. This gives the I.M.F. a pool out of which loans can be made. Borrowing is made in gold or convertible foreign currencies in return for an equivalent amount of the member's own currency. The maximum that can be borrowed is twice the quota, less any amount of the borrowing country's currency already held by the Fund. A member can draw from the I.M.F. as of right the equivalent of its gold tranche position. In addition, members may also negotiate stand-by credits beyond this amount, that once agreed may be drawn upon as soon as required. Anything beyond this has to be with the agreement of the Fund. Loans must be repaid within 3–5 years and there are small interest and service charges. Repayment is made by the member buying back his own currency with gold and convertible currencies earned through external surplus.

Although members must adhere to exchange rate stability around an adopted par value, they can in certain circumstances adopt a new par value, the degree of prior consultation with the I.M.F. depending on the extent of the change. If the country's payments imbalance, whether continuing excessive surplus or deficit, does not respond to corrective policies within a reasonable time, then it may be held to be in 'fundamental disequilibrium', due usually to its rate of inflation being out of line with other countries. In these circumstances of fundamental disequilibrium the approved remedy is to adopt a new par value of exchange. The adoption of a lower par value, that is fewer U.S. dollars for each unit of its currency, is called devaluation; the adoption of a higher rate is revaluation. Changes in par value not exceeding 10 per cent may be carried out by the member without consultation with the I.M.F.; between 10 and 20 per cent the I.M.F. must be consulted but has to give a quick answer. Changes of over 20 per cent obviously require more detailed consideration.

OTHER BORROWING ARRANGEMENTS

An ancillary I.M.F. borrowing facility is the General Arrangements to Borrow which was negotiated in 1962. This is also known as the Paris Club or Group-of-Ten, consisting of ten leading industrial nations: Britain, North America, Common Market, Sweden and Japan, with Switzerland as an associate member. When an I.M.F. member requires certain currencies of which the Fund has an insufficient supply, it can call upon the Paris Club countries to provide additional quantities of their currencies, provided it is in respect of a loan to a member of their Group. The maximum amount that the Group-of-Ten will lend to the Fund in this way is $6,000 million. The Paris Club countries need only respond if they feel that the loan is justified and those who are themselves in balance of payments difficulties can opt out.

When Britain was in balance of payments deficit from 1964 onwards, the Paris Club countries also extended directly massive short-term loans to stave off speculative attacks on sterling.

Many short-term (three to six months) borrowing facilities were evolved during the sixties, mainly to help Britain out. When sterling came under pressure in the Spring of 1961, following revaluation of the deutschemark and the guilder, the Basle arrangements were brought into existence, being so named after the location of the Bank of International Settlements in Switzerland, at which the governors of central banks of eight European countries meet each month. When a member country's currency is under pressure the other seven agree to hold it and to extend loans of foreign currencies for periods of three months at a time. The Bank for International Settlements was founded in 1929, primarily for the purpose of supervising the Young Plan that was concerned with Germany's reparation payments after the First World War; but it was also intended that the B.I.S. would serve to promote closer collaboration between central banks. The Bretton Woods Agreement called for the winding up of the B.I.S., but it has continued in existence to play a useful role in international monetary co-operation, serving as an informal meeting place for central bankers. As well as being associated with international borrowing exercises, the B.I.S. has also at times co-ordinated official intervention in the euro-dollar market to prevent international interest rate levels fluctuating too sharply.

Another form of short-term international lending that developed during the early sixties was a system of swap credits arranged by America's central bank (the Federal Reserve) with the central banks of other countries. This system involved mutual exchange of currencies between two countries to increase their international reserves and thus their ability to defend existing exchange rates against balance of payments and speculative pressures.

It will be recognised that the I.M.F. system is still gold-based, since borrowing rights are related to quota, a quarter of which has to be subscribed in gold. From time to time quotas have been increased, but this has also involved additional gold subscription. In that they are repayable, loans from the I.M.F. have not represented permanent additions to international reserves.

Furthermore, the Fund's loanable resources have until only quite recently consisted entirely of its member nations' currencies and official holdings of gold; the I.M.F. itself not creating any international liquidity or money supply.

SPECIAL DRAWING RIGHTS

All this changed at the beginning of 1970 when Special Drawing Rights were brought into being. These are a permanent addition to international reserves, in the same way as newly-mined gold (and also, but more questionably perhaps, U.S. dollars accruing to other central banks as a result of America's external payments deficit). In this sense these Drawing Rights have been referred to as 'paper gold', also justifying this description in being gold-backed, although not gold-based. Their exchange value is guaranteed in terms of the present gold value of the U.S. dollar, so that any future change in the dollar price of gold would increase by the same proportion the value of S.D.R.'s in terms of foreign currencies. S.D.R.'s cannot however be converted into gold. Unlike I.M.F. borrowing rights, S.D.R.'s are not gold-based, since they are simply brought into being by a decision of the Fund members, with no gold subscription requirement, although the share-out of the quantity created is based on I.M.F. quotas. In 1969 the Fund agreed to create $9,500 million of S.D.R.'s, $3,500 million being distributed at the beginning of 1970 and $3,000 million at the beginning of each of the two following years. The distribution to member countries takes the form of a credit entry in a special account kept by the Fund. When a country uses its S.D.R.'s its account is debited, with that of the country receiving them being credited. Average net use of Drawing Rights over a three to five year period cannot exceed 70 per cent of the allocation; while the receiving country must accept S.D.R.'s up to three times its own allocation. The user country pays interest to the Fund, a receiving country earns it. Upon receiving S.D.R.'s most countries treat them as additions to their reserves.

FLEXIBLE EXCHANGE RATES

The post-war system of adopted par values has meant that for much of the time the strain of international payments imbalance has had to be taken on the reserves, rather than on exchange rates. This also meant that domestic economic policies have of necessity been geared to the external position. For a deficit country deflationary measures have been required in order to discourage imports and encourage exports; for a surplus country the acceptance of a higher rate of inflation has been necessary. Such policies have been politically unpopular, particularly those of a deflationary nature. To delay taking them for as long as possible, deficit countries attempted to finance their trading deficit by attracting short- and long-term capital inflows and in addition drew fully upon a wide variety of specially evolved international borrowing arrangements.

In more recent years, the view has been pressed strongly that all this could be avoided if the international monetary system returned to a regime of more flexible exchange rates. International payments imbalance would be automatically corrected by exchange rates depreciating in the case of deficit countries and appreciating in the case of surplus countries. A falling rate would make imports expensive and exports more competitive; an appreciating rate would have the reverse effect. Governments would therefore be free to pursue domestic objectives, like growth and full employment, without all the time having to look over their shoulder at the external payments position.

The most extreme of the flexible rate suggestions is that of a completely freely floating rate, determined solely by the forces of supply and demand in the foreign exchange markets, with no official intervention. Some advocates would, however, allow some degree of the latter in order to prevent too violent fluctuations, particularly when due to speculative factors. Those that probably stand a better chance of adoption are the more modest proposals for 'wider bands' of permissible fluctuation around the par value; or a 'crawling peg', a continuing gradual adjustment of the par value itself. The first of these envisages a change from the present 1 per cent on either side of par, to a somewhat larger percentage. But once the country's exchange rate reached the upper or lower limits of this widened band the adjustment process would cease. In this respect, more useful would be a par value or 'peg' that moved up or down by say a $\frac{1}{4}$ per cent per month.

The opponents of exchange rate flexibility fear that free market

o

movements in rates would set off speculative pressures that would carry these movements much further. This criticism is not quite so valid against the more modest proposals, but then these also might be criticised as not being sufficiently flexible to bring about a correction of imbalance in trade. A more sophisticated objection to rate flexibility queries whether in fact it would achieve external payments equilibrium. In the case of a depreciating rate, due to a higher degree of inflation than in other countries, the discouragement of imports and encouragement of exports might, in the absence of sufficient surplus productive capacity, reduce the supply of goods available in the home market, thus making for a greater rise in their price. In the case of essential imports, like foodstuffs and raw materials, these would probably continue to come in, but at a higher price, thus having a cost-push inflation effect. These inflationary forces could eventually put the country once again into adverse balance of trade, setting off further exchange rate depreciation. Devaluation can have the same effect.

Despite the I.M.F. requirement that member countries adhere to a pegged rate, there have been occasions when countries have allowed their exchange rate to float, but generally when their currencies have been strong enough to float upwards. Canada did so throughout the fifties, right up to 1962, and more recently again from the middle of 1970. The deutschemark was allowed to float for a month, just before it was officially revalued towards the end of October 1969; another period of upward float began in the spring of 1971.

INTERNATIONAL CAPITAL MARKETS

Over the last dozen years two private (non-official) international capital markets have grown up: the euro-dollar and the euro-bond. The volume of international short-term lending and borrowing increased greatly with the development from 1958 onwards of euro-currency markets, notably that of the euro-dollar, but, to a lesser extent, also euro-sterling. The continuing U.S. balance of payments deficit gave ownership to those outside America of a growing volume of dollar balances with U.S. banks, private non-residents however usually passing these on to their own banks in return for local currency. Non-resident banks could either transfer their balances with U.S. banks to time deposit

(deposit account) or they could keep them as demand deposits (current account) but lend the use of these to other non-resident banks, by placing them in the euro-dollar market. The borrowing bank would therefore have a liability to repay denominated in U.S. dollars; thus a euro-dollar would be created, being defined as a deposit liability on the books of a bank outside America, denominated not in its own currency but in U.S. dollars. In fact, there is a good deal of on-lending by one Euro-bank to another, before the ultimate end-use, so that there can be a multiple of euro-dollars created on the basis of a non-resident owned U.S. bank deposit.

The ultimate user may keep the euro-dollars and use them, for example, for trade financing (as an alternative to bills of exchange) or they may be swapped into another currency to add to the supply of domestic credit and capital. In Britain, euro-dollars have at times been switched into sterling by merchant banks for lending to local government authorities and hire purchase finance companies. Doing so, of course, is profitable only when rates paid for deposits in these areas are sufficiently above the euro-dollar rate to meet the cost of forward cover. (The poorer exchange rate on the basis of which the funds are to be switched into dollars again at the end of a lending period.) When banks in America were subject to restrictive official monetary policy, to evade the effects of this, they themselves, through their overseas subsidiaries, have at times been substantial borrowers of euro-dollars.

London is the main centre of the euro-dollar market (that of euro-sterling is in Paris). It is a highly sophisticated market, conducted between banks and for large amounts, so that euro-dollars are an extremely volatile form of short-term capital, highly responsive to changes in arbitrage and speculative factors. The magnitude and consequences of 'hot money' flows have therefore been greatly increased with the growth of the euro-dollar market, now estimated on a net basis (excluding mere on-lending) to be of the order of $40,000 million.

Following the same sort of terminology, the private international capital market for long-term funds has been designated the euro-bond market. As in the case of the euro-dollar, the prefix does not, of course, mean that the participants are restricted to Europe. A euro-bond is a fixed interest loan, denominated in a currency of recognised stability and widespread acceptability, like the U.S. dollar or the deutschemark, but sold to investors in countries other than that in whose currency the bond is denominated. These bonds are issued simultaneously in several countries by international syndicates composed of half a dozen leading banks and then spread over a larger number of financial institutions who act as underwriters. Thus, the euro-bond can tap several national capital markets, this facility being especially important for large companies whose issues would be beyond the absorptive capacity of any one capital market.

Euro-bond issues blossomed rapidly from 1963/64 onwards, for at that time foreign borrowing in the U.S. capital market was discouraged by the Interest Equalisation Tax, adding 10 per cent to borrowing costs. At that time also the U.K. balance of payments moved into deficit, making the British monetary authorities unwilling to see foreign borrowers shift from New York to London. In 1965, and to an even greater extent at the beginning of 1968, the American Government restricted capital investment abroad, U.S. corporations therefore having to finance their overseas operations locally and they thus became substantial issuers of euro-bonds.

WORLD BANK

The World Bank is not really a bank, it is an international loans fund for development projects. It exists to provide long term capital, particularly for those areas that would have difficulty in attracting private funds on bearable terms. Its alternative title better reveals this function, namely, International Bank for Reconstruction and Development (although the 'Reconstruction' part is now out-of-date, since it related to recovery from the devastation of the Second World War). Like the I.M.F., the I.B.R.D. was set up following the Bretton Woods Conference, and the Bank actually began operating in 1946. The World Bank is owned by just over a hundred member governments of the I.M.F., who subscribed its initial capital. The other sources for funds it lends are: bond sales on the capital markets of the Western World, sales to private investors of parts of loans it has guaranteed and from the reserves it builds up out of its received interest and other charges.

The World Bank grants loans at conventional rates of interest (about 1 per cent above the rate at which the Bank itself can borrow) for periods as long as 20–25 years, with repayment of principal usually beginning after 3–4 years. Repayment has to be guaranteed by the Government of the recipient country, and in many cases it is the Government itself that is the borrower for some large public sector construction project like an irrigation scheme, highway, etc.

The World Bank has two offshoots: International Finance Corporation (founded in 1956) and the International Development Association (in 1960). The first of these (I.F.C.) exists to provide loans for private projects in underdeveloped countries, these loans not being guaranteed by governments. The I.D.A. provides interest-free and very long-term (50 years) loans for low income countries, but these do have to be guaranteed by the Government of the country concerned. Like those of the World Bank itself loans given by the I.F.C. and I.D.A. can only be for well-prepared projects of high economic priority, each application being carefully vetted by a visiting World Bank team of experts.

PART FIVE

Strategy of the Firm

16

Economic Cycle and Business Planning

ALLOWING FOR STOP-GO IN BUSINESS PLANNING

What may be regarded as the 'anatomy of the economic cycle' was examined in some detail in Part Four. The cycle was first of all described in terms of the sequence of cause and effect that economic theory as well as common sense would lead us to expect. Then, to show that it usually worked out that way in practice, the economic happenings between 1961 and 1971 were narrated. We will now look more closely at the relationship between this economic background and business planning. There are in fact few management decision areas which are not in some way influenced by the economic background. Certainly, all the major operational activities of a firm—such as purchasing, production, selling and finance—are very much affected by economic events. We will also consider how the individual firm can attempt to gear itself to the ever-present likelihood of economic fluctuation. It is, of course, possible in this, as in many other spheres, to be sceptical. How does one know what is going to happen? Even if one does, what can be done about it? And anyway it may never happen!

To start with this last argument. Although politicians are always ready to promise that next time it is going to be different, the experience of the post-war years suggests that it is safer in business planning to assume that economic fluctuations are not abnormal, but are in fact the natural order of things. What we have, therefore, got to do in our day-to-day business activity is to learn to live with them; or, at least, learn to minimise losses and maximise gains. Having faced up to the fact that the economic cycle, in some form or other, is always going to be with us, we must then watch out for those indicators which signal the onset of a 'stop' or a 'go' phase. Knowing in advance which way the economic wind is likely to be blowing enables us to make anticipatory adjustments in our business planning, in order to get the most out of the 'go' periods and to reduce losses as much as possible during the 'stop' phases.

ADVANCE WARNING INDICATORS

As we have seen, governments generally embark upon restrictive measures when there is evidence of increasing inflation and a deterioration in the balance of payments. Usually these two features are present at the same time, the former giving rise to the latter. The period from 1969 onwards was unusual in this respect by having a massive balance of payments surplus despite a high and accelerating rate of inflation. The reasons for this paradoxical situation were dealt with earlier. But in any case even where the problem is inflation by itself, governments will feel impelled to take corrective action when this begins to assume sizeable proportions, of say between 5 to 10 per cent. A rate under this can probably be tolerated, providing it is not giving rise to deterioration in the trade balance. When, on the other hand, the problems facing a Government are rising unemployment and stagnation, then it will move to more expansive fiscal and monetary policies. Once more the period 1969/70 was unusual for reasons earlier described. Normally it can be expected that rising unemployment will reduce wage-push and inflationary pressures in general, leading as well to an improvement in the balance of payments, so that it will be possible for the Government to be more expansive in its policies.

The peculiarity of the 1969/70 situation did not, of course, alter the problems themselves. In any case, as already indicated, there are reasons for believing that there will be some return to customary relationships between these problems and therefore traditional official policy responses can once more be anticipated. The key advance warning indicators of the onset of restrictive or expansive phases in the business cycle remain therefore those concerned with inflation, balance of payments and unemployment.

With wage-push induced inflation, attention centres upon the percentages in which claims are being couched and settlements made. The bargaining force behind these will normally be lessened by a rising unemployment percentage and falling number of unfilled vacancies; increased by a declining unemployment percentage and a rising number of unfilled vacancies. The actual rate of wage-push engendered will be shown up by the indices of wage rates, average earnings and the degree of wage drift. Demand pull inflation will also reflect the employment situation and will be evidenced by lengthening order books and rising imports. The rate of inflation is revealed by indices for retail and wholesale prices.

In assessing the trend in the balance of payments, attention is focused upon the monthly figures for imports and exports of goods. It is the balance of merchandise trade that largely determines Britain's overall balance of payments position. Our invisible trade in services shows a surplus of the order of £40 to £50 million per month. The long-term capital account is invariably in deficit to the extent of some £100 to £200 million a year. Short-term capital movements are extremely volatile and can be of massive proportions. They are not readily forecastable, since they depend upon a multitude of factors: U.K./O.S.A./N.S.A. balance of payments relationships, exchange rate movements (either current or speculative) and interest rate differentials. Only the visible trade figures are published monthly; all the other items of the balance of payments are recorded on a quarterly basis, not becoming available until some months later. Imports and exports are shown separately and on a seasonally adjusted basis in order to better assess their trend, that of imports being generally the most crucial. The difference between the two is the visible trade balance: an excess of imports over exports representing a deficit; and on those rare occasions when exports are greater than imports there is a surplus on visible trade. With invisibles running at £40 to £50 million a month, the visible trade deficit can be of these proportions before the current account balance of payments is in deficit. But since some surplus is generally required to offset the net outflow of long-term capital, the visible trade deficit, to be satisfactory, ought to be no more than £20 to £30 million a month. All this of course leaves out of account any repayment that may be required of outstanding international indebtedness; and to this extent the current account surplus will need to be that much larger and therefore the tolerable visible trade deficit that much smaller. This may also mean that the government will have to pursue a restrictive policy for a longer period to ensure the continued earning of an external payments surplus out of which to make debt repayments.

As long as there are no inflation and balance of payments problems, governments will be eager to pursue expansionary policies. There is less need therefore to define limits of tolerance in respect of unemployment. In fact, views as to the unacceptability of unemployment levels have shifted somewhat in recent years; from 1966 onwards 2½ per cent came to be accepted as a normal level of unemployment, whereas in the early part of the sixties it would have indicated a recessionary situation. It can still be said that when national unemployment gets above 3 per cent this entails such high figures in certain regions that the position becomes politically unacceptable. The Government will then be subjected to considerable pressures to reflate. A declining unemployment percentage strengthens the forces of wage-push and when it goes below 2 per cent this itself provides an advance warning of the likely acceleration of inflation (but in most recent years of course this has happened even with unemployment rising above 3 per cent). The level of employment shows a regular seasonal pattern, being higher during the summer months (with the hotel and catering industry active) than in the winter months (when certain industries like construction may be adversely affected by weather conditions). A truer assessment of the trends of unemployment is derived from seasonally adjusted figures, although these still do not exclude irregular variations. Due to the existence within the unemployment statistics of 'unemployables' or 'voluntary unemployed' it is sometimes thought that the 'unfilled vacancies' figure gives a better indication of the true state of the labour market.

There are of course countless other statistics that could also be watched. What has been given here is, however, a sufficient guide to which way the economic wind is blowing. It is the trend in these indicators that is important: if this shows continued deterioration it will be wise to ignore all the attempted explaining away, not only by the government of the day but by the incorrigible 'growth' economists.

Economic Cycle and Business Planning

From what has been said so far, it will be obvious that the task of economic forecasting is neither impossible nor time-consuming; and certainly not beyond the capability of the average manager. Having said this, we now come to the much more important question: What do we do about it? Since we have already described the features of economic fluctuation, the strategy to be adopted by the firm should be fairly self-evident. Nevertheless, for the sake of completeness, it will now be gone into in some detail.

A STRATEGY FOR ECONOMIC CYCLES

In taking into account economic fluctuation the underlying basic precept is that individual business planning should aim to be counter-cyclical. It should be based on the belief that neither the expansion nor the restriction can last for more than two to three years. It follows from this principle that when everyone else is talking of expanding, the clairvoyant manager should be thinking of pulling in his horns. Conversely, when all his fellows are deep in gloom and despondency, our clever manager should be getting ready for the expansion which he knows is just around the corner. Of course when everybody gets enlightened, a new strategy may be required; but until then that which will now be outlined holds good.

PURCHASING

Raw material price movements, as well as the general availability of such materials, depend upon the state of industrial demand, which in turn springs from the general level of economic activity. If the materials used are world commodities, the demand for them will reflect the tempo of industrial production in the major manufacturing nations of the world (U.S.A., Germany, Japan and Britain), as well as strategic factors and events like the wars in Korea and Vietnam. While the latter events cannot always be foreseen, managers can at least be on the alert for their economic consequences—in the shape, for example, of rising world commodity prices. Sooner or later suppliers will pass on these higher costs; although when the special factors disappear, the onus may be on the purchasing officer to suggest some return of prices to their previous level.

Upturns in the general level of world industrial production can be more readily anticipated. It requires an economic awareness of which of the major industrial nations of the world are about to enter expansionist or restrictionist phases. There is of course no natural law which ensures that they all expand and contract together. It is true that an expansionist climate in one country may provide a buoyant export market for its neighbours, but rising exports do not necessarily indicate that a country is in an expansionist phase; Britain's best export performance has often been in deflationary years. Sometimes the course of events may, however, get retarded in one country and accelerated in another, with the result that there will be times when the economic expansions of major industrial countries take place at the same time, causing a concentration of demand for raw materials and later for capital goods, as well as for capital itself.

RESEARCH AND DEVELOPMENT

While a company's research and development activity is undeniably more a matter of science and technology than economics; nevertheless, the latter is a factor not to be neglected when considering new product development. Indeed, in the initial selection of areas of scientific search or the type of new product to be developed, long-term economic and social trends ought to be a starting point. Furthermore, a broad appreciation of the general structure of the economy will indicate likely markets: their size and characteristics, as well as the outside factors having a major influence upon them. The timing of new product launching should as far as possible be set to coincide with a period of expansion, either in the economy generally or in the industry sectors likely to provide a market for the product. Industrial customers will be less interested in new products during deflationary periods, unless these offer significant cost savings—and how many new products initially do this?

SALES PROMOTION

Major promotional expenditures to aid sales expansion on existing products will similarly stand a better chance of success (and give a better return per £ of marketing expenditure) if these are also timed to coincide with an expansion phase, rather than a period of downturn. While such convenient timing may not always be achievable in the case of new product development, there is no excuse for sales expansion programmes not coming at the right moment. And yet how many of the major promotional pushes begin to get dreamed up in the second year of a consumer goods expansion that everyone assumes is going to continue indefinitely? When the fanfare of trumpets is sounded, it is generally completely drowned by the crash of the severe 'stop' measures.

The depths of the deflation is the time for planning, so that the great leap forward can be made as soon as the lights are 'green' again. Although promotional expenditures tend to be cut-back during the deflation (and this may be right and proper) planning at such times costs little. It is only when the plans are put into operation that the major expenditures have to be made; and that will be when expansion comes along and when people do not in any case mind spending money. Market share enlargement is also easier when the market as a whole is expanding, for when it is contracting existing suppliers are grimly determined to keep what share of the market they already have. Under such conditions, unless things get so bad that some firms go bust, market share capture is not easy.

INVESTMENT

Launching new products, or attempting major sales increases with existing products, often involves the creation of enlarged plant capacity. The speed and cost with which this can be carried out will again be determined by the economic conditions of the time; by the demand on the engineering and construction industries, as well as by the availability and cost of credit. In deflationary periods, prompt delivery and keen prices will be offered by plant manufacturers. It may also be possible, during such times of deep business pessimism, to buy factory space and machinery from manufacturers who suddenly discover that they have over-expanded. Expansion by the takeover of other companies and their facilities may be achieved more cheaply during such a period, in which share prices are usually at a low level, perhaps even below the net asset value of the company expressed on a per share basis.

FINANCE

Certain developments in the economic cycle put a squeeze on company profitability. But if these can be anticipated, action may then be taken in good time to safeguard profit margins. We saw in Part Four how strong cost inflationary pressures arise in the second year of the expansion phase, being reflected in an upward pressure of wage demands. To compensate for this rise in costs prompt pricing action should be taken while demand is still buoyant and before the Government attempts to enforce price stabilisation.

A traditional weapon of government restrictive policies is high interest rates and reduced availability of credit. One effect of this is to make the raising of long-term capital expensive, at a time when in any case the demand for capital is usually running at a high level, due to an upturn in fixed capital formation. It would thus be far better if businessmen took steps to obtain the necessary money while interest rates were still low; by doing so they might raise new capital at 2 per cent less in interest charges. In the same way new equity finance (ordinary shares) may be raised more cheaply (in terms of cost of annual dividend) if this is done while share prices are still high and yields low, before restrictive measures adversely affect company profitability and cause a decline in the stock market. Although all this might mean that companies obtained finance long before they needed it, since Britain has perhaps the best developed short-term capital market in the world, there should be no difficulty in finding interim employment for the money until it is required to pay for the new plant and machinery. Frequently, of course, companies have not gone to the market earlier simply because at the planning stage they did not envisage any need for external finance: the trouble in such cases lies in over-confident cash flow forecasting, based no doubt upon over-confident sales forecasting.

With a high Bank rate, working capital is costly, again at a time when there is a greater demand for it, for stocks are likely to be accumulating due to a downturn in sales. To avoid this it is important to make anticipatory moves by way of lower production schedules and run-down in stockholding. The cost of working capital is also a factor to be considered when planning purchasing and sales strategy during the expansion periods.

INDUSTRIAL RELATIONS

A firm's industrial relations and training policy should also take into account the present and future economic climate. The pre-expansion phase can be used to recruit and train new personnel before the labour market becomes tight again. When the un-employment percentage is very low, in the latter part of an expansion phase, labour relations will be very much dominated by the strong bargaining power of the unions in such a situation. Management must therefore expect strike threats, intensification of pressure for higher basic wage rates and an increasing degree of wage drift. Allowance should be made for all this when estimating forward labour costs. While acceding to wage de-mands during an expansion period, management may attach conditions to improve efficiency and factory discipline; but there will probably be greater scope for this during a period of down-turn in the economy, when unemployment is higher.

What has been outlined above gives in very broad terms some indication as to how the manager should respond to economic fluctuation when making decisions in the major business planning areas. It is extremely important that management should cultivate the habit of taking periodic economic looks to ascertain what stage the economy is at in the cycle, what the prevailing climate is likely to be over the coming years and what action should be taken in various parts of the organisation in the light of this. Of particular importance in the last few years has been the right strategy to adopt during highly inflationary periods. Some in-dications of what this should be have already been given, in Chapter 9, when we described the gainers and losers from in-flation.

17

Determination of Price and Output

In dealing with the strategy of the firm, consideration has been given as to how it can best react to the realities of the economic cycle. In the remaining chapters of this part we leave aside the impact of these fluctuations and examine instead the economic principles underlying the normal everyday behaviour of the firm.

It was earlier seen that one way of allocating the factors of production is through the operation of the price mechanism. We now look in more detail at how 'price' results from the interplay of the forces of supply and demand in the market. In economic theory 'the market' is a mythical place to which buyers and sellers come and, as a result of what Marshall described as the higgling and bargaining of the market', a price is fixed which leaves neither unsatisfied buyers nor unsatisfied sellers. This market mechanism formed the cornerstone of classical economics. Today its controlling force over economic affairs is more limited and in many areas it has been found to be no longer adequate in regulating our modern economic requirements. But the principles exhibited in the operation of 'the market' still provide a useful explanation of much of our economic behaviour, helping to predict the likely sequence of cause and effect. So, although it has long been traditional to study the operation of the market mechanism, it is by no means entirely irrelevant to our modern requirements to continue to do so.

LAWS OF SUPPLY AND DEMAND

The greatest of the laws of economics is that of supply and demand: it is by way of being a universal explanation for a wide variety of economic happenings. This law gives an explanation of how price, any price, is arrived at in the market, on the assumption that there exists perfectly free competition and that other things remain the same. This latter proviso is of course seldom present

216

in practice, and free competition has also become rarer. Further-more, the word 'price' is used in a wide sense, not just to cover the price of finished goods, but also materials, as well as the cost price of the factors of production. Free competition involves not just price-cutting between producers, but also perfect market knowledge on the part of the buyers, who must also compete, as well as free movement of the factors of production in response to changes in their price. On the basis of these definitions, which are also assumptions, the law of supply and demand states that a greater increase in demand than in supply will cause price to rise; while a greater relative increase in supply will cause price to fall. We will now look at how this happens.

The interaction of supply and demand in the market to establish a level of price can be illustrated by way of a graph, as well as in words. Unlike many of the mathematical presentations of economics this one is readily intelligible to the layman. The shape of the curves reflects the essential nature of the forces of supply and demand; although once more we are in the realm of general-isation, which if not 100 per cent true, is at least true in the majority of cases. This is all that can be claimed for any economic law.

The normal behaviour of demand in the market situation is that the higher the price of the article, the smaller will be the quantity demanded; while the lower the price, the more will be demanded. A lower price may encourage existing consumers to buy more, if it is that sort of product; or alternatively there may now be more people who can afford the product at the new lower price. A higher price works in the opposite way; to reduce the quantity demanded.

On the supply side, the higher the price the greater the quantity manufacturers will be willing to supply; the lower the price the less they will be willing to supply. This behaviour of supply accords with the law of diminishing returns we encountered earlier. Additional output involves the working of existing plant and labour more intensively, which may also be less efficient or more costly; or additional output may require the creation of new capacity. Therefore, a higher price may be a very necessary condition for any enlargement of supply.

Supply and demand curves may be plotted on a graph (Fig. 1), along the horizontal axis being scaled the quantity of the product consumed, and up the vertical axis the range of price. On the basis of generalisations already made regarding the behaviour of supply and demand in relation to price, it follows that the demand curve (DD) will slope downwards to the right; while the supply curve (SS) will slope upwards to the right. The two curves intersect at a point, known as the point of equilibrium (P), to which in given conditions price will always move. This is the only price where the quantity demanded (OC) will equal the quantity producers will be willing to supply (again OC). At any higher

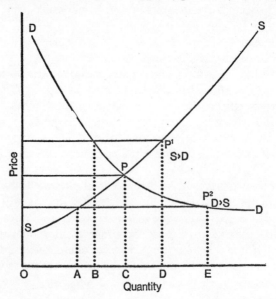

Fig. 1: Equilibrium level of price at which demand and supply are equal

price (P¹) the quantity supplied (OD) would be greater than consumers were willing to buy (OB); while at a lower price (P²) the quantity demanded (OE) would exceed that which manufacturers were willing to supply (OA) at that price.

Thus, moving up or down the price scale will result in an increase or decrease in the quantity demanded or supplied. It should be noticed that this is a different concept from the one we will now consider. Our analysis so far has been rather static. To make it more dynamic we look at what happens to price when there is a shift upwards or downwards in either demand or supply, or both. In other words, we consider the effect of an increase or decrease in the level of demand and supply, rather than, as we have done so far, the quantity demanded or supplied at various levels of price.

SHIFTS IN SUPPLY AND DEMAND

What happens to the curves when there is a change in the general level of demand or supply is illustrated in Fig. 2, but to

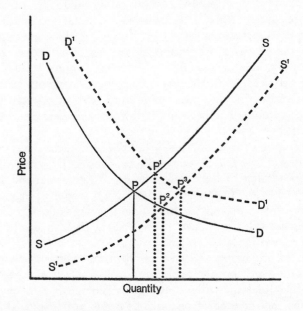

Fig. 2: Effect on price of increases in demand and supply

avoid confusion only *increases* in demand and supply are actually shown. In the case of demand, an increase is represented by an upward movement of the curve to the right (D¹D¹), but if demand contracts the movement is downwards to the left. With supply movement is in the opposite direction: an increase in supply is represented by the curve moving downwards to the right (S¹S¹), and upwards to the left when supply is curtailed. We can now look at what happens to price as a result of independent movements in demand or supply, as well as combined movements.

If the demand for a product increases to a greater extent than the available supply, a situation of scarcity will arise. The eager buyers will bid against one another and this will force up the price (from P to P¹). This higher price of course provides an incentive for producers to increase the supply, by bidding higher for the factors of production and installing more machinery, thereby bringing supply more into equality with demand. The higher level of price will also naturally react upon demand; some of the clamouring buyers will be put off by the higher price and therefore equality will also be achieved by a reduction in demand, as well as an increase in supply. As supply increases and demand becomes more and more price conscious, price will cease to rise and may even fall back a bit, but not to the original level.

When the change in the demand/supply relationship is in the form of a fall rather than a rise in demand, with supply remaining the same, or not falling by as much, then equality between the two will be brought about by a fall in price. Producers will compete with one another to secure the smaller available demand by cutting their prices. The fall in price will be arrested by some of the suppliers ceasing or curtailing production because at the lower price some of the production activity is no longer as profitable. The lower price may at the same time increase consumption, so that demand will rise to meet falling supply, thereby also helping to arrest the price fall.

Changes in supply relative to demand will also lead to equilibrating movements in price. A fall off in supply, due possibly to product hold-up, without any equivalent change in demand will have the same effect on price as a rise in demand: that is, price will tend to rise. An increase in supply relative to demand will cause price to fall (P²), much as in the case of a downward shift in demand. Since this also causes a reduction in profitability, it may eventually lead to some producers going out of production, so that supply will drop back to a lower level.

Thus, when the existing equilibrium is disturbed by a change in either supply or demand, with no matching movement in the same direction on the other side, there will be a price change, which itself will act to bring supply and demand into equality again. The level of price at which this happens is the new equilibrium price. When both supply and demand move to the same extent and in the same direction, then price of course remains the same (P^3).

Movements from the side of either demand or supply inevitably, as we have noted, set up a reaction on the other side. As a result, it may take some time before price really settles down again—if it ever does, for in the real world other things seldom remain the same. There may in fact be a series of equilibrium prices as we go through time. To illustrate this, let us consider an upward shift in demand. The first effect will be to put up price, since it is unlikely that supply can be adjusted immediately, unless stockholding in the industry has been high. However, arrangements will be made in the medium term to squeeze out more production from existing capacity. When this becomes available, it will tend to bring price down slightly from the scarcity level; although it will not come back all the way to the level prevailing before the upsurge of demand. For one thing, the extra output will very probably have been obtained at a higher cost. In the longer term, additional capacity will be created: either by firms already in the business or by new entrants. When the new production capacity comes on stream, assuming no further increase in demand, this will occasion a further softening of price, although it will still probably stay some way above the original level.

ELASTICITY

It will have been noticed that, not only do changes in demand and supply influence price, but these forces themselves are influenced by price. The degree to which demand or supply react to price changes is termed 'elasticity'. This concept of elasticity is most frequently used with reference to demand. Elasticity of demand is the degree of responsiveness of demand to price changes. If demand decreases or increases by the same proportion as the price increase or decrease, so as to give an unaltered total sales revenue, then such demand is held to have an elasticity of unity. If instead, the price reduction gives rise to a greater proportionate increase in demand, with a resulting larger total sales revenue, demand is said to be elastic, that is having an elasticity greater than unity. Where demand increases very little, following a reduction in price, such demand is deemed to be 'inelastic' in character and the total sales revenue will be less as the result of the price reduction. When the price movement is in the opposite direction, namely upwards, then the implications of elasticity in the demand for the product in terms of total sales revenue are somewhat different. An inelastic demand will result in a higher sales revenue following a price increase; whereas when demand is highly elastic consumers will be put off by the higher price.

Whether demand is elastic or inelastic will often depend on the nature of the product. If it is an essential item like salt (which people must have, but need in only a limited quantity) then no matter what happens to the price, demand will remain pretty much the same. In the case of a product for which there are many substitutes, and which people need not have, but which can be consumed in a wide range of quantities, the demand for such a product will usually be highly elastic. Elasticity of demand will also reflect the degree of price consciousness on the part of the consuming public, which of course may vary according to the prosperity of the times. The concept of elasticity is obviously of great importance to management in deciding what pricing action should be taken to achieve maximum profitability.

'Elasticity' can also be applied to supply, although it is less usual to do so. When the supply of a product can be readily altered in response to price changes, it may be regarded as elastic. Where it takes a long time to increase supply, or where supply cannot easily be discontinued (as for instance in the case of jointly produced products), such supply is deemed inelastic. With products where this is the case, a price rise following an increase in demand will tend to remain more permanently at that level. Similarly, when demand slackens and price falls, the absence of any corresponding adjustment from an inelastic supply will cause the price fall to be greater and more lasting.

The degree of elasticity and inelasticity in the case of both demand and supply can be represented by the shape of the curve: a gentle slope denotes elasticity; while steepness reflects inelasticity.

HOW PRICES ARE ACTUALLY DETERMINED TODAY

To those actually responsible for fixing prices all that has gone before must have appeared to bear very little resemblance to the reality of our modern industrial society. In some spheres, markets, in the higgling and bargaining sense, still of course exist and in these prices do result from the interplay of demand and supply—the stock market being an example of this, as also are the markets in commodities and agricultural produce. But, as far as manufactured products are concerned, there is little higgling between buyers and producers, except perhaps in the case of the supply of materials and components by one company to another. With products sold by a company to the ordinary consumer, the producer tends to fix and publish the price, or since the abolition of resale price maintenance, perhaps we should say the producer 'recommends' the price.

This recommended price is worked out mainly on the side of supply, paying some regard of course to buyer's possible reactions to it. But the price is not determined by moving along any hypothetical demand curve and reading off the quantity likely to be demanded at various levels of price: for how can the manufacturer construct such a demand curve? Instead, the price is built up from some sort of starting point, such as cost of production.

In the past economists have tended to dislike the cost of production explanation of price. Where there are many producers with varying efficiencies, whose cost, they ask, is to be taken as the basis for price? This particular objection can be readily answered: the cost of production of the marginal producer can be taken as fixing a level for price, giving the more efficient producers, with production costs below this, an additional profit. A traditional objection has been that the cost of production approach does not explain the price of objects whose value lies primarily in their scarcity and where there is little or no cost of production, or where the cost was incurred many years ago. Such goods however are a distinct category and are small in number by comparison with the huge volume of manufactured goods.

When calculating price, businessmen do therefore tend to start with the production cost and to this they add the required profit margin, in terms perhaps of a minimum acceptable return on capital employed in producing a product, and this gives the final build-up of price. It should be noted that when we talk about an acceptable return on capital, the cost of capital has already been included in production costs, either in the form of amortised machinery costs or working capital in the form of wages and raw material costs. The return on capital is additional to all this and is in fact the reward for risk and enterprise. The price which has thus been built up on the basis of cost of production and return on capital has of course to be compared with the price of near enough equivalent competitor products, if these exist. The price of a particular product may even be pitched in relation to that of another product made by the same company, as in the case of standard and de luxe models.

The actual price behaviour of manufacturers is also frequently very different from that portrayed in the theoretical operation of supply and demand in the market. In the real world prices are published and therefore not very frequently altered. When there is an increase in demand, but no immediate matching increase in supply, the result is usually a 'waiting list' rather than an increase in price. Another behaviour pattern, which goes against economic teaching, is that in some cases in the face of falling demand manufacturers will put up, rather than reduce, their price, in order to protect profit margins.

The product pricing methods actually employed by business-men are therefore very different from the theoretical economist's description of the interaction of supply and demand in the market. In the real world these influences are present all right, and the generalisations about tendencies and reactions remain valid. But in the real world demand and supply curves cannot in fact be constructed and therefore it is not possible to estimate beforehand demand and supply reactions or the extent of price movements. Generally, it is the producer who must take the initiative in deter-mining price: the buyer can react to this, but cannot usually him-self make any price suggestion. Answers to questions about how much will be bought or sold at this or that price can be derived only from trial and error, within a very narrow empirical range. And even then the answers will be valid only in the given set of circumstances, which are unlikely to remain for long unaltered.

OUTPUT DETERMINATION UNDER PERFECT COMPETITION

Even with price established, either by the producers or by combined forces of supply and demand, individual manufacturers still have to decide how much they will produce at this price. Many firms, especially if they are sales dominated, usually just sell as much as they can produce. Maximisation of sales, rather than maximisation of profit, is in such cases the determining principle; and indeed there may even be a complete unawareness of any possible conflict between these two objectives.

While there is a consciousness that greater volume brings down unit costs by spreading overheads, it may still not be recognised that there is also a point at which it becomes less profitable to sell more, because the law of diminishing returns is operating in a variety of guises. There may be increasing customer and competitor resistance to further sales penetration and to overcome this marketing expenditure may have to be proportionately greater in relation to the hoped-for sales increase. On the production side, additional output may be obtainable only by using machines more intensively, possibly also less economically, and by employing less proficient labour. Thus, unit costs at various levels of output will vary greatly; initially reducing as overheads get spread over greater volume and as the economies of large-scale production are reaped. Eventually, however, unit costs will stop declining and even begin to rise, because of the operation of some of the factors mentioned above.

To assist in determining the optimum level of output, at which profitability is maximised, there are certain cost concepts used in economic theory. Although these may not be employed in practice, this is not because the principles are incapable of being applied, but simply because businessmen are preoccupied with other goals. We have already touched upon the two broad categories: namely, fixed and variable costs. Fixed, or overhead costs, are present regardless of the level of output and are such items as rent, depreciation, development and design expenditure. Variable costs are those increasing with the level of output, but not incurred should there be no output at all. The major items in this category are wages and material costs.

The line of differentiation between fixed and variable costs is not sharp: for example, if skilled labour cannot be laid off during a temporary slack period, then the wage cost of such labour assumes the character of a fixed overhead. Similarly, in the long run many fixed costs can become variable: for example, surplus factory space may be disposed of and there may also be a disinvestment of machinery by ceasing to make provision for depreciation.

AVERAGE AND MARGINAL COSTS

When overheads are added to the variable costs incurred in producing a certain quantity and the total then divided by that quantity, the result is average cost per unit. Where there are heavy fixed charges to be recouped, this results in very high average cost at low levels of output. At higher levels of output average cost is lower, not only because the amount of fixed cost to be carried by each unit is smaller, but also because variable cost per unit may also reduce, due to the economies accruing from large-scale operations.

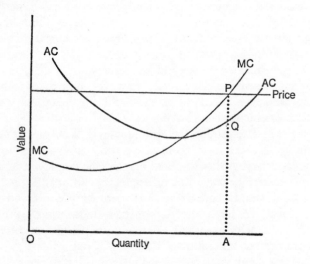

Fig. 3: Output determination: perfect competition

With the decline in variable cost, the cost of the extra or marginal unit will naturally get smaller. Marginal cost is the extra cost incurred in producing an additional unit of output. Since fixed costs are 'fixed', marginal cost is in effect the addition to variable cost resulting from the production of the marginal unit.

In graphical presentation (Fig. 3), the average cost curve (AC) will tend initially to slope very steeply downwards, as rising volume in the early stages greatly reduces the per unit allocation of overheads. The curve of marginal cost (MC) may also at first slope downwards, if economies of large-scale production are reducing variable cost, but the initial downward slope of this curve is unlikely to be as steep as that of average cost. At low levels of output the average cost curve will be well above the marginal cost curve, since the latter represents variable cost only, while average cost includes variable and also the very large element of fixed cost.

When diminishing returns set in, the marginal cost curve will begin to rise and it will eventually intersect the average cost, particularly since the direction of the latter may still be downwards. But this point of intersection will represent the minimum level reached by average cost and also reflect the fact that rising marginal cost now exactly cancels out the beneficial effects of overheads spreading. From this point onwards the effect of the continued rise in marginal cost is greater than overheads spreading and therefore pulls up average cost with it.

When the level of price is at the point of intersection of the average and marginal cost curves then there is neither loss nor excessive profit. At this point it should be explained that economists include 'normal profit' as an item of cost. A firm making normal profit will be content to stay in business, but no new entrants will be attracted. In the short run, if adverse trading conditions are expected to be only temporary, a firm will stay in business even if price is below this breaking even point. As long as the price obtained covers the minimum average variable cost it is perhaps worthwhile continuing to keep the production activity in being, and accepting a loss with regard to overhead cost. But if price falls below minimum average variable cost, the firm will cease production to avoid making any further loss on top of that already incurred by overhead cost. This is known as the shut-down point.

The most profitable level of output for the individual firm is that at which marginal cost is equal to price (see Fig. 3). To go beyond this point (OA) would mean selling the marginal unit of output below cost, so that total profit would be reduced. In the same way, stopping short of the point of equality between marginal cost and price would represent a failure to engage in the production of units whose marginal cost would still be below the level of price and therefore on whose production extra profit could be earned. If this point of equality between marginal cost and price is well above the intersection of the marginal and average cost curves, there will be a sizeable excess profit for the firm at that price, to the extent of the difference (PQ) between average cost and price.

In a competitive situation the existence of such an abnormally large profit will attract new entrants or cause existing producers to instal additional capacity. If there is no matching increase in demand, this expansion of supply will exert a downward pressure on price, bringing it nearer to the point of intersection of the average and marginal cost curves, this being the break-even point, where there is neither excessive profit nor loss.

The theory of output determination in a situation of perfect competition can be summed up in three propositions:

(*a*) A firm maximises profit by producing up to the point where marginal cost equals price. If, at this level, price is well above average cost, there will be a greater than normal profit.

(*b*) With price at the level where marginal and average costs are equal, also the point of minimum average cost, a firm is merely breaking even, making neither an abnormal profit nor a loss.

(*c*) Competition will tend to exert pressure to bring price down to a point where marginal cost equals minimum average cost.

OUTPUT DETERMINATION BY SOLE SUPPLIERS

The principles of output determination for maximum profitability described so far have been those applicable to perfect competition. But completely free competition is not at all common in real life. Manufacturers are more usually, to a varying degree, in a position to determine price; indeed as early as the planning and design stage they often have a definite price in mind. The sole supplier or monopolist must by the nature of things fix his own price; and this is also true of manufacturers whose product is somehow different from all others, or is made to appear different. There is thus a wide range of possibility with regard to price and output; the sole supplier having to determine that price, and its corresponding level of output, which will give him the best profit. Although he would undoubtedly like to, he cannot simply opt for a high price and a large output, for the consumer's reaction to price is also a determining factor. The producer can, however, choose from a wide range of possibility between high price/small output on the one hand and low price/large output on the other.

The solution to the problem of output determination in the case of the sole supplier is not, however, too far removed from that of the competitive situation. It will be remembered that under perfectly free competition, with price given, production goes on up to the point where the revenue obtained from the sale of the marginal unit equals the cost of producing it. This has been described as the point of equality between marginal cost and price; since the price is identical for every unit sold regardless of the level of output, it is obviously also the same thing as marginal revenue. But, for the producer who has some control over price, the latter need not be the same thing as marginal revenue. Marginal revenue is that addition to total revenue achieved by the sale of the marginal unit. Although the price obtained for the marginal unit will be the same as that for all other units of output, this price itself will depend on the level of output. Generally speaking, the higher the price the lower will be the volume demanded; while the lower the price the greater the volume demanded. Increased output may therefore be possible only if price is lowered. The revenue lost as a result of reducing the price must therefore be taken into account when calculating the additional revenue obtained from the larger sales volume achieved by the price reduction.

An example will perhaps make this clearer. A producer may be able to sell 50 units at 50p each, giving a total revenue of £25. In order, however, to sell an additional unit he may have to reduce his price by $\frac{1}{2}$p to $49\frac{1}{2}$p, so that total revenue from the sale of 51 units will be £25·24$\frac{1}{2}$. The marginal revenue obtained by selling one unit more is therefore 24$\frac{1}{2}$p, although the price at which it was sold was $49\frac{1}{2}$p. Marginal revenue and price can therefore be two separate and distinct things. If the cost of producing the extra unit is less than 24$\frac{1}{2}$p, there will have been an addition to total profit. And the producer can keep on increasing his profit through larger sales induced by price cuts right up to the point where the extra revenue achieved is the same as the extra cost incurred. To go any further than this would reduce total profit.

In the sole supplier situation, profit is therefore maximised at that level of price and output where marginal revenue is equal to marginal cost. Again this can be illustrated graphically (Fig. 4).

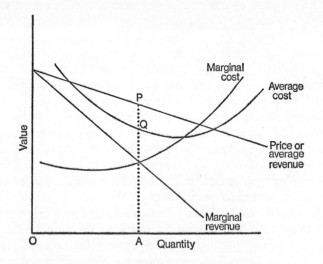

Fig. 4: Output determination: sole supplier

The price or average revenue curve is in fact the more familiar demand curve, showing the quantity that can be sold at each level of price. The point of intersection of marginal cost and marginal revenue curves shows the quantity (OA) and, by extending up to the average revenue curve, the price (P) which will give the greatest profit. The extent of this profit is the difference (PQ) between the average cost and the average revenue curves.

USEFULNESS OF MARGINAL ANALYSIS

Although we have concerned ourselves mainly with output determination, marginal analysis can also be useful as a basis for choice in a wide range of business decision areas. It can help decide, for example, the worthwhileness of selling additional output, where extra costs have to be incurred in doing so, or where something lower than the standard price has to be offered. Marginal analysis is particularly useful in export pricing; fixed cost being left out of consideration altogether and only the extra variable cost being taken into account when fixing the overseas price. In selective pricing, if the price obtained in any particular market is at least marginal cost then no loss will be suffered; and, if it can be slightly higher than this, there will be some contribution towards covering overheads.

Marginal analysis is also useful in making production decisions. A decision to instal a new process, supplanting existing machines, can be justified if average cost under the new process is still less than the marginal cost under the existing one. In periods during which firms have to operate below capacity, work should be shared out among the production units so that their marginal costs are the same. For, with an upward sloping marginal cost curve, concentration of total production in one installation would be on the basis of a higher marginal cost than if the available work was spread over two or more. Where the installations have varying efficiencies, it obviously pays to use exclusively the most efficient, but only for as long as its marginal cost remains below the level of the minimum marginal cost of the second installation. When this point is reached, work should be allocated between them in such a way as to keep their marginal costs in step.

18

Competition and Monopoly

COMPETITION

Free competition is not only a basic condition for the successful operation of the pricing mechanism; it is also an essential safeguard against exploitation of the consumer by the producer. Indeed, from society's point of view, the capitalist free enterprise system is only acceptable if there exists free competition. Where this is absent, the state may have to step in to protect the consumer and then enterprise becomes not quite so free. Free competition also provides flexibility and adaptability in the economy, by ensuring that production responds to consumer preference, as indicated by price.

The basic premise of the free market system is that the consumer is king. This follows from the fact that the goal of all production is consumption; either directly or indirectly through investment. The economy should therefore ideally be operated in such a way that the consumer gets the best product at the lowest possible price. The pricing mechanism, operating on the basis of free competition, brings this about. Competition between producers will ensure the price is not unreasonably high and that extra supply is forthcoming should demand require it.

Free competition is a state in which no single producer (or for that matter no single buyer) is in a position by himself to influence price. For this to be so, each producer should account for only a small portion of the total industry output; so that any variation in his supply will be readily offset by other producers and will have little repercussion on price. The market price, in other words, is something which the individual producer just has to accept. The same is true from the side of demand: no one buyer must be so significant in the total market demand that by withdrawing his demand he can influence price. Free competition also implies that neither buyers nor sellers act in concert, but operate and compete independently of one another.

MONOPOLY

The opposite of such a system of free competition is monopoly. The extreme form of monopoly is where there is only one producer or buyer, in which case he very obviously is in a position to dictate price. In reality, of course, perfectly free competition and absolute monopoly rarely exist. Absolute monopoly is rare because there are few things in this world for which there are no substitutes. A monopoly situation can, however, be regarded as existing when a producer or buyer is so dominant in the market that his behaviour can influence price. A situation in which there are a few dominant producers exerting an influence on the market is termed 'oligopoly'. Where there is one large dominant buyer this is call 'monopsony'.

Absolute, or less than absolute, monopolists, generally seek to influence price in an upwards direction by limiting output; that is by creating a position of scarcity. They may also, however, agree prices, without any limitation of output. Their ability to do this depends to some extent on the elasticity of demand; which in turn may depend on the nature of the product and the availability of substitutes. Elasticity of supply is also important. Of course, the object of the monopolist may be to make supply inelastic and his chances of doing this are greater when the trade is one into which entry is difficult, either because of the know-how necessary, or because the initial costs of setting-up production are sizeable.

NATURAL MONOPOLIES

Not all monopoly situations arise from malice aforethought; from a desire by one, or a few producers, to create a condition in which they can exploit the public. Quite often a monopolistic situation develops because it is inevitable in the circumstances; there is a 'natural' monopoly rather than a consciously contrived one. The only chemist shop in the village will unavoidably have a monopoly of pharmaceutical sales in that immediate area. Even over a wider geographical area the demand for a specialist product may be so limited that the total national requirement still justifies only one producer—this being so in the case of certain chemical additives and auxiliaries, used only in very small quantities. A monopoly position may be enjoyed through ownership of the only source of supply of a raw material or of a unique site.

There are cases where it is clearly wasteful, and not to the public advantage, to have more than one supplier. This is broadly so in the case of the public utility type of activity: in the provision of water, power, transport, etc. Even if such activities are not provided by a national authority, public utility undertakings generally have at least a local monopoly. Too active competition in some of these areas has in the past not only been wasteful, but also a danger to the public. The tale is often told how before the formation of the London Passenger Transport Board private bus companies used to race one another to the bus stops, in order to be the first to pick up the available passengers. In the public utility sphere a degree of competition may, however, still exist, as for example between types of fuel and power, or means of transport.

Not all monopolistic tendencies are either natural or logical. Even without going as far as combining with one another or squeezing out competitors, there are many activities in ordinary business practice which tend to diminish competition and which are therefore monopolistic in character, although in each case this would probably be indignantly denied. Goodwill, whether as an item in the balance sheet or through the old boy net, is incompatible with the concept of free competition. Advertising, which insists that brand X is different from all other brands, or which by some 'giveaway' builds up brand loyalty, is again an attempted creation of a state of unfree demand—the creation of a 'sole supplier' situation for the producer of brand X. The award of patent protection is a more open, and indeed intended, method of creating for a period of years a sole supplier situation in respect of the patented article. Another way in which the state can create a monopoly situation is by nationalisation, with the state enterprise becoming the monopolist. Trade union practices restricting entry into a particular occupation also limit supply and therefore affect price. Among such practices are apprenticeship and craft regulations, as well as insistence on a 'closed shop'.

These are some of the everyday aspects of the business world which we all accept, but which nevertheless tend to restrict competition and therefore have a monopolistic taint. More readily associated with monopoly and restrictive practices are certain actions by firms, either singly or more usually combined, which limit competition—keeping price artificially high, and above what would be the equilibrium price in a completely free market. Probably the most tacit of these is the phenomenon of price leadership, in which the pricing policy of the dominant producer is followed as a matter of course by the other suppliers to that market, but without any formal discussion or agreement between them. There are many areas where suppliers simply refuse to compete on the basis of price; instead preferring to win customers by the service they offer. The commercial banks are perhaps the most outstanding and unashamed example of this. Even in the so-called highly competitive motor industry, price bands can be clearly distinguished and all manufacturers' models falling into these categories are only a few £s removed in price from one another. Nor is this really surprising; as we saw in the previous chapter, the fixing of a price has to be done with reference to one's competitors. In order to facilitate this unconscious co-ordination in the pricing activities of independent suppliers price lists have been exchanged 'for information'. Suppliers have in the past gone further than this and through their trade associations actually 'recommended' prices to their members.

CARTELS AND TRUSTS

When producers get together regularly to fix prices, and in times of over-supply even to share out the market on an agreed quota basis, this sort of arrangement is called a 'cartel'. This is a fairly loose affair, which rarely lasts. The participating firms maintain their separate corporate identities, discipline being achieved by a system of levies and fines. The levies are to provide compensation for under-utilisation of capacity. Where the temptation to exceed quota is not resisted, fines are imposed. Cartels usually spring up during depressed periods characterised by a good deal of over-capacity in industry; but during which producers do not want to indulge in a cut-throat competition, from which only the strongest and most efficient will survive.

A more permanent form of combination between suppliers is

the 'trust', a term more familiar in America, where legislation against monopolies is in fact termed 'anti-trust'. The trust brings companies together under a common controlling financial interest, usually in the form of a holding company, vested in which are controlling shareholding interests in the companies embraced by the trust.

The enormous resources needed today to produce certain products, as well as carry out research and development, necessitates large company units and the number of these competing in any given market must as a result be small. This is particularly true, for example, in atomic energy and aircraft manufacture. With long-term development projects, price has to be calculated well in advance by the producer, since upon it much planning rests: therefore the producer has to be in a position to dictate price.

There are, of course, sectors where this is not so and where therefore something approaching the classical market mechanism can continue to function. But even in these areas, individual producers may be anxious to achieve a dominant market share. In striving for this, they may use tactics expressly designed to force their competitors out of business, perhaps bringing out unbranded cut-price products, known as 'fighting' brands, in order to wage price war without damaging the image of their traditional brands. When a firm has achieved a quasi-monopoly position, it may, however, attempt to hide the fact by marketing its products under different brand names, not readily recognised by the ordinary members of the public as all coming from the same company. This semblance of competition may also be fostered by keeping alive the brand identity of firms taken over by the dominant supplier. This practice is also useful in retaining brand loyalty, and this may be how it is justified to the public. It may also happen that once a supplier has achieved a dominant position in a market he will be at pains to keep in existence what few remaining, harmless small competitors are left. This enables him to argue that technically there is still competition.

'COUNTERVAILING POWER'

In the modern tendency to combine, and therefore towards monopoly, there are certain safeguards for consumers. For one thing, in the case of industrial products the consumer himself may be a large firm enjoying a position of monopsony, quite capable of dealing on equal terms with dominant suppliers who try to hoist prices too high. Sometimes indeed it is the suppliers who have to band together to defend themselves against dominant buyers (such as public bodies, like the Post Office and the CEGB). Even where the consumer is an ordinary private person, the growth of consumer associations, and the banding of consumers into groups which demand preferential terms for their members, are all helping to compensate for getting-together on the side of supply. Certain large retail chains have a powerful monopsony position in relation to the firms supplying them with consumer products; these often being made to the retailer's precise specification and carrying his brand. The supplier firms may in fact have their production almost exclusively geared to the retail chain's requirements, and indeed are often lured by the chain organisation into such a position of dependence. It should not be overlooked, however, that these monopsony retailers are often at the same time furthering the interests of the consumer, and may even be regarded as his champion and agent in the ceaseless fight against the constant tendency of certain producers towards exploitation of the consuming public. Further back in time, the growth of the trade union movement can be seen as representing a combination of suppliers of labour to improve their bargaining position and working conditions in the face of a few large buyers of labour. All these defensive combinations, which have grown up in the face of monopoly position on the other side, are well described by Professor Galbraith* in terms of a theory of 'countervailing' power; or, as he hesitated from labelling it, 'countervalience'.

In addition to countervailing power there are other safeguards against monopoly. Some dominant suppliers exercise a self-discipline and do not in fact abuse their position to charge a monopoly price, lest this should evoke accusations of monopoly power and invite state intervention. Where a monopoly situation has grown up, which is in danger of being against the public interest, this has always been recognised as one of the justifications for state ownership, particularly in the case of public service industries. More recently it has been suggested that, as an

* *American Capitalism*, by J. K. Galbraith (Hamish Hamilton 1957).

alternative approach in such cases, the state may resurrect competition; either by setting up a competitor enterprise or by taking an interest in, and encouraging, such a project. Even although the degree of competition between suppliers within a country may lessen, the development of free trade areas, such as E.F.T.A. and the E.E.C., as well as tariff reductions negotiated under G.A.T.T., all serve to increase the degree of international competition, which can also keep in check the monopoly power of national producers.

The official attitude to monopoly in this country has always been more tolerant than has been the case in certain other countries. Since 1948, however, there has been a gradual development of more and more effective monopolies and restrictive practices legislation and this we will now consider in the remaining part of this chapter.

MONOPOLIES AND RESTRICTIVE PRACTICES LEGISLATION*

Passing laws against monopolistic and restrictive business practices is a comparatively recent activity in this country, unlike the United States which has always had a vigorous tradition of 'trust bustin', the early American legislation going as far back as the Sherman and Clayton Antitrust Acts of 1890 and 1914. In Britain, however, monopolies were regarded as not necessarily bad in themselves and legal supervision of business agreements was substantially left to the law of contract, although there was in addition a traditional hostility to activities constituting a 're-straint of trade'. The first piece of specifically anti-monopoly legislation in this country was the Monopolies and Restrictive Practices (Inquiry and Control) Act of 1948, but since then state supervision of those business activities tending to restrict competition has undergone continuous development and definition. Only the latest position will be described here, the superseded features in the main being omitted.

It may, however, help understanding to begin by outlining very broadly the general course of developments over the past

* An excellent article on 'Monopoly Legislation in Britain' contained in the November 1965 issue of the *Midland Bank Review* was most useful in compiling this section.

twenty years. The 1948 Act, as can be seen from its title, dealt with monopoly situations as well as restrictive practices indulged in by firms not necessarily holding a monopoly position. The official attitude towards each of these two categories differed. Monopolies were from the start regarded as only being bad if they operated against the public interest. Restrictive practices were considered as undesirable in themselves, unless they could be proved by those operating them to have advantages to the public greatly outweighing any disadvantages. In recognition of this differentiation in official viewpoint, the 1956 Restrictive Trade Practices Act separated restrictive practices from the scope of the Monopolies Commission and subjected them instead to judicial enquiry and legal sanctions under the Restrictive Practices Court. Later, the list of restrictive practices to be subject to this review was extended to include resale price maintenance and information agreements. The scope of the Monopolies Commission was similarly broadened to cover not only the consideration of existing monopolies but also those about to be created through mergers; while the definition of a monopoly situation was widened to include services as well as trade in goods.

The Monopolies Commission, originally set up in 1948 and later modified in 1956 and 1965, is a statutory but not a judicial body. The maximum size of the Monopolies Commission nowadays is twenty-five, but it can split up into groups. Its function is to investigate and report on monopoly situations referred to it by the Department of Trade and Industry. The area of investigation is defined in terms of a particular good or service, where at least a third of the trade in the U.K. is supplied to or from one source. The task of the Monopolies Commission is to ascertain whether such a monopoly situation operates against the public interest. If it does, the findings of the Commission may be enforced by an Order issued by the Department of Trade. Originally, the firms adversely reported upon had only to give undertakings that they would cease to operate in a way that was detrimental to the public interest; but since 1965, there has been power to dissolve a monopoly. Furthermore, the Commission can now act to prevent a monopoly situation arising, through its power to investigate recent or proposed mergers. This power was given to the Commission by the Monopolies and Mergers Act 1965, which provided that the Department of Trade could refer a merger to the Monopolies Commission either within six months of it taking place or as soon as a merger was proposed. Such mergers are liable to be referred to the Commission if they are likely to lead to, or strengthen, a monopoly position and involve assets to be taken over of a value in excess of £5 million. Once a reference to the Monopolies Commission has been made the government has the power to hold up a merger. As in the case of monopolies, the task of the Commission is to report on whether a merger is likely to operate against the public interest. If it finds that this is so, the Department of Trade will prevent the merger.

The supervision of restrictive practices is currently on the basis laid down by the 1956 and 1968 Restrictive Trade Acts and the 1964 Resale Prices Act. The 1956 Act stipulated that restrictive practices were to be regarded as operating against the public interest, unless they could be successfully defended by the parties concerned before the Restrictive Practices Court. All existing agreements, whether oral or written, concerning restrictions on prices, quantities, description, terms, places, persons and conditions of trading were to be registered with the Registrar of Restrictive Trading Agreements. These agreements were then to be either abandoned or defended before the Restrictive Practices Court (a court of law with power to issue orders preventing the continuation of the restrictive practice, as well as the making of a similar one). The proceedings of the Court take place in public, except that export agreements may be considered in private if there is a danger that information divulged will be of use to foreign competitors. The grounds upon which restrictive agreements may be justified are numerous. It may be argued that they protect the public from physical injury; or that their removal would deny the public of certain benefits; or that they counteract restrictive measures taken by others; or are necessary for the negotiation of 'fair' terms in the face of a dominant buyer or seller. A restrictive practice may also be upheld if there is a danger that the abandonment of it would lead to unemployment in a particular area or would adversely affect export business. Lastly, an agreement may be continued if it is ancillary to any other restrictive practice already approved by the Court. In all these cases, it must be shown that the benefits accruing to the public from the retention of the restrictive practice exceed any possible detrimental effects. Within a few years of the Restrictive Trade Practices Act being passed a very large proportion of the agreements originally registered ceased to exist; the majority being abandoned, while a smaller number were unsuccessfully defended before the Court.

The 1956 Act had banned collective resale price maintenance, but in doing so had recognised the right of an individual manufacturer to enforce his prices upon retailers. It was necessary therefore in 1964 to pass the Resale Prices Act in order to prohibit resale price maintenance entirely, except in cases where special exemption was granted. Claims for exemption had to be registered with the Registrar of Trading Agreements before the 16th November 1964; and from 30th April 1965 there was a general prohibition of any new agreements in the sphere of resale price maintenance. Registered agreements could continue to be operated until the Restrictive Practices Court had considered them. The grounds upon which exemption could be claimed from the general prohibition had to be argued before the Court. They were not quite as numerous as those laid down under the 1956 Act. Once again, the benefits of retention of resale price maintenance had to be proved to be greater than the advantages accruing to the public from its abolition. Resale price maintenance could be continued if in its absence there was likely to be a substantial deterioration in the quality of goods available for sale or a reduction in the number of shops handling them. Resale price maintenance could also be justified if its absence could be expected to lead to a general increase in retail prices in the long run, through a reduction in the number of competing retailers. In areas, such as pharmaceuticals, resale price maintenance might be defended as being necessary on health grounds. Manufacturers could also submit that the abolition of resale price maintenance would lead to a reduction in necessary after-sales services.

One category of agreements between manufacturers, not specifically included in the 1956 Act, was those relating to the sharing of information. It was found that, after price fixing agreements had been ruled illegal by the Restrictive Practices Court, in some cases manufacturers were replacing these by giving advance notice of price changes to their trade associations and this was having the same effect as the previous price fixing agreements. In the summer of 1965 such an evasion was held to be in contempt of Court: because of this the F.B.I. warned its members against the circulation of information on proposed price changes. The 1964 White Paper on Monopolies, Mergers and Restrictive Practices indicated that future legislation would be taken to bring information agreements within the scope of the 1956 Act.

The 1968 Restrictive Trade Practices Act brought about the necessary tightening up on this point by giving the Department of Trade and Industry power to call for any 'information agreement' to be registered, although in practice only those potentially detrimental to the public interest. This Act also, however, added new categories to the list of those agreements that need not be registered, such as those in support of prices and incomes policy and agreements about standards; while temporary exemption may be extended to agreements made for the modernisation and rationalisation of industry, particularly those receiving encouragement from the N.E.D.C. An additional ground on which agreements could be defended was that they did not *materially* restrict competition. The 1968 Act improved the enforcement of the 1956 Act, by stricter time limits for registration of agreements and penalties for non-registration.

19

Demand Analysis

Demand analysis is a comparatively recent management staff function. After the Second World War, there was for many years little need to analyse demand: it was there and it was insatiable. All that was produced could readily be sold; so there was no need to worry about finding out what people really wanted, or trying to forecast how much they would want. This happy state of affairs lasted almost right up to the beginning of the sixties; quite a remarkably long period of seller's market.

The prolonged buoyancy of demand was due to several factors. First of all, there was a great deal of wartime consumers' starvation to be satisfied. At the end of the war, there was certainly plenty of purchasing power in the form of war savings and service gratuities to make this demand effective. When these savings were exhausted, the level of purchasing power still remained high, due to the continuation of the state of full employment into the post-war years, coupled with governmental policy favouring a redistribution of wealth from the savers to the spenders. The growing adoption of transatlantic living habits provided the public with plenty of ideas for spending and also gave the opportunity for the development of vast new consumer durables industries. The extension of the hire purchase facility, particularly from 1954 onwards, dispensed with saving as a necessary precursor to spending and allowed demand to blossom forth at a rate even greater than the rapidly growing industrial earnings. Sooner or later, of course, these forces were to play themselves out; they had in fact done so by the beginning of the sixties. The post-war seller's market gave way to a buyer's market and once more the consumer was king. From that moment onwards demand analysis became a serious and necessary subject for study.

Demand analysis is carried out for at least three major purposes. It enables the producer to learn how he can please the customer better, and thereby increase his sales. A knowledge of how much is being spent in a particular area, and on whose products it is being spent, gives top management its only really objective assessment of sales performance, one which is infinitely preferable to being told by the sales manager how well the sales force are doing. Lastly, demand analysis provides information about the market that enables a scientific attempt at sales forecasting to be made. Upon this sales forecast a great deal of management planning hinges.

SALES FORECASTING

Sales forecasting is generally the responsibility of the sales manager; although he is by no means the only person who suffers if his estimate of the future should prove wrong. Sales forecasting is not simply a way of setting targets for the sales force. Much more important, it forms the basis of the factory manager's production schedules and chief accountant's cash forecast. If the sales manager's boundless optimism, and desire to prove his selling virility, result in a sales forecast which actual sales do not live up to, then stocks will accumulate in the factory and workers may stand around idle. The chief accountant will be faced with a growing liquidity problem, as more money gets tied-up in stocks and creditors grow faster than debtors. The dangers in over-forecasting are therefore very real, particularly since the sales manager's prime concern will always be that he should never be in danger of losing a sale through lack of supplies. He will therefore tend to make sure that there is always enough, even if this means running the risk that there will often be more than enough.

Longer term sales forecasts are required to assess the need for the creation of additional production facilities in relation to existing plant capacity. This longer term forecast will also show up labour requirements and enable recruitment and training to be planned well in advance. The accountant makes longer term cash flow forecasts to determine whether any proposed expansion can be financed from the company's own resources or whether resort will have to be made to the capital market. An essential basis of new product planning is some estimate of expected sales volume, so that initial development and capital costs may be adequately amortised and unit cost determined.

Demand Analysis

Sales forecasting techniques have developed an increasing degree of sophistication as the tempo of competition has increased during the buyer's market of the sixties. At first, the methods employed by many firms were exceedingly crude. The crudest of these involved the application of something slightly better than last year's achieved percentage increased to get next year's expectations. This technique required only a very elementary facility in arithmetic and a degree of optimism, both qualities well within the capability of the average sales manager. There were the more enlightened others who paid some attention to the market. They had informal chats with their customers and quite happily generalised from these individual instances. For firms whose products were usually ordered by customers well in advance the problem of forecasting was considerably easier. In such cases all that was necessary was to plot cumulatively on a graph 'orders received' and 'actual sales' made. Orders would always of course run ahead of sales, but the average observable distance between the two graphs gave a time-lag, representing the number of months it took sales to attain the level of orders outstanding. From this could readily be estimated the expected monthly sales volume.

Such forecasting techniques were still primitive, and certainly seem so to us today. Reliable forecasting required to be more sophisticated: to be based on the size and growth rate of the particular market, and the share of it which the producer hoped to obtain. Such data called for the employment of many investigatory techniques, forming the subject matter of a new management science called 'market research'. It will be noted that although the classical economists' concept of the 'market' is not really adequate to explain large areas of business activity today, nevertheless the word 'market' has not entirely gone out of use. It was quite remarkable how many firms there were in the fifties who quite successfully sold their products without having any very precise idea of the value of total expenditure in their market, nor the growth rate of that market, nor the factors upon which that growth depended. There was understandably greater ignorance of how that market was shared out among the firms competing in it and of recent trends in market share capture or loss. Indeed, even today precise information of this kind is still lacking in certain areas. To fill in all these gaps in knowledge has been the task of market research.

With the development of national planning from 1962 onwards, the work of the N.E.D.C. has been something of a catalyst in this search for market information. It also extended considerably one of the earlier informal techniques, namely consultation with customers as to their future likely requirements. The national plans themselves provided a good deal of data in this respect. A forerunner of this type of enquiry could be found in the investigations carried out in 1957 by the Iron and Steel Board, in planning a major expansion of the iron and steel industry. In such exercises there are, however, still dangers lying in wait for the forecaster and he should be on his guard against them. One of these is what may be termed the 'compound optimism' factor. One's customers, in giving estimates of their future requirements, may be allowing for that little bit extra, much as the sales manager does when future production schedules are under consideration. Furthermore, the customer industry's estimate of requirements may in turn be based on his customers' estimates, which again may have a 'contingency' allowance built-in. And to make matters worse, the whole thing may be based on an over-optimistic growth rate for the economy!

When hoped-for national growth rates do not materialise in practice, businessmen may feel the need to carry out their own more realistic economic forecasting. This is particularly important in the case of those industries upon whom economic cycles tend to have exaggerated effects; such as those whose sales depend on the availability of credit, which may suddenly blossom forth or equally suddenly contract. Consumer demand based on 'credit' is always much more volatile.

NATURE OF PRODUCT DEMAND

In the previous chapter, when considering the operation of demand and supply in the market, the aspect of demand with which we were concerned was the reaction of demand to price movement. We saw that, generally speaking, as price rose the quantity demanded tended to fall. We also saw that the extent to which demand reacted in this way to price changes, resulting from changes from the side of supply, depended upon what is termed in economics the 'elasticity' of demand. The degree of this elasticity quite often derives from the type of product. In dealing with demand analysis we are also very much concerned with the type of product, for upon this depends the sort of demand analysis to be used, and particularly the research techniques to be applied.

Demand analysis is concerned with the size of the demand for a product; where it lies, what are the attitudes and techniques in the customer industries, as well as the outlook for these industries against the background of broad social and economic developments. This is, by any measure, a wide range of enquiry and each one of these aspects merits a book on its own. The remainder of this chapter will, however, concentrate on the more quantitative aspects, where the science of economics can be of some help to the manager in analysing the market and the factors impinging upon it.

Products can be very broadly divided into two major categories: consumer or industrial. Consumer goods may be split into necessity or luxury items. Underlying the demand for consumer goods are such important factors as population changes and the redistribution of wealth. While these factors may have some effect on the demand for luxury items, they are of much more importance in relation to necessity items, like food, clothing and housing. In the demand for luxury goods fashion plays a more dominant part, as also in some cases does the availability of credit: for example, with consumer durables like cars and domestic appliances. Industrial goods may be components supplied to an industry assembling them, which in turn may sell the assembled product to consumers. Industrial goods may also be capital goods: either working capital, like consumable materials; or fixed capital, like plant and machinery. The varying nature of all these types of product implies that different factors must be taken into account when assessing the demand for them, although some of these factors will be common to more than one type. Since the end object of all production is consumption, even in the case of investment goods the demand for them always is to some extent a derived demand for consumption.

POPULATION TRENDS

The factor of population is perhaps worth looking at in some detail. Overall population growth rates are usually small and seemingly insignificant percentages. In Britain's case the annual population growth rate is only three-quarters of 1 per cent. However, within this, there are some trends of proportions significant enough to have an influence upon the demand for consumer goods as well as broad implications for government taxation and social benefits policy. Looking between now and the end of the century there are several discernible and interesting population movements. Over the next thirty years our population will gradually grow at a faster rate. The total will rise from our present 56 to 67 million: in each of the next three decades increasing by 3, 3½ and 4 million respectively. The vital force in this growth will be the 20 per cent increase by the 1990s in women of child-bearing age, although the number each will have is expected to stay at the present 2·5 children. As a result of this factor, together with the high and low birth rates of past periods, the average age of our population will be getting younger. Changes in the numbers in each broad age group simply reflect past differences in birth rates: the high rates of the Victorian and Edwardian period up to 1911 and also from the Second World War onwards; the low birth rate during the First World War (and the effect of casualties) and the depressed twenties and thirties.

Since the Second World War the working population in this country has grown very slowly, but between now and the end of the century it will increase much faster, rising by about 20 per cent. This will be favourable for Britain's growth prospects. The actual increases over the next three decades will be 1, 2 and 3 million respectively. Ultimately this growth in the working population will improve the 'dependency ratio': that is the number of retired people and children under fifteen there are per thousand of working population. Over the next five years the number of retired people will increase twice as fast as the working population, so that the ratio will rise a bit further, probably reaching a peak of 680 by 1981; thereafter it will fall to around 640 by the end of the century. From 1976 onwards the working population will be rising strongly; while the number of retired people will increase much more slowly.

Obviously of much more immediate concern for business planning is what is going to happen over the next decade, by comparison with age group growth rates that have occurred over the past ten years, as shown in the table below. Four significant changes of trend over the next ten years are clearly highlighted. The school-age population will not be growing nearly as fast. The much talked about 'teenage bulge' is now entering the 25–39 age group and causing a very sharp rise in its numbers. The only declining population group, the middle-aged, will contract even faster. While not growing as fast as over the past decade, the number of retired people will still be a close second fastest group, after the 25–39 age category.

U.K. POPULATION (*thousands*)

Age Group	1961	1971	% inc/dec	1981	% inc/dec
Under 5	4,273	4,582	+7	4,924	+7
5–14	8,074	8,957	+11	9,153	+3
15–24	7,150	8,175	+14	9,087	+11
25–39	10,357	10,344	nil	11,761	+14
40–64	16,877	16,779	−1	15,837	−6
Over 65	6,204	7,258	+17	8,141	+13
TOTAL	52,935	56,095	+6	58,903	+5

Source: Annual Abstract of Statistics, H.M.S.O.

MARKET RESEARCH SURVEYS

In addition to readily available published data, demand analysis for consumer goods requires market research in the form of surveys of public spending habits, obtained either by shop audits or shoppers' interviews. These provide data on the total value of spending in particular categories, market shares enjoyed by the various suppliers, as well as consumer reaction and attitudes to products. The number of shops that can be audited, out of the total number of retail outlets in this country of nearly half a million, is naturally limited. Similarly, only a small sample of the total consumer population can be reached. Nevertheless such surveys often involve interviewing large numbers, the factor limiting the number of interviews being cost in relation to the marketing value of the information to be obtained. Because of the lengthy interviewing time, motivational research programmes must obviously be conducted on the basis of very much smaller samples.

Demand analysis in the sphere of industrial products usually involves a smaller number of interviews and requires a good deal more information than is available in published statistics. Sometimes global market size is not difficult to build up, for with specialised products the total number of users may be quite small. As already indicated, industrial products may be put into three categories: consumable materials, components and machinery. Estimating future demand in such areas involves a good deal of technical and scientific knowledge, as well as some understanding of the structure of British industry, particularly in terms of the location of firms and their product range.

As regards consumable materials, total usage can be estimated on the basis of a knowledge of production processes in user areas, as well as the national output statistics for the products manufactured. More detailed information is available in the Census of Production, about which more will be said later in this chapter when dealing with statistical sources. Looking now at components. Much of British industry is engaged primarily in assembly, a notable example of this being motors, a large proportion of the value of whose output consists of parts bought from other firms. This is also true of the shipbuilding industry. Again total demand for such components may be derived from national output figures for the products concerned. The demand for both consumable materials and components is largely dependent on the level of activity in the consumer goods industries. Fluctuations in the requirements for materials and components will therefore be caused by the same factors that give rise to variations in the demand for consumer goods.

We turn now to our third category of industrial products: machinery. In describing the features of the economic cycle, we have already seen how an upturn in demand for capital goods, like machinery and industrial buildings, follows after the first year to eighteen months of consumer goods expansion. Expenditure on fixed assets is largely for the provision of enlarged production capacity, rather than for the replacement of obsolete capacity, although the Government would like to see more of the latter happening. The extent to which an upturn in investment takes place following an expansion in consumption therefore depends on how far below capacity is the level of actual operation in consumer goods industries. Some investment demand of course derives from other capital goods industries, but these supply in turn consumer goods industries: as in the case of engineering firms constructing steel-making plant for the steel industry, whose requirement for such plant depends on the needs of other industries like motors, shipbuilding, etc. When considering national income determination, we saw how the need for extra capacity on the part of certain manufacturers caused a very much greater increase in the level of activity of the engineering industry. We also saw how this higher level of demand seems to come from all directions at once and is often too great for the capacity of U.K. engineering industry, with the result that a good deal of foreign machinery is imported; a cause for particular regret when a few years later the British engineering firms find themselves with insufficient orders.

The total amount spent on fixed capital formation in a year, such as 1970, can be as much as £8,700 million. Just over half of this, namely £4,700 million, represents the investment carried out by private industry; the remainder being the spending on capital assets by public authorities, including local authorities, nationalised industries and public corporations. In terms of type of asset, the 1970 total breaks down: plant and machinery £3,400 million; building and works £2,900 million; dwellings £1,400 million; vehicles, ships and aircraft £1,000 million. Public sector investment has a much higher proportion in the form of 'bricks and mortar', amounting to 70 per cent of the total as, against only 40 per cent in the private sector. Only £2,000 million of the capital investment actually took place in manufacturing industry, this being under half of total private sector investment. A very sharp upturn occurred in manufacturing industry investment in 1961, a large element in this being the expansion programme of the iron and steel industry. In addition to manufacturing, almost as much spending on capital assets takes place in the distributive and service industries, where in an expansion period the level of investment appears to turn up earlier than in manufacturing. Although, like manufacturing, distributive and service industry investment is subject to cyclical fluctuations, there has in this area in recent years been a long-term upward trend, which has done much to support the level of investment during periods of downturn, thus reducing the violence of the fluctuations.

TECHNOLOGICAL DEVELOPMENTS

Sometimes the major influence on the demand for products, particularly industrial ones, is not economic and social factors, but technological change. As modern industry becomes increasingly scientific, with firms selling more and more to other firms rather than to the final consumer, the technical factor in demand analysis looms larger. The iron and steel industry can once again be drawn upon for the purpose of illustration: this time to show how technical change in an industry can affect the types and quantities of materials used by it.

It has already been noted that the expansion programme of the steel industry, carried out in the late 1950s and early sixties, increased capacity by nearly half as much again and this meant a good deal of business for steel plant producers like Davy-Ashmore and the Wellman Engineering Corporation. A large proportion of the additional capacity installed took the form of the new L/D and Kaldo steelmaking furnaces, the essential feature of these being their use of oxygen to speed up the combustion process, whereby iron is refined into steel. Some of the older open hearth furnaces were also converted to use oxygen.

This change in steelmaking technology had repercussions for some of the other suppliers to the steel industry, apart from the plant manufacturers. With the rate of oxygen usage in the new processes being as high as 2,000 cubic feet of gas per ton of steel, total consumption of this gas by the iron and steel industry expanded between 1959–66 alone from 7,000 million cubic feet to 35,000 million cubic feet. This meant tremendous growth in industrial gas business for the dominant British supplier, the British Oxygen Co., as well as for the more recently set up British subsidiary of the American firm, Air Products and Chemicals.

Growing oxygen usage also had implications for the producers of the refractory bricks, with which steel furnaces are lined. Notable among producers of these bricks are the Steetley Co. and General Refractories. At first, the change in steelmaking technology was rejoiced in as being favourable to refractory producers, for the use of oxygen involved higher temperatures in the furnaces, and therefore called for a better quality and more expensive refractory brick. However, it was later found that even in the case of open hearth furnaces, and certainly more so with the new converters, the higher rates of output being achieved through oxygen usage were also resulting in a substantial reduction in refractory consumption per ton of steel produced; and this more than outweighed the benefits of the shift to higher quality bricks.

For the firms involved, such a technological change in an industry can obviously have greater repercussions on the demand for their products than all the economic and social factors put together. In the example considered, it was the demand for existing products that was affected. However, scientific discoveries can result in the creation of entirely new products and new markets, prime examples of this being the plastics and electronics industries.

SOURCES FOR DEMAND ANALYSIS

There are in existence today many companies concerned solely with the provision of market information for use by other companies. Some of these are independent organisations carrying out market investigations and surveys, either in the consumer field or in what is known as industrial market research, or sometimes in both these areas. Many of the larger advertising agencies have research subsidiary companies, providing services not solely for the agency's clients but for any other firms who care to use them. These market research organisations carry out regular surveys and audits into the public's opinions or spending habits, making the results available on a subscription basis. Such syndicated services have the advantage of being available to interested firms at a lower cost than if they had to be specially commissioned. More specific tailor-made research projects are also undertaken, particularly in areas unlikely to be of wider interest and especially in the field of industrial market research.

In addition, a large and steadily increasing volume of published information is available to managers to help them determine future demand patterns in their markets. Some of this information is distributed separately by trade associations, but much of it is included in the statistics circulated by the Government, and particularly the Central Statistical Office. This published information may be considered in two groups. Firstly, there are the routinely issued statistics, mainly relating to output, and secondly there are economic forecasts, both official and unofficial. There is a wide range of statistical publications and we will consider them in their order of frequency, starting with the most frequent. As many of the figures become available, through press releases, they are reported in the daily press. In addition, however, *Trade and Industry,* which appears every Thursday, contains most of the official statistics released during that week and often has them in fuller detail—among such are statistics of retail spending, by product and outlet, and engineering orders and deliveries. In addition the Department of Trade has a special *Monitor* subscription service, giving regular monthly statistics for particular industry sectors and containing a good deal of past history for comparison and identification of trends. Official statistics are brought together in the *Monthly Digest of Statistics,* covering the whole economy. There is a sister publication called *Financial Statistics,* which concentrates on the financial and monetary side of the economy, with statistical details of the operations of financial institutions. Much of the information in these two monthly publications is at the end of the year consolidated in the annual *Abstract of Statistics.*

Another interesting official monthly publication is *Economic Trends,* a major feature of this being the graphical presentation of trends over the past ten years in production, fixed investment and stockholding. This publication also contains special articles, sometimes giving the summarised and provisional results of surveys in the field of population and industrial input-output analysis. Another useful feature of Economic Trends is the graphical plotting of cycles of industrial production and investment, showing the peak, trough and timing of current cycles in relation to previous ones. It is in Economic Trends also that detailed quarterly balance of payments information is given.

There are two official yearly publications which go in great depth into certain areas. The first of these is the *National Income and Expenditure Survey,* known colloquially as the 'blue book'. This breaks down gross national product into its major categories, as well as giving the latest generalised information on industrial input and output. Most of the data contained in this publication is shown both on a current price and constant price basis, so that the effects of inflation can be circled out if desired. There is a detailed breakdown of personal expenditure into various categories and trends in the pattern of consumer expenditure over the years can be identified. Another section of the 'blue book' gives global company accounts information, showing the trend in profits and the allocation of earnings as between depreciation and other retained income and payments to shareholders. The trading profit information is also broken down by industry sector. The 'blue book' contains the most detailed information available on total investment in both the public and private sectors of the economy, this being broken down by type of asset and, in the case of the private sector, by industry.

Another annual official publication contains considerable information on consumer spending—*The Family Expenditure Survey*. This publishes the results of a survey of the spending habits of a large number of households, showing what is in effect their average weekly expenditure on a multitude of items. This information is also displayed in terms of size of household and income category, so that working, middle and upper class expenditure habits can be distinguished.

There are two detailed censuses taken by the Department of Trade of manufacturing industry and the retail trade. The *Census of Production* currently in use is that for 1963 and covers nearly one hundred and thirty distinct industry sectors, with a separate report issued for each and others serving as introduction, index and summary. Each individual industry report shows the number of companies and separate working establishments contained in it, as well as the number of employees. Since this is also expressed by size category, the degree of concentration or dispersion of the industry is revealed. A total figure for sales and net output is also given, while the value of stocks is broken down in terms of finished products, work in progress, materials, stores and fuel. The sales values of the principal products are also listed. Capital assets are distinguished in terms of buildings, plant and machinery, and vehicles. The next of the detailed 5-yearly censuses will be that for 1968; but from then on the census will be carried out on an annual basis, starting with the year 1970.

The latest available *Census of Distribution*, covering goods and services supplied through the retail trade, is that for 1966. The

Census gives the total value of sales in each retail category, such as grocery, boot and shoe, etc., with a separate figure for independents, multiples, and co-operative societies. In addition to total sales, details of numbers employed, purchases, stocks, capital expenditure and gross profit margins are given. Gross margins as a percentage of turnover are shown, as also are stock-to-turnover ratios.

In 1963 a detailed analysis was made by the Central Statistical Office of what went into industries and what came out of them. This was eventually published in 1970 with the title of *Input-Output Tables for the United Kingdom 1963*. This looked at seventy different industry and commodity groups and showed on the input side the payments made by each industry for services rendered by the factors of production and the sources of raw materials and components used (in terms of U.K. industry sectors or imports). On the output side, each industry's total sales were broken down in terms of the other industries to which its intermediate products went, as well as sales to final buyers such as private individuals, public authorities, investment and exports. Provisional input-output tables for 1968 were published in the January 1971 issue of *Economic Trends*.

ECONOMIC FORECASTS

Apart from this great wealth of information about the past, recent and not so recent, there are available also many economic forecasts, both long and short term, conducted by official and unofficial bodies. These can be helpful to the manager in anticipating future demand conditions for both consumer and industrial products. One short-term indicator of the general level of economic activity which is available before many of the official statistics is the total number of *bank cheque clearings,* this being reported in the daily financial press. The number of cheques being cleared naturally increases and decreases with the volume of transactions in goods and services and this gives an indication of the general level of activity in the economy.

Every quarter the *National Institute of Economic and Social Research* issues a review assessing recent developments in the economy, as well as giving a forecast for some eighteen months forward. The forecast is understandably in broad terms, looking at the possible level of imports and exports, and internally at the level of consumer expenditure, investment and employment. Investment is shown separately in terms of stocks and fixed capital formation. The second part of each review contains a useful statistical summary going back for some years. Quarterly figures are given for the most recent years and these are often more useful than monthly ones when making historical comparisons and identifying trends.

Among the longer term forecasts available are those prepared by the *Government Actuary and Registrars General* as to the future total size, and breakdown by age and sex, of U.K. population. These population forecasts go as far ahead as the year 2001 and are contained in the annual Abstract of Statistics. From time to time, revised population forecasts in terms of regions and working population appear in Economic Trends.

Official longer range economic forecasting used to be embodied in the *National Plans*, usually issued for five-year periods. There were three of these National Plans and they contained a review of general government policy, as well as the growth expected for the economy and in the various industry sectors. A similar exercise to the National Plan was carried out independently under the auspices of the National Institute of Economic and Social Research, the body which publishes the Quarterly Review. Their plan, entitled *The British Economy in 1975*,* was produced by W. Beckerman and Associates. The book aimed at presenting a comprehensive statistical picture of what the British economy would look like in 1975, provided a somewhat faster rate of growth was achieved in the meantime.

* Cambridge University Press 1965.

20

Growth of the Firm

As has been remarked in an earlier chapter, the subject of growth has been much thought of and talked about in recent years. But long before this consciousness about growth was in national economy terms, indeed from the very beginning of our industrialisation, growth has been the natural course of development of the basic production unit in the economy, namely the firm. The tendency for firms to want to grow has indeed been one of the vital forces in the economy. In some cases the speed of this growth has been quite remarkable. Although this country has been industralised for nearly two centuries now, many of today's industrial giants were only born in the thirties; and there are even some large firms today which have grown from nothing in the last twenty-five post-war years.

MOTIVES FOR GROWTH

Following the modern fashion of enquiry into motivation, we begin by looking at the compelling forces leading to growth by the firm. Perhaps the principal of these is the driving ambition of the man at the top, who may in fact have been the founder of the business. If he is still the sole or substantial owner, then the desire for more and more wealth will be allied to the non-financial aspects of personal ambition. But even where there is no proprietorship motive the driving force of personal ambition may be just as great by itself. In his own, and in the world's, eyes a man's importance will be closely identified with the growth of the organisation he heads. The same kind of motivation applies further down the line. Departmental managers, just as much as managing directors, feel that their status, and perhaps their remuneration, increases with the growth of the departments over which they have charge. Thus growth becomes a dominant motive, perhaps even coming before maximisation of profit.

Indeed physical expansion, by saddling the business with a higher depreciation charge, may act to reduce the amount of profit available for distribution to shareholders. All this may explain why sophisticated methods of optimum output determination are little used; growth of sales and establishments being what the professional managers are really seeking. The motivation of the manager is therefore not the same as that of the shareholder; the latter being interested in maximum profit, and growth only if it improves profitability. The manager wants growth, since he sees little of the profit. Provided enough profit is earned to pay the dividend and to permit its occasional increase, the professional manager will in the main be allowed to pursue growth, without too many questions being asked by the generally passive proprietors. To bring about a closer identity of interest between the manager and the shareholder, many firms, particularly in America, give their senior management shares in the company, not just as an additional element of remuneration but to give them a stake in profitability.

Growth can be justified for a variety of reasons. It may arise from the extension into other activities, to provide an added security for employees and proprietors alike by not having too many eggs in the one basket. Diversification may also be defensive, in the sense of being enforced, if traditional markets are contracting or have little growth prospect. Growth may also be defensive in the sense that a firm may have to keep on growing to keep up with its competitors, or to avoid being squeezed out or taken over.

ECONOMICS OF LARGE SCALE

Probably the most respectable, and positive, motive for growth is the desire to reap the economies which come from doing things on a large scale. Being 'economies', they should improve profitability, so that in this desire for growth the interests of the shareholders will also be served. Firms are often initially led into expansion to obtain certain technical advantages. If all the stages of production can be carried on by the one firm and on the same site then there will be obvious savings in the reduction of transportation and avoidance of heat loss. The bigger the concern, the more worthwhile it becomes to employ costly, but labour saving, machinery. Where machines are already in use, growth in output will justify using larger machines, requiring perhaps no greater number of operatives than the smaller ones. Large production units are generally also more economical in the use of power. There are certain fixed assets available only in a 'king' size, so that an organisation has to be big to use them at all. It is often only a large organisation which can afford adequate research and development facilities and therefore participate in innovation.

Apart from these technical advantages of large-scale operation, there are also ultimately managerial advantages. In small enterprises the man at the top has to be a managerial jack-of-all-trades. But in a large company the task of management can be divided up amongst specialists, each trained and experienced in his particular sphere. The managerial 'capacity' of such a team will obviously be greater than that of one man. The strategy of business planning is also easier in the case of a big organisation. Thanks to the law of large numbers, forecasting will be more accurate, since swings and roundabouts tend to cancel out. Uncertainty can also be reduced by gaining control over supply sources or sales outlets. A captive market provides not only a guaranteed outlet but one which can be integrated with the total organisation planning.

There are also financial advantages in size. A large purchaser is always in a stronger bargaining position to extort price and other concessions. His suppliers will be willing to tailor-make to his requirements without extra charge, partly because the scale of his order makes it feasible for them to do so, quite apart from any arm-twisting ability of the large purchasing organisation. A well-known firm can obtain capital more readily, and at a lower rate of interest, than can a smaller enterprise, which is inevitably regarded as riskier. Banks in granting overdrafts also take the size of their customer into consideration when determining the amount allowable and how much above Bank rate to charge to what they term 'prime borrowers'.

WAYS OF ACHIEVING GROWTH

The desire for growth is most gratified when it assumes physical form: like a larger factory, or another factory, or a bigger and more impressive looking office block. In some business spheres the growth-wish can be satisfied by steeply climbing sales, or 'billings', or copies sold. And it is on such things that physical growth must itself be based. Greater sales have to be made to justify the larger factory. Growth therefore springs from increased sales of existing products or by the addition of new items to a firm's product range. The first method depends on the growth rate of the market or on the possibility of increasing market share, which is perhaps doing it the hard way. Easier and more spectacular growth can be achieved either by the acquisition of other firms or by merging with them, provided one's own company is clearly the dominant partner.

Acquisition is probably the most usual and most successful method of growth. If the firm to be taken over is a private one, it requires persuasion of the present owners to sell. This, for a variety of reasons (including death duties), they may be willing or forced to do. In the case of a publicly owned company an offer, with or without prior consultation with its directors, must be made to the shareholders to purchase their shares from them, either with cash or the offer of shares in the bidding company, or a mixture of both. The price offered must usually be well above the current valuation in the stock market, which may still not truly represent the company's net worth. Sometimes this discrepancy arises from a failure of the directors to enlarge share capital by scrip issue to keep pace with growth in the firm's assets due to a policy of high retentions. Depressed market conditions, over which the directors have no control, may also result in the firm's share being quoted at a price well below the value of net assets per share. Either way, a company may become an attractive take-over prospect, particularly if it has large holdings of cash and investments, resulting from the directors' decision over the years not to invest any further in fixed assets in the traditional business of the company.

Industrial combination, whether by take-over or merger, may proceed in one of two directions: by what is termed in economics 'horizontal' or 'vertical integration'. Horizontal integration represents further involvement in the firm's existing activities and inevitably means combining with competitors. Vertical integration is growth either by extending backwards to supply sources or forwards to sales outlets, the latter involving

Economics for Executives

wholesalers, retailers, or customer industries. Both horizontal and vertical integration can also, of course, be achieved by starting from scratch—by setting up supplying organisations or sales outlets.

WHY SOME FIRMS REMAIN SMALL

Despite the economics of large-scale production and all the possible ways in which firms can grow larger, there are many that stay more or less as they are in terms of size. The proprietor may not want his business to get any larger than he is capable of managing by himself or with his family. The rate of growth may be limited to what finance can be found from retained profits or the proprietor's own personal fortune. The proprietor may not wish to risk losing financial control by going public. Apart from the personal quirks of the man running the firm, its size may remain small because of a limited market—either in geographical terms or due to the specialised nature of the product. For some products, even nationally the total requirement is small. This is particularly true of certain speciality chemicals, used in very small quantities as auxiliaries in the plastics industry, whose market may be limited to one particular plastic, made perhaps by only one or two manufacturers.

DISECONOMIES OF LARGE SCALE

A limit to growth may come from the fact that if a firm gets any bigger certain diseconomies begin to operate—apart from the possibility that the state may look askance at any further growth, as we saw when describing monopolies and mergers legislation. Great size poses certain organisational problems and there develop the sort of tendencies which Professor C. Northcote Parkinson has humorously, but also unerringly, described. There is duplication and overlapping of functions, plus a good deal of empire-building, which only the occasional economy campaign manages temporarily to demolish or hold in check. Large organisations tend to have a certain ponderousness. They lack flexibility and quickness to respond to changes. There is too much money tied up in existing activities for them to be abandoned lightly. When, during a deflationary phase of the economy, the level of industrial activity drops, the burden of overheads tend to weigh more heavily in a large organisation and cannot readily be lightened, and the depressing effect on profits is all the greater.

Some of the organisational rigidities of a large organisation can be got round by decentralisation. This represents a dispersion of what may have been a too concentrated power of decision-making at the top. Decentralisation can be brought about by major organisational separations. Policy-making is hived off from day-to-day operations, with top management being assisted in the formulation of policy by central staffs. The latter also carry out functional supervision of operational activities coming within their area of specialisation: for example, the cost accountants in the central finance staff will keep a watching brief on cost accounting activities in the group's factories. This separation of policy-making from operations creates what is termed a 'staff and line' organisation. On the organisation chart a bold thick line connects the heads of the operating divisions directly with top management. The staff departments are out on the side and do not interrupt the direct line communication. Their function is not to control operations but to advise top and operating management. The operating divisions will as far as possible be self-contained entities, perhaps responsible for the manufacture and sale of a complete product or model. In the U.S. motor industry, for example, the product divisions manufacture, or more accurately assemble, one particular model. The heads of these decentralised parts of a larger group are given profit maximisation responsibility, their area of command being designated a 'profit centre'. In fairness, and so that there will be no alibis, it follows that the manager of the profit centre must have at his command all that is necessary for him to fulfil his obligation to maximise profit, and this sometimes extends to allowing him to buy outside the group products made within the group, provided he can show that he does so more cheaply and to the benefit of his own profits.

FINANCING GROWTH

A firm's growth has to be financed, even if it is only by the provision of more working capital by the bank to enable the carrying of the higher level stocks necessary to support a greater sales volume. When expansion of fixed assets is involved as well, the need for finance is even greater. For really large companies, major expansion programmes will involve the expenditure of amounts as much as £50 million. The capital to finance such projects derives from two major sources: the company's own earnings or the savings of investors.

CASH FLOW

Few companies pay out each year the whole of their profits to the shareholders. Some people argue that they should do so, thereby forcing companies to subject their capital expenditure projects to the acid test of the capital market. However, companies in this country now retain about 60 per cent of their earnings. Some of the finance for growth may therefore be found from undistributed income, including the annual allowance set aside for depreciation to provide for the replacement of existing machinery, when wear and tear, or obsolescence, requires this. This money need not be rigidly tied to the exact replacement of existing plant and machinery, but is generally available as part of the firm's pool of internally found capital.

Depreciation and retained earnings together make up what is called 'cash flow'. This should be compared with the firm's outstanding capital commitments to assess to what extent internal funds will be sufficient, or whether resort may also have to be made to the capital market. After the initial flotation some companies have never again had to go to the market. By pursuing a high retention policy, perhaps to the detriment of the shareholders, these firms have managed to self-finance all their capital projects.

Before going on to examine the way in which outside capital may be raised, two other sources of funds for investment should be recognised. Although bank lending is primarily short term, being designed to cover working capital needs, nevertheless bank borrowing is sometimes used as interim finance for fixed investment. Indeed, on the Continent banks have long been providers of medium and sometimes longer, term finance for industry. Another source of money for investment is from the Government, as tax allowance for depreciation or as cash grant.

OFFICIAL INVESTMENT INCENTIVES

In 1966 a new system of investment incentives was introduced in the form of cash grants. These largely replaced the previous method of giving tax relief in respect of investment expenditure through what were termed 'initial' and 'investment' allowances. Cash grants were introduced partly because the Corporation tax, by taxing the company itself more lightly, had rendered the existing system of allowances less valuable. It was also argued that the previous system had been too indiscriminate, giving tax relief for all sorts of investment expenditure, regardless of national interest. Manufacturing and extractive industries were given cash grants of 20 per cent of the value of expenditure on new plant and machinery. Service and construction industries were excluded from the grant system, but had their initial allowances increased. Ships were eligible for cash grants, as also were purchases of computers anywhere in industry and commerce. In its mini-Budget of October 1970 the Conservative Government announced the abolition of the cash grant system and return to the giving of tax allowances to encourage investment.

THE CAPITAL MARKET

When depreciation, retained earnings and cash grants are still not sufficient to meet the cost of a firm's capital expenditure programme, recourse has to be made to borrowing from the investing public. Such borrowed funds may come from existing shareholders of the company or from other investors, and in both cases will undoubtedly include large institutional investors, like insurance companies and private pension funds. The main occasion when capital has to be raised by a company is, of course, when it is first formed, either from scratch or by a private company 'going public'. But apart from this, there may be times when a company must enlarge its share or loan capital to finance expansion programmes.

There are two major categories of capital which may be raised by a company: loan capital and equity capital. The preference share is a third in-between form nowadays little used. There are in addition many sub-species of these major types. Broadly, the distinction between equity and loan capital is that the former confers ownership, whereas the latter is merely a loan at a fixed rate of interest. Many features of these two classes of capital follow from this distinction.

The holder of an equity, or an ordinary share as it is more commonly known, is entitled to vote and to elect the directors of the company at the annual general meeting. After all of the obligations to creditors, loan stock and preference shareholders have been satisfied, the ordinary shareholder has the residual claim. The directors, whom he elects, decide how much of the profits will be paid out by way of dividend to the ordinary shareholder, this being expressed as a percentage of the nominal value of the share. According to whether profits are good, not so good, or downright bad, this percentage can be increased, reduced, or even be nil. If the company has to be wound up, the ordinary shareholder comes last in the ranking of claims on realised assets, and he may lose his 'share' in the company altogether. The ordinary shareholder is therefore the risk-taker.

A loan stock holder, on the other hand, is fundamentally a lender of capital, being a creditor rather than an owner of the company. He has no say in the company's affairs unless there is default either on the fixed annual rate of interest he is due to receive or, if the stock is redeemable, on the eventual repayment of the sum lent. The loan stock holder's claim on the company ranks before the ordinary and preference share holders. The most common form of loan capital is the debenture.

Preference shares are nearer in character to loan capital; although they rank after it in priority, but before the ordinary shareholder. Preference shares carry no vote and unless specified as 'cumulative', the dividend paid on a preference share may, in a bad year, be passed over; and only in the case of a 'participating' preference can something more than the fixed dividend be given in an extremely good year.

Before concluding this section on the capital market, a brief and very general description will be given of the mechanics of new issue of stocks and shares. The forms which these may take have already been described above and the choice is generally made by the company in conjunction with its financial advisers, usually a merchant bank acting as an issuing house. The issuing house acts as an intermediary between companies requiring capital and savers with funds to invest; most new issues made are dealt with in some degree by issuing houses, who can attend to the legal and administrative matters connected with the issue, as well as provide underwriting. The Bank of England has to be consulted as regards the timing of any new issue over £1 million in value.

Where an existing public company wishes to raise more ordinary capital, it is expected to give its existing shareholders the first option of taking up the new shares. A circular is sent offering the new shares by way of 'rights issue', giving the opportunity to subscribe for them in a fixed proportion to existing holdings, for example, one new share for every four held.

A different procedure has to be adopted where a private company 'going public' issues shares to the public for the first time. This procedure will also apply in the case of existing public companies wishing to make something other than a further issue of ordinary shares, for example, an issue of preference or loan stock. When issuing a loan stock, a public company, while offering the stock to the public, may also give priority to applications from existing shareholders.

A firm wishing to make an issue to the public must produce a prospectus, containing a considerable amount of detail about the company, and advertise it in at least two national newspapers. Applications for shares may go direct to the company concerned, with the issuing house acting only as underwriter. (Underwriting guarantees that any part of the issue not subscribed for by the public will be taken up by the issuing house and institutional investors acting as sub-underwriters.) Alternatively, the issuing house can buy the new securities, and also any existing ones, from the company and itself act as principal, offering them to the investing public, this method being known as an 'offer for sale'.

Fixed interest issues, particularly if they are likely to appeal only to institutional investors, are often made by way of a 'placing'. Permission is given by the Stock Exchange to place blocks of stocks with institutional investors, no invitation to subscribe being extended to the public; but at least a quarter of the value placed must be made available to jobbers, so that the public may buy on the Stock Exchange. 'Introduction' is a method of getting a quotation on the Stock Exchange, without any substantial sale of existing securities to the public, and is not therefore really a means of raising money.

INDUSTRIAL AND COMMERCIAL FINANCE CORPORATION

Firms too small to be able to issue shares to the public have to find their finance from other sources. Traditionally, this has come from 'ploughed back' profits and from the private wealth of the owners, although the latter ability has been considerably diminished by present-day levels of taxation and death duties. Certain private financial institutions make money available to small industrial and commercial firms; among these are merchant banks. Holding companies are often prepared to take an equity interest in growing new businesses.

A body set up after the Second World War, specifically to provide finance for small and medium size businesses, is the Industrial and Commercial Finance Corporation. The Corporation is owned by the Bank of England and the joint stock banks. Most of its lending is on a fixed interest basis, the Corporation charging the borrower about 1 per cent above the current yield on British government securities. It has not in the past been usual for the I.C.F.C. to take an equity interest in the companies to which it lends, although in recent years it has begun to do so more frequently. Nor, unlike some of the other financial institutions, does it insist on appointing a representative to the board. A subsidiary of I.C.F.C., Industrial Mergers, assists small and medium sized companies wishing to merge.

INDUSTRIAL REORGANISATION CORPORATION

To improve the competitiveness of British industry, particularly with regard to export performance, the Labour Government wished to see greater concentration and rationalisation in many sectors. It therefore announced in 1966 the setting-up of the Industrial Reorganisation Corporation whose function was to encourage mergers, acquisitions and regroupings, in a more active way than could be done by private financial institutions like merchant banks. The funds used by the Corporation came from the Exchequer, and in return the I.R.C. made fixed interest or dividend payments to the Exchequer.

The Industrial Reorganisation Corporation was given very wide ranging powers to facilitate reorganisation of either the whole or a part of an industry sector. It made capital available to private industry, either as a loan or by taking an equity interest. It also set up new companies, by itself, or in partnership with private enterprise. The Corporation had the power to purchase capital assets and make them available to new industrial groupings, if necessary on a leasing basis. Finance was not intended to be provided by the Corporation on a perpetual basis, for the more it could circulate its capital, the more projects it was able to undertake: it was therefore expressly given the power to *sell*, as well as buy and hold company securities. Thus, the Industrial Reorganisation Corporation provided an alternative mechanism to nationalisation for state intervention and participation in industry. The I.R.C. was brought to an end by the Conservative Government.

Index

Index

Index

Index

Index